THE MASTER SPEAKS

Other Writings of Joel S. Goldsmith

Joel S. Goldsmith

THE
MASTER
SPEAKS

A CITADEL PRESS BOOK
PUBLISHED BY CAROL PUBLISHING GROUP

Carol Publishing Group Edition - 1993

A Citadel Press Book
Published by Carol Publishing Group
Citadel Press is a registered trademark of Carol Communications, Inc.

Editorial Offices: 600 Madison Avenue, New York, NY 10022
Sales & Distribution Offices: 120 Enterprise Avenue, Secaucus, NJ 07094
In Canada: Canadian Manda Group, P.O. Box 920, Station U, Toronto,
Ontario, M8Z 5P9, Canada

Queries regarding rights and permissions should be addressed to:
Carol Publishing Group, 600 Madison Avenue, New York, NY 10022

Manufactured in the United States of America
ISBN 0-8065-0912-0

Carol Publishing Group books are available at special discounts
for bulk purchases, for sales promotions, fund raising, or
educational purposes. Special editions can also be created to
specifications. For details contact: Special Sales Department,
Carol Publishing Group, 120 Enterprise Ave., Secaucus, NJ 07094

15 14 13 12 11 10 9 8 7 6

Except the Lord build the house, they labour in vain that build it.

Illumination dissolves all material ties and binds men together with the golden chains of spiritual understanding; it acknowledges only the leadership of the Christ; it has no ritual or rule but the divine, impersonal universal Love; no other worship than the inner Flame that is ever lit at the shrine of Spirit. This union is the free state of spiritual brotherhood. The only restraint is the discipline of Soul, therefore we know liberty without licence; we are a united universe without physical limits; a divine service to God without ceremony or creed. The illumined walk without fear—by Grace.

THE INFINITE WAY

Contents

8

9

INTRODUCTION

In many parts of the world, in many universities and churches, an interest in so-called spiritual healing has sprung up in the last twenty-five years.

Actually, many of those who have pursued this interest have touched true spiritual healing. However, that which is being so widely written about as spiritual healing is, for the most part, psychological healing, sometimes with faith in an unknown God added. The difference between this type of healing and spiritual healing is as vast as the difference between darkness and light.

Psychological healing is primarily an activity of the human mind and intellect. Spiritual healing is the activity of the Soul faculties: it is always performed without mental activity, without the necessity of the physical presence of the patient, and often without his cooperation beyond that of giving his consent—and often not even with that.

The Infinite Way Writings contain the letter of truth through which is developed the spiritual consciousness that heals, reforms, redeems, and saves. These writings are textbooks which may be used by individuals, groups, or organizations desiring to practice and to further spiritual healing.

This very book, *The Master Speaks*, based on the teachings of the Master, Christ Jesus, is ideally suited to the purpose of serving as a textbook for the

teaching of spiritual living and spiritual healing—
and may be used by any church denomination, any
university healing activity, or by any other group
interested in this subject.

*Once the difference between psychological and faith
healing and the healing by spiritual consciousness is
recognized, a new era will begin in human history.*

JOEL S. GOLDSMITH.

Box 5308,
Honolulu,
Hawaii.

CHAPTER ONE

ONENESS WITH GOD

SPIRITUAL teaching is an unfoldment of the activity of the Spirit of God in individual consciousness as revealed by the Master, Christ Jesus. Every spiritually illumined teacher throughout all ages has recognized that out of the depths of the silence, out of the depths of the Infinite Within-ness, come the joy, the peace, and the harmony of our daily lives.

The Infinite Way differs from many other metaphysical teachings. In those teachings we find that the emphasis is placed on the term "wrong thinking," and we learn that we, as seekers, have been held responsible for our disease or for our lack of healing. In some way or other, it was our wrong thinking that was responsible. But that is not true. The error is never ours. The error was here long before we appeared on the human scene; and if we are not careful and if we do not help to eradicate it, it will be here for somebody else to be victimized by long after we are removed from the human scene. It is always an impersonal error, a universal belief.

We can never lose true teaching, after it has become a part of our own being. Once we understand this teaching, once it really becomes a part of us, it cannot be lost; and if the whole world said that we were wrong, our own demonstration of it would be

13

the proof that it was right. But until that time when it is ours—when we know that we really have it—let us hold on to it within ourselves. The Master said to the leper who was healed: "See thou tell no man."[1] After it is really ours, we can go and show the priests, but until that time comes, let us wait a while, and let it solidify within us.

We have books to read which help us in our unfoldment—books of a spiritual nature, dealing with spiritual subjects. We have Scripture. And more and more we should learn our Bible, because the Bible is the Book of Life. Much of the world has missed the mark by reading the Bible from its historical and literary points of view; whereas it is filled from cover to cover with the very bread of life, the very water, and the very wine of life, when its teachings are spiritually discerned. It does not help much to recite the 91st Psalm, and then to think that because we have recited it or memorized it, we shall be protected by its teachings. The Bible as a book is not our protection or our security. The Word is protection and security. And when we know the meaning of the 91st Psalm—when we really know that it is true that "he that dwelleth in the secret place of the most High"[2] is protected—we have made the 91st Psalm our own. Most of the 91st Psalm tells us what will happen when we have learned to abide in "the secret place of the most High." That first sentence is undoubtedly the most important part of it.

When we learn to abide in spiritual truth, in spiritual consciousness; when we learn to "pray

[1] Matthew 8:4.   [2] Psalms 91:1.

14

without ceasing"; when we learn to live in the atmosphere of God as the only cause and creative power; when we learn to live in the atmosphere of God as omnipresent; then, the rest of the 91st Psalm becomes true in our experience. Reciting the fact that a thousand shall fall at our left and ten thousand shall fall at our right, or that these evils will not come nigh us, will not do any good. The evils will not come nigh us when we have fulfilled the message of the 91st Psalm which is: Dwell in the secret place of the most High; dwell in the consciousness of God; dwell in the consciousness of God as a living Presence, as an infinite Power, as Truth, Itself.

When we dwell in and with and through these truths, so that they become the very embodiment of our being; when, for instance, we accept the truth that even our body is the temple of the living God, we no longer have to fear what evils will come nigh us. This means, literally, that we are setting God up as the one Presence and the one Power and the All-Power and the only Power, that we are acknowledging nothing less than Omnipresence.

Universality of Truth

We find confirmation of this truth in the Old Testament and in the New Testament. In the Old Testament, we read:

Thou wilt keep him in perfect peace, whose mind is stayed on thee.[1]

In all thy ways acknowledge Him, and he shall direct thy paths.[2]

[1] Isaiah 26:3.   [2] Proverbs 3:6.

All through Scripture we find emphasized the necessity for acknowledging God as the reality of our being. When we come to the Master, we find him saying:

I can of mine own self do nothing.[1]
My doctrine is not mine, but his that sent me.[2]
The Father that dwelleth in me, he doeth the works.[3]

And Paul tells us:

I can do all things through Christ.[4]
I live; yet not I, but Christ liveth in me.[5]

This is like the beginning of the 91st Psalm: "He that dwelleth in the secret place of the most High." Then the other things—all the evil things— will not come nigh unto him, and all these good things will. We shall find that the truth in which we are abiding, and which we are permitting to abide in us, becomes the fortress; it becomes the rock. We do not need steel linings in our Bibles; we do not need a suit of armor; we do not need money in the bank; we do not need an inheritance of bonds or stocks. I do not mean that we should not have wealth; I mean we do not need it. We come to a place in consciousness where we realize that this truth actually becomes our shield and buckler; it becomes our fortress; it becomes our steel lining; it becomes our bank account, our source of supply, and our very supply itself.

Now, watch. Back in Deuteronomy we find the first commandment:

And thou shalt love the Lord thy God with all

---

[1] John 5:30. [2] John 7:16. [3] John 14:10.
[4] Philippians 4:13. [5] Galatians 2:20.

thine heart and with all thy soul, and with all thy might.[1]

With all your heart, love the Lord. And have no other gods before Him. Acknowledge only the one Presence. Then we turn to Leviticus, and we read: "Love thy neighbour as thyself."[2] Here we have two commandments from the Old Testament which have become the very foundation of Christianity; because when Jesus was asked about the commandments, he gave that very First Commandment, and then he added to it the second: "Love thy neighbour as thyself."[3] He made these two Hebrew laws the foundation for the Christian teaching.

Why is it necessary and important for us, first of all, to know these two commandments; and secondly, to know that they are Old Testament teachings as well as New? There is a very important reason for it. It is important to know the commandments themselves, regardless of where they came from, because they explain the foundation of all our work, which is the *allness of God* and the *universality* of that truth. In other words, all that is true of God, is true of individual being. This individual being is every Jew and every Gentile; it is every Protestant and every Catholic; it is true of every Hindu and every Moslem; it is every person in the universe whether white, black, or yellow. If we do not accept the universality of this truth, we shall again lapse into the error that has caused every war in history, and

[1] Deuteronomy 6:5.   [2] Leviticus 19:18.
[3] Matthew 22:39.

17

that will continue to cause all the future wars, discords, and diseases. This error is the belief that we are something separate and apart from God; or that even if we are not, some other person is.

In the book, *Spiritual Interpretation of Scripture*,[1] you will come across the place in which I have repeated the Golden Rule from the Sermon on the Mount, which is popularly stated: "Do unto others as you would have them do unto you."[2] I have shown in this book, from the records that are actually in existence, that this Code of Conduct did not have its beginning either in the Christian era, or even in the Judaic era. It goes as far back as there are recorded manuscripts and recorded time. We have this teaching: "Do unto others as you would have them do unto you" in Hebrew Scripture and in Oriental Scripture. We have it repeated in Greek literature and in Roman writings. From the beginning, philosophy has repeated the teaching: "Do unto others as you would have them do unto you."

Are we, then, to accept this exclusively as a Christian teaching, or as a God-revealed teaching unto men throughout time? We shall never outgrow the narrowness of orthodox religion until we come to that point of accepting God as the revelator of Its own Being, revealing the truth about, and unto, all men, in all scripture.

It is an impossibility for us as metaphysicians to receive a telephone call or a telegram for help, and

---

[1] By the author (Willing Publishing Company, San Gabriel, California, 1947).
[2] Matthew 7:12.

to be able to give that help instantaneously and spiritually, if we stop for one second to consider whether the call comes from a Catholic, a Protestant, a Jew, or a Hindu; whether it comes from a German, a Japanese, a Russian, or whoever it is that is the enemy at the moment. Unless our thought responds instantly to the fact that God is the only life, that God is all there is to individual being; and unless in our heart and Soul we truly believe that, we cannot be spiritual healers. We might do some mental healing with a little mental pounding, here and there, but we shall never be spiritual healers until every call for help brings out in us a sense of love. This will be a sense of love that comes not as love for a person. In the normal course of events, we shall never know one-tenth of those who call on us for help; we never shall meet one-tenth of the people who will call on us for help, once we achieve this spiritual awareness of being. The calls will come from all over the world, and they will come by mail and telegram and telephone. We shall not know whether it is a metaphysician calling, or whether it is a Catholic or a Protestant, or whether it is a prisoner in a dungeon. And it is better so, since our immediate response must be: "This is the very Christ of God appearing to me as an individual call for help, as an individual person, or as an individual claim. All that can ever be accepted in my consciousness is God—God, and the Christ of God, which is God appearing as the individual, whether that appearance comes as person, place, or thing."

Until we can stand on that ground and on that rock, we shall not be able rightly to interpret, "the

place whereon thou standest is holy ground."[1] Why
is the place whereon I stand holy ground? Because I[2]
am standing there; that is what makes it sacred.
Could we, by any stretch of the imagination, first
stop to ask who it is that is standing there, or what
his name or race or religion or creed is? Not in this
great revelation of God—God appearing as individual
you and me. That breaks down in our consciousness
all emphasis on religion or race or bigotry.

Let us remember this: As human beings, you and
I are no more Israel than the people who walked in
Galilee. It is only those who, in some measure,
arrive at spiritual consciousness, at spiritual awareness, who are Israel. When we speak of Melchizedek,
without mother, without father, we speak of you
and me as we come to the realization of our true
identity as children of God, or God made manifest.
No mortal could be Melchizedek; no human being
could be Melchizedek; but only that which is
greater than Abraham, only that which is greater
than all or any degree of human good—in other
words, pure Spirit. And we are Melchizedek, when
we have acknowledged that we were never born and
that we shall never die; that we are the very I, the
reality and substance of God's Being; and that God
is the substance and reality of our being. That is
Melchizedek; that is the Christ. To say that that
which appears as any individual is anything less than
Allness is sinning against the Holy Ghost.

It is the same old sin that the Hebrews tried to
perpetuate in making everyone first become a

[1] Exodus 3:5.
[2] Wherever "I" appears in italics, the reference is to God.

20

Hebrew, before he could become a Christian. Let us not repeat these mistakes now. The only way we can avoid them is to begin here and now to forget our human birth, to forget the human birth of everyone on earth, and to go right to the center of being, and there recognize Christ, the Spirit, the presence and power of God. As we do that, we do not heal human beings; we do not enrich them, although that is the way in which it appears to the world. What we do is to bring to light their spiritual identity—that which has always been there, but which, as in the incident of the prodigal, has seemed to have disappeared.

Opening Consciousness to Truth

The reading of books and the study of Scripture is the first step of the way by which we open our consciousness to the inflow of spiritual Truth. The second step is our association with those who are on the path, and especially with those who have gone even one step further than we have. In and of themselves, these steps are not Spirit, but they lead us back to the kingdom of God within our own being. They keep reminding us of our true identity, leading us back from the mesmerism of the world which would try to pull us down into the beliefs of humanhood. These steps that we take are aids and helps toward holding us to the center of our being, until ultimately we arrive at that place where we can walk on the water, with no outside help.

The ultimate of our work is to arrive at that place where the Comforter can come to us, not through a book or a teacher, but *through the unfoldment and revelation of our own inner being*. We, in this work, must avoid the necessity for the statement that Jesus had to make to his followers: "If I go not away, the Comforter will not come unto you."[1] In other words: "As long as you are relying on me, as a person, as long as you insist on coming to me with every patient you cannot heal, or with every claim you cannot meet, and keep looking to me to do it for you, the fullness of this revelation will not come to you." We must realize our true identity as the allness of God made manifest.

There is a further step and that step is the step of meditation. It is in and through meditation that we, ultimately, touch the kingdom of God within our own being. Most of our lives we have talked about God; we have talked about Spirit; we have talked about our Soul; and we have even talked about the Christ. But very few of us have actually made the acquaintance of God, Soul, or the Christ. To most of us, these are still terms for something separate and apart from our own being, something which we hope, ultimately, to realize or to attain. In this work, we try as soon as possible to make an end to this thought about God as separate and apart from our being, to the continuous talk about Christ, or praying to Christ or God; and we try to come as rapidly as we can, to the realization of God—to an actual God-experience.

For God can be experienced here and now. God is an actual reality, a living being. God is not something far-off. As the poet tells us: "God is closer

[1] John 16:7.

22

than breathing, nearer than hands and feet." It is not necessary that we go through life talking about God, hoping, praying for the day we shall meet God —sometimes even praying that we shall die in order that we may meet God. No, no, no! God can be realized here and now. God is a living Soul. God is a living being. God is a living light. In spite of all of the universality and impersonality of God, God can become intimate and personal to us. For that reason, Abraham was able to know God as Friend, and Jesus was able to know God as Father. Many of the great Hindu masters realized God as Mother, and present-day metaphysicians refer to God as Father-Mother. All of these reveal God in an intimate way, and yet as the inner reality of our being.

Neither "Right Thinking" nor "Wrong Thinking" Is Power

In this work we depend, not so much on the truth we know, as on the truth that is unfolded to us, revealed to us, within our own being. In the work that we are doing, the human mind becomes an agent, an avenue of awareness. It becomes that through which we become aware; it is not a creative power. The thoughts we think are not creative power. We do not make a power of our own thinking and of our own thoughts. "All power is given unto our Lord, on Him we place reliance."[1] God, the real Being, our real being, is the power; and It reveals Itself to us in Its own way. "For my thoughts are not your thoughts, neither are your ways my ways,

[1] Martin Luther.

23

saith the Lord."[1] If that is true, all of the thinking that you and I do, does not really constitute spiritual thinking at all. What constitutes spiritual awareness, spiritual knowledge, is what comes to us from the "still small voice,"[2] the impartation which comes to us from God.

So we, as we go on, do much less talking truth, thinking truth, reading truth, and much more receiving truth. Sometimes that impartation comes through in words. But in this work, one of the main points on which we stand is that our thinking—even our good thinking, even our good thoughts—will not help anybody. Only God, divine Reality, is our help. And God reveals Itself to us—sometimes in words, sometimes in thoughts, sometimes in feelings. Sometimes we sense the very presence and power of God, and that is It.

Recognize God as the Source of All Good

Building the consciousness of Omnipotence, of Omnipresence, is our work. Let us always remember to carry out, if necessary a hundred times a day, the work that is outlined in the chapter on "Meditation" in *The Infinite Way*.[3] That is where, on waking in the morning, we begin to acknowledge our oneness with God, in the way that a wave is one with the ocean. Let us consciously bring ourselves to the remembrance of the truth that "I and my Father are one,"[4] and that that one is really God. God is all

[1] Isaiah 55:8.   [2] I Kings 19:12.
[3] By the author (Willing Publishing Company, San Gabriel, California, 1956).
[4] John 10:30.

24

there is, and all that the Father hath is ours. All that God is, I am. And then, let us remember to acknowledge God as the source of all good: whether we are receiving some form of good or whether we are expressing some form of good; whether it is money incoming, or money outgoing; whether it is food that we eat; whether it is an invitation from a friend; whether it is even the weekly allowance from a husband or father or an estate—let us immediately recognize God as the source.

In this work, we have come to a great realization, the realization that nothing that exists out here in the realm of form or effect is substance or supply. We have come, in this revelation, to see that it is the consciousness of my being, the very life of my being, the very Soul, which is my supply; and to know that that supply appears outwardly as dollars, patients, students, income, or clients, as opportunity, sales, purchases. Whatever form of human existence we are experiencing, God, the Spirit of our being, appears outwardly as that form. Therefore, it is not of too much consequence whether a customer moves away or a patient leaves us; we are not concerned with that, because God, the substance of our being, is appearing outwardly every moment in the form necessary to our demonstration or unfoldment.

What happens out here in this world becomes of no consequence. There should be no reason now why we do not form new organs and functions of the body, if that should be necessary to our unfoldment. It is only the universal belief that tells us that a hand cannot grow again if we need one. When fortunes

25

are wiped out, people jump out of windows, because they believe that that is all the money that is left on earth. They forget that the very Intelligence that brought them money will bring it back again and again and again. They forget how many times currency has been wiped out in the world, all the way back from Roman currency to German currency. And yet men have gone on and have become wealthy again.

It does not make any difference what happens in this so-called external world, or to it—your consciousness will form it anew. It does not make any difference if an atomic bomb wipes it out—your consciousness will form it anew. God is your individual consciousness. God is individual consciousness, and individual consciousness is forever creating and revealing Its own Self, as the infinite forms necessary to your demonstration or unfoldment.

So, whether your good is appearing to you today as a gift from someone, or as a salary, please learn to look through it, to the actual Source, so that you do not become dependent on it. Never become dependent on it. Never become dependent on your salary, on your job, on your dividends, on your husband, or on your wife; even while they may be the avenue through which your good is appearing at the moment. Learn not to be dependent on them, but to look through them and see God as the Source of your good unfolding to you.

We, in our work, must find our complete oneness with God, so that *all* that the Father has makes itself manifest as our individual experience, regardless of what is going on in the world around us—

whether or not it blows up, or whether or not there is enough rain for the crops. We must find our oneness with God.

I call to your attention this statement of the Master: "I have meat to eat that ye know not of."[1] Regardless of what seems to be going on in the outer world, I have an inner source of supply. It is an invisible Substance, it is true. But it appears outwardly as loaves and fishes, with which to feed the multitudes. It appears outwardly as a piece of gold with which to pay taxes. It appears outwardly as healthy bodies, where sick bodies seem to have been before.

Let us remember again that this Substance, God, which is individual consciousness, is forever expressing Itself and manifesting Itself as the things of this world. Therefore, we never have to worry about what happens to the things of the world. We must live and dwell in the secret place of the most High, dwell in the secret knowledge that we have meat the world knows not of, that we have within us a well-spring of water that will spring forth into life eternal:

I, the divine Consciousness of my being, am the infinite spiritual Substance of that which is to appear outwardly as an opportunity, as a sale, as a purchase, as a home, as a companion, as a husband, as a wife. Regardless of what the seeming human need may be, this Infinite Invisible of my own being is forever manifesting Itself in the form necessary, in all the forms, as all the forms, necessary to my unfoldment.

[1] John 4:32.

27

In this work, we learn to dwell in the secret place of the most High. We learn to abide in the consciousness of God, unfolding and revealing Itself as our daily experience. We learn to become completely independent of the world, and to realize that every one else in the world is just as independent, when awakened to his true identity. The secret is *true identity*. "Know thyself," the Greeks said. Find within your own being the realization of God as your being, as your substance, as your life, mind, and body, and then you will find that the whole world is free. As men awaken to that, they come into this same freedom from mortal, material, human limitation, from the sense of finiteness. And all of this comes, not through the intellect—not through intellectually hearing this—but through, and only through, the *spiritual discernment* of it.

CHAPTER TWO

REALITY OF SPIRIT

THE most important part of our work is finding the answer to the question, What is God? So long as we think of God as some kind of a super-man sitting on a cloud or a man on a cross or some unknown and mysterious being, we do not bring even a small amount of spiritual power into our experience.

Gratitude, appreciation, and recognition are a natural part of spiritual revelation and realization. Nevertheless, we might repeat over and over, "Thank you, Father" from now until doomsday; but unless we actually understand *what* God is, *who It* is, and *what It* is we are thanking, and *why* we are thanking *It*, such outward expression is of little value. What is It that we are acknowledging; what is It we are thinking about; what is It we are seeking as the source and foundation of our unfoldment? God—but what *is* God? For thousands of years God has been considered as something separate and apart from us. Today, however, we are no longer willing to accept a far-off God, because we have come to understand that God is the Soul of our being; God is the Mind, the Spirit, the very Substance of which we are formed. God is the center of our being. God is the infinite consciousness of our being. Our "Thank you, Father" is, therefore, not only an expression of gratitude, but it is a recognition and realization that the Father, or God, is the divine consciousness of our very own being.

The value of that recognition is that whatever we find to be true of God is universally true. It is true of us and it is true about every individual, everywhere, and at all times. "His mercy endureth forever."[1] This truth is universal and eternal throughout all generations. Whether we are thinking of people who, to our human sense of things, have passed on or whether we are thinking of people who are now on earth or those who are yet to come, remember this: God is their very own consciousness and they are always under divine protection, divine guidance, and divine illumination. We have no personal responsibility, therefore, toward them. To understand *what* God is, is to see God as the very life of individual being. If we realized God as the life of individual being, we would never again be concerned about whether anyone is, to appearance, alive or dead; because we would know and understand life as the only reality.

Conscious Awareness of the Presence of God Is Necessary

This leads us to another very important element in this work. The only benefit we derive from any truth teaching is through the activity of our own consciousness. Therefore, unless we understand every word of truth we declare, we are deriving no benefit from it. We must be consciously aware of the truth

1 Jeremiah 33:11.

of every statement we use. We must not be satisfied to be human beings walking up and down the street, believing that afar off somewhere there is a God with whom we can leave our problems. To say glibly, "Oh, well, I am going to leave it to God," as if there were a God out there to whom we could shift our problems is of little value. But we *can* leave our every problem to God, when, through a correct understanding of the revelation of truth, we rise to an understanding of the true nature and character of God. When we have a conscious awareness of the truth of being, God becomes the very activity of our being and we can then leave everything to God. In themselves, the statements, "Thank you, Father," or "I and my Father are one," are of no value; but the conscious awareness—our conscious knowledge of the meaning of those statements— makes them God-power in our experience.

Consciousness is God—your consciousness and my consciousness. One infinite, indivisible Consciousness, which appears individually as your consciousness and mine—this is God. It is the activity of your consciousness and mine which results in the fruitage of our harmonious daily experience. We cannot sit with a dull, sleepy, or thoughtless mind and believe that there is a God-power acting somewhere for us. God-power is the activity of our consciousness. This God-power appears as the activity of our consciousness. God-power is our consciousness at work, and it it is our consciousness when it is imbued with truth, an awareness of truth, and not merely the declaration of truth.

It is on this very point that truth students have

made some of their greatest blunders. They have believed that the recitation of these truths is a virtue or has power. This is an incorrect assumption. It is not the activity of the human mind that is power; it is the consciousness imbued with a knowledge of truth that is power. Jesus said, "And ye shall know the truth, and the truth shall make you free."[1] He did not simply say, "The truth will make you free." He could have said just that. A study of the words of the Master shows how sparing he was in his use of words and how very careful he was in his choice of words. He could have saved several words by saying, "The truth will make you free." But he did not do that. He went to the trouble of saying, ". . . know the truth, and the truth shall make you free." If we are to follow his teaching, we must become aware of the meaning of the truths that we read and declare and make these truths an active part of our consciousness, of our conscious awareness. Then they bring a *feel* with them, and that *feel* is the power made manifest.

Since Spirit is God, Spirit is real; Spirit is vital, alive; Spirit is allness. Spirit is totality. But although this is true, there must be a conscious awareness of the reality of Spirit. In that conscious awareness, we have the power that produces the harmonies of our daily experience.

Even before 1492, the oceans existed, and beyond the seas, rich and fertile lands. But to those who believed the world was flat, to those who accepted appearances for reality, the total extent of the ocean was only about eight miles. They looked out and saw

[1] John 8:32.

where the sky and the ocean met and, of course, seeing that, they believed that they could not go beyond that point. This limited sense, based wholly on appearances, actually bound them to the limitation of their own little country and the waters nearby.

All this time, in reality, there was no such limitation. Never once did the sky touch the water. The oceans, the seven seas, were always open and free for travel, and yet, for centuries, every person sat in his little corner, a prisoner to the idea of the sky's meeting with the ocean in the distant horizon. All this was changed by one man who was not blinded by appearances, but who, in turning away from appearances, reached the conclusion that the world was not flat, but round. Of course, if the world is round, the sky does not come down and touch the water, nor does the water rise up to the sky. The sky is always in its own place, and the water is in its own place. Neither one is a barrier to the other. That one man, through the activity of consciousness, through his unlimited vision, refused to be hypnotized by everybody else's belief. He, able to think independently, unhypnotized and free, caught the vision which enabled him to sail forth opening up new worlds.

So it is with us. If we sit back and give credence to the beliefs of the world just because people have believed them since time began, then we, too, are limited. Today most of us are limited by our sense of body; we believe that wherever we are at this moment is the extent of our being. Actually, that limitation has as little foundation as the limitation imposed on those who believed the earth was flat. A few have had the actual realization that they are not confined to a body. In that realization they can instantaneously be anywhere in the world: as a matter of fact, they are already there, only not consciously aware of it. We, as infinite individual consciousness, can be anywhere and everywhere in this world; but we have not as yet gained the conscious awareness of that fact.

It should not take very long to prove that we are not *in* the body. Let us look at our own feet, and then ask ourselves two questions, "Is that foot I?" or "Is that foot *mine?*" Let us wait until we have a distinct answer within ourselves. Let us not go any further away than our feet, and see if we can really find ourselves in our feet. If we are not there, then at least we shall have discovered that we are not confined somewhere down in our shoes or in the bones or flesh of our feet. Through this kind of an exercise, we shall come to the realization that that foot is not I, but *mine*. I *possess* my foot, but I am not *in* my foot.

Let us continue the journey and go to the legs. Are we in the legs or are they our legs? Are they not our vehicle, our possession, our instrument, the instrument we use at this moment for the purpose of walking? Let us be sure that we understand that we are not doing this just as a pastime. We are doing it because this little idea contains within itself the entire secret of life as it has been revealed for thousands of years. The fact is that we are not body and we are not *in* a body.

We go from the legs all the way through every

34

member of the body, until we reach the topmost hairs of our head. As we proceed, let us not hesitate to stop, at any or every point, and ask ourselves if this is I or if this is mine: Am I there? Am I in the muscles, the nerves, the stomach, or the solar plexus? Am I in the heart, liver, or lungs? Am I even in the brain, or is all of this *mine*? Is all this merely an instrument for my use? As we continue the search to find in what part of the body we are localized, searching tirelessly, the revelation finally comes to us, "I cannot find myself in this body. There is not a particle or part of this body in which I can find myself entombed. I am not there at all! All the time that I thought this was I, it was *mine*. I thought that when I looked in the mirror I saw myself. I never did. I saw only my body; I was not there."

We must understand this basic premise thoroughly because merely rehearsing it or agreeing with the author that we are not in the body will not be of much benefit to us. We, ourselves, must have the conscious awareness that we do not exist *in* the body; that we are not to be found inside the body, search though we may, from our toenails to our topmost hair. Having reached this conclusion, the next thing we must ask ourselves is, "Since I am not in the body, where am I?" Yes, that is the great mystery: Where am I? Who am I? What am I? One thing we shall immediately be sure of, and that is that we are not confined even to a room, and we are not confined to a body.

The next thing that must come to us is, "Since I am conscious of my body, and I am conscious of this room, and I am conscious of this building, and I am

35

conscious of my home, and I am conscious of my family, and I am conscious of my friends, and I am conscious of my business; then it seems to me that all I find is that I am conscious of this; I am conscious of that; I am conscious of the other. *What is there to me but consciousness?"*

Proceeding along these lines we find that our business is our consciousness of business; our home is our consciousness of home; our body is our consciousness of body. None of these things exists separate or apart from our consciousness. None of these things exists outside our consciousness. None of these things exists outside the government and the power of our consciousness. We learn, moreover, that the body exists only at the standpoint of our consciousness. If we were not conscious of the body, we would not have a body, or it would not be of any value to us, because we would not be conscious of it and, therefore, would be unable to use it.

Only that of which we are conscious is important in our experience. When we have no consciousness of body, it is as if we did not have a body, and we lose all interest in it. If we have no consciousness of our bank account, it ceases to be of any use to us. All the money we might have in the bank would be of no avail, if we did not have the conscious awareness of that bank account, where it is, and what its purpose is. Without this awareness, even a bank account would be of no value to us.

If we do not have a conscious awareness of the presence and the power of Spirit, It does no healing work for us. That is the reason one person is able to do successful healing work, while another fails. The only difference is that one has a conscious awareness of the Spirit which does the work, whereas the other has not yet attained that conscious awareness of the Spirit. It takes a *conscious awareness* of the Presence to do the work. Everything in this life is dependent upon our conscious awareness. It is logical, therefore, to say that *all there is to us is consciousness*. All we are is consciousness.

Developing Spiritual Consciousness

Our great purpose in life should be the development and unfoldment of our spiritual consciousness or spiritual awareness. For that purpose it becomes necessary for us to begin with the knowledge that we are not feet, legs, or torsos, but that *we are a state of consciousness*, appearing to the world as body. We are infinite consciousness; we are divine consciousness. Apart from consciousness we are nothing, but as consciousness, we are *infinite*. This we must understand. It is absolutely necessary first, to understand that we exist as consciousness; and secondly, to become conscious of this reality of existence.

As we look out through our human eyes and see only so much bone or so many pounds of flesh, then, of course, we cannot be satisfied with ourselves or with life. As we learn, however, through our developed spiritual consciousness, our awakened consciousness, to behold Him as He is, then we shall begin to see that we are not flesh and bone; we are consciousness. We can be satisfied with that likeness. That is the reason The Infinite Way teaches us

37

never to look at a person, but to look through him, especially through the eyes, where we can catch glints and glimpses of that light, which is the reality of being. We are consciousness: you are consciousness; I am consciousness. In proportion as we become conscious of one another—as we really are—then we enjoy one another, and each one of us takes his rightful place in the scheme of things.

Physical or mental healing is based on the belief that we exist somewhere between our feet and our head, and it attempts to do something about a physical existence. Spiritual healing has an entirely different basis. Spiritual healing is dependent on the individual's becoming consciously aware of the truth that we do not exist *in* the body or *as* the body, but that we exist as infinite, divine consciousness.

Jesus did not say that he was the body. He said, "I am . . . the life."[1] He did not say that he knew the truth. He said, "I am . . . the truth."[2] When we begin to understand what this means—I am life eternal; I am truth—then, we can also see that the body or anything else—music, paintings, sculpture, literature—can be the subject and the object of our consciousness;[3] and we can come into an awareness of it as it is, not as it appears to be to the unillumined or ignorant sense, but as it really is.

Here is the great wonder of this world and of this work: *There is a Christ.* Whether we call It the Christ of the Christians, Immanuel of the Hebrews, or Tao of the Chinese; there is a Christ. That Christ is

[1] John 14:6.   [2] John 14:6.
[3] This subject is dealt with more fully in the author's *The Art of Meditation*, Harper and Brothers, New York, 1956, pp. 123-29.

infinite, invisible presence and power. It is actually the seat of our being, the center of our being. It is the one divine, individual reality of each one of us. But to experience the presence and power of the Christ, it is necessary to be consciously aware of the Christ as the reality of our being, as the seat and source of our intelligence, our eternality, and our immortality.

From this time on, it will be less than useless for us to talk about the Christ, or about God, or about Spirit; or even to read inspiring writings about God, or about the Christ. We have been through thousands of years of hearing about God and praying to God and expecting to meet God in the next world. From this point on, the time has come for the actual realization and demonstration of God. We are making an about-face and we are recognizing the I-Amness of the Christ. We are recognizing the presence of eternal Life here and now—not in some future event, and certainly not in some past event which has gone beyond the possibility of recapturing. Our work lies in attaining the I-Am-ness of the infinite Christ. Christ has always been the infinite, invisible divinity, but we now come to the conscious awareness of the Christ as the foundation of our health, as the foundation of our wealth, as the foundation of the happiness of our home.

Realization of the Christ Appears as Form

In my work the treatment is always this: *realization of the Christ.* When I sit quietly and peacefully in a receptive state of consciousness, sooner or later,

I feel something within that I know to be the divine Presence, the Christ; and I find that It, that Presence, that Christ, meets these claims, whether they are mental, moral, physical, or financial. It, Itself, enters into human relationships, bringing peace where there was strife—that is, when that peace is desired. Many times people do not want the peace of the Christ. They want their own human will satisfied. They may want to see a fight settled amicably, but they want it settled on their own terms. A person may want his health, but he wants it, not the way by which the Christ may bring it to him. In anyone the Christ touches, It always dissolves the elements of sensuality, envy, jealousy, or malice. The Christ very often operates in our consciousness to dispel even inherited or environmental traits which are not conducive to spiritual living; but many people do not want that to happen to them. They want to hold on to their lust for power, their lust for place, their lust for money, or their lust for something else—and yet expect to get their healing, too. They want the healing, but they do not want to surrender the personal sense of self.

This does not mean that in our practice of The Infinite Way an attempt is made to discover what is erroneous in an individual's thought and then try to correct it. No, no, no! Never would we be guilty of trying to find out what error lurks in another person's thought. But, by abiding in this spiritual sense of truth, harmony, and peace, whatever of material or mortal sense exists as a state of thought is dissolved. The treatment, therefore, for anything and everything, is "Peace, be still." That is all. Just those words, "Peace, be still!" are enough if they come from a state of consciousness which is at peace and which has found the center of its being.

If I were to try to correct something in your mind or body, the treatment would fail. If, however, I forget the world and what is called form, and find my center of being—find my peace, the realization of the Christ—then quickly the answer comes, "I have been helped," or "I am healed." It was not anything which I knew, or any power which I, of myself, possessed; it was this Christ.

If we do not have this consciousness of the presence of the Christ, we lack the one element which does the healing work. The Christ is always present with us; the Christ is the reality of our being; but the need is for the *conscious awareness* of the presence of the Christ. We develop that through studying and hearing the Word, coming together with other students on the path, and the revelation within our own being brought about through meditation. Reading, association with others on the path, and meditation bring us to that state of consciousness where all of a sudden the inner realization comes, and the Christ unfolds and discloses Its glory to us.

Our consciousness of truth appears outwardly as form. This Christ, which is Spirit, appears tangibly as form. It may appear as a new heart or liver or lung for somebody; It may appear as a new bone in his body; It may appear as husband, wife, or companion; It may appear as an opportunity; It may appear as a parking place on the street. It appears in the tiniest forms—a little pin, if that is what is needed at that moment. We do not sit back and try to form it. We do not sit back and sigh that we are going to need the pin, parking place, or a new piece of flesh. Our only responsibility is to attain the consciousness of the presence of the Christ, the awareness of our oneness with the Christ. We sink back into our inner being; we feel ourselves at the center; and out of It flows the infinity of God. We do not direct It any place. We are just a center of peace, a center of Christ activity, a center of love, and a center of life. The more continuously we maintain that attitude, the more does that love appear outwardly as money, patients, students, customers, or whatever the need may be.

Our consciousness of truth appears outwardly as form; but we do not have to outline what that form shall be. We are required only to live and move and have our being in Spirit—to live as Spirit, as Soul, as Consciousness. We are responsible only for maintaining our spiritual integrity, and this is attained and maintained in the degree that we see Soul, Spirit, and purity, as the life and harmony of every individual. This means every individual, not every mortal.

We are not dealing with the mortal picture. We are not looking at it or trying to improve it. We are looking through it to the reality of being, with our spiritual wisdom, with our intuitive sense. Who, by searching, can find out God? Nobody. We never can find God with the intellect, our human sense, or our reasoning power; we find God only in our inner, intuitive, spiritual consciousness. In a moment of awareness, something within suddenly says, "No, it is not I, but He. I am He." Something within gives us the feeling of a divine Presence, of oneness. As we realize this, we spiritually discern the reality of our neighbor's being—even our enemy's being, since we are told that it really does not do us any good to know all this truth about our friends only; the scribes and the Pharisees did that. We, who have taken the name of Christ, must see that this is true, even of what appears to human sense as our enemy. Many of us think of an enemy as a person, but we have no greater enemies than death and disease. Ultimately, we must come to see through the illusory picture of death and disease to life eternal, and then we shall not experience death.

The world will go on experiencing the death of the body until, in consciousness, it overcomes the belief of death. In other words, as long as we entertain an awareness of death, that awareness will appear in the form of death. Our inner awareness appears outwardly as form. When we have the inner awareness of life eternal, it will appear outwardly as immortality, spirituality, harmony, peace, joy, power, and dominion.

Evil a State of Hypnotism

Does wrong thinking, then, appear outwardly as sin, disease, and death? No, it does not. It comes to us merely as an appearance or a belief, and we accept that appearance or belief as if it actually were an external form. Can a person who is hypnotized into believing that there is a white poodle on the hypnotist's platform, ever produce a white poodle there? No! All the hypnotized thinking in the world will not produce a white poodle. It will only produce an appearance or a belief which the victim claims is a white poodle. Wrong thinking will never produce sin, disease, or death. We are not creators; God is the creative principle, and It creates only Its own image and likeness. Our wrong thinking and the world's wrong thinking, therefore, will never produce sin, disease, or death. Such wrong thinking will only objectify the belief as an illusory picture like our "white poodle" and then look at it and say, "How am I going to get rid of it?" It is not even here, so how can we get rid of it? There is no such thing as sin, disease, or death; and all the wrong thinking in the world that we can do will not produce such things. But the universal belief in a selfhood apart from God does produce these erroneous pictures which we see as claiming to have substance, law, and reality; but which they do not have. All such pictures are as unreal as the white poodle which the hypnotized man believes he is seeing. Let us remember, he is not seeing it; he *believes* he is seeing it.

There is no way to remove that white poodle except to awaken the subject out of his state of hypnosis. How do we do that? One with God is a majority. If there were one person of spiritual vision in the audience who could laugh out loud and say or even think that there is not a white poodle to get rid of, the hypnotized man would awaken out of the dream. It is only because everyone is in agreement with him—the blind leading the blind—that it happens. If someone would consciously realize that he is merely witnessing a form of hypnosis, such a realization would quickly awaken him to the fact

44

that hypnosis is not a power. It is a *belief* in a power apart from the one Life.

Whenever we are confronted with any form of disease, sin, death, lack, or limitation, let us be quick to realize, "This is a hypnotic picture, and I do not have to do anything about it." In this way, we can very well have an instantaneous healing. Even if the healing is not instantaneous, our holding to that truth will ultimately reveal the harmony which already is.

We must realize that there is no disease: there is only hypnotism; there is only a hypnotic picture appearing as disease. Spiritual healing is not using truth with which to overcome error. It is not using the power of good to overcome the power of evil. Jesus answered the impotent man: "Rise . . . and walk."[1] This was not using a power to heal disease; it was saying, in effect, "There is nothing to be overcome." He did not use the power of God to do something to Pilate or to ward off the Crucifixion. He said, "Thou couldest have no power at all against me, except it were given thee from above."[2] Then he let the Crucifixion proceed and he proved life eternal.

A spiritual healer is not a person who develops a technique of using truth to overcome error or of using treatment to overcome disease. A spiritual healer is that state of consciousness, which knows that God alone is the reality of all being, and that anything else is a state of hypnosis. The recognition that he is dealing with a state of hypnosis, rather than with a person or with a condition, is the healing consciousness.

[1] John 5:8.   [2] John 19:11.

45

CHAPTER THREE

SEEING AND HEARING

The same day went Jesus out of the house, and sat by the sea side.

And great multitudes were gathered together unto him, so that he went into a ship, and sat; and the whole multitude stood on the shore.

And he spake many things unto them in parables, saying, Behold, a sower went forth to sow;

And when he sowed, some seeds fell by the wayside, and the fowls came and devoured them up:

Some fell upon stony places, where they had not much earth: and forthwith they sprung up, because they had no deepness of earth:

And when the sun was up, they were scorched; and because they had no root, they withered away.

And some fell among thorns; and the thorns sprung up and choked them:

But other fell into good ground, and brought forth fruit, some an hundredfold, some sixtyfold, some thirtyfold.

Who hath ears to hear, let him hear.

And the disciples came, and said unto him, Why speakest thou unto them in parables?

He answered and said unto them, Because it is given unto you to know the mysteries of the kingdom of heaven, but to them it is not given.

For whosoever hath, to him shall be given, and he shall have more abundance: but whosoever hath not, from him shall be taken away even that he hath.

Therefore speak I to them in parables: because they seeing see not; and hearing they hear not, neither do they understand.[1]

SPIRITUAL truth, when it is sown in the human mind, in the intellect, is not effective. A great many people. with highly developed intellects, many physicists and physical scientists, believe that God is a necessary adjunct to a well-rounded life and that the practice of religion is desirable. Few have had an actual religious experience in which they have felt the presence and power of God. Most of these intellectuals do not have the spiritual awareness which would make God a demonstrable reality; they are convinced that God is a necessity, but they are not yet convinced of God.

Truth, received through the intellect and remaining on the level of the human mind, regardless of how logical or reasonable it may sound, is not spiritual awareness. Even though we have ears—and we all have ears, physical ears—but do not hear spiritually; even though we have eyes with which to read all the books of spiritual wisdom which have ever been written; if we are unable to hear or see spiritually, we are missing the mark; we are missing the entire spiritual path. Truth remains a seed, that spiritual seed which is dropped on the barren soil of either material consciousness, mental consciousness,

[1] Matthew 13:1-13.

47

or intellectual consciousness, and it cannot spring forth into spiritual fruitage.

And in them is fulfilled the prophecy of Esaias, which saith, By hearing ye shall hear, and shall not understand; and seeing ye shall see, and shall not perceive:[1]

In this you see why this teaching is an entirely different teaching from other metaphysical teachings in the world. The Infinite Way is not just a method of acquiring a greater knowledge of truth; it is not merely knowing more truth. This teaching does not rely on any truth that we may know intellectually. Even in our treatment or healing work, the truths that we know with the human mind or the words that we declare with our lips are not power. Until we come to see that our good thoughts are not spiritual power, we shall not see that even the world's evil thought is not power.

There is only one power and that power is spiritual consciousness. God, divine consciousness, "hath not given us the spirit of fear; but of power and of love, and of a sound mind."[2] God has given us a consciousness, a Spirit, a sense of power—not mere words to declare. When we are confronted with problems of our own or those of others, let us not be too quick to try to find out what is true or what is false about the problem. It does not make much difference what the truth is or what the lie is. The letter of truth will not do the work. Intellectually knowing more truth will not help. It is the Spirit, the consciousness we entertain, that does the work. It is

[1] Matthew 13:14.   [2] II Timothy 1:7.

the ability, when looking at a human being, to perceive that which is not apparent to the human senses, and in that perception see through the individual to the Christ of his being. All of our work is the development of spiritual consciousness. It is not knowing more truth.

For this people's heart is waxed gross, and their ears are dull of hearing, and their eyes they have closed; lest at any time they should see with their eyes, and hear with their ears, and should understand with their heart, and should be converted, and I should heal them.[1]

Here is the whole story of the human world. It does not want its dollars, power, or position taken away from it. The world is afraid to listen to this message for fear that it might become convinced that war is not a necessity or of the needlessness of panics and depressions. It turns away from any truly spiritual message for fear that it might be convinced of its truth and then would have to discard such unethical business practices as misrepresentation or unfair competition. The men and women of the world are afraid to learn about spiritual truth, because they know that once they have been touched by the Spirit, never again could they do the same things in business, or in their home life, never again could they be the same to their families. Those who do turn to this path must not only receive this message through their ears and through their eyes, but they must be willing to perceive it spiritually, and then to live so as to carry it out into actual expression.

[1] Matthew 13:15.

But blessed are your eyes, for they see: and your ears for they hear.

For verily I say unto you, That many prophets and righteous men have desired to see those things which ye see, and have not seen them; and to hear those things which ye hear, and have not heard them.[1]

There are many sincere, earnest people, who try hard to catch some degree of spiritual awareness, and yet are not able to respond to the spiritual impulse. They may hear what we are saying or read what we have written; and yet, the truth does not take root in their consciousness. They want to feel the quickening of the Spirit; they have a deep love for God. I have seen many tears shed by people who have said despairingly, "I see it; I hear it; but why can I not *feel* it; why can I not understand it within me?" That is tragedy. That is sad. Ultimately, these people, if they can be patient and persistent in their search, if they will stay on the path, will find that their consciousness does open, and they will grasp spiritually what they now hear only with the ears and see with the eyes.

There are those, however, who have caught a spiritual glimpse of "I, if I be lifted up . . ."[2] These will find that all those who touch their lives, will, in a measure, be lifted into that consciousness also. When we are fed entirely from within, then we can go out and "feed the sheep," feed the others, feed those who are not yet ready for the experience themselves. Let us drink in the truth through the eyes and through

[1] Matthew 13:16, 17.   [2] John 12:32.

the ears, until it does open up the Soul, the consciousness, the spiritual awareness; and then, after that, we shall be ready to go forward.

Parable of the Sower

Hear ye therefore the parable of the sower.

When any one heareth the word of the kingdom, and understandeth it not, then cometh the wicked one, and catcheth away that which was sown in his heart. This is he which received seed by the wayside.[1]

There are many students who are able to understand spiritual teaching and to follow the spiritual path faithfully until a real problem touches them—and I mean real in the sense of depth, that is, a problem of health, loss, lack, or limitation—and then they fall away. That is when it becomes evident that the message has not taken deep enough root and that their consciousness has not responded to it. The spiritual sense has not unfolded sufficiently to enable the student to remain steadfast until the truth of the message is proven.

He also that received seed among the thorns is he that heareth the word; and the care of this world, and the deceitfulness of riches, choke the word, and he becometh unfruitful.[2]

This passage does not need explanation, does it? Our own fear of lack or limitation—the fear of the loss of our wealth, supply, or any form of materiality;

[1] Matthew 13:18, 19.　　　[2] Matthew 13:22.

or our fear of what may happen to our body, that it might lose its sense of well-being, suffer, or die—these are the fears which would choke the spiritual impulse and destroy it.

> But he that received seed into the good ground is he that heareth the word, and understandeth it; which also beareth fruit, and bringeth forth, some an hundredfold, some sixty, some thirty.[1]

We cannot hope to be the good ground which "bringeth forth, some an hundredfold, some sixty, some thirty," if we attempt to bring Spirit into earthly matters, to sow Spirit with the flesh. We must be that seed, that droppeth as the kernel of wheat that drops into the ground and dies, before the spiritual fruitage can be brought forth. We must die daily by giving up some fear or some sense of materiality. We can rise above earthly concerns into the Spirit, and watch the discords and errors of human existence fall away; but to try, for instance, to use Spirit for material purposes, is to miss the way. We cannot and we must not use Spirit to enhance our human existence. The human sense of existence must fall into the ground and die. Our prayer should be the same prayer as that of the Master, "Glorify thou me with thy glory." In other words: Show forth, through me and as me, spiritual perfection, spiritual life, spiritual peace, spiritual harmony.

The message of the Master was never for the glorification of the earth or earthly things. To seek only to make the body healthier or the purse richer

[1] Matthew 13:23.

would be to glorify humanhood, making it better humanhood, healthier humanhood, greater humanhood. No man loved his people more than Jesus loved the Hebrew people of his day. No one would have done more to bring them into their freedom than he would have done, and yet he made no effort to free them, either from Rome or from their own materialistic church. He said, "My kingdom is not of this world."[1] His efforts were all directed toward teaching them a spiritual message—a message which they could not learn through their ears. And Jesus warned against "vain repetition," hearing with our ears and speaking with our tongues. Rather we must listen for the still small voice and receive in the inner ear the spiritual message, the joy of the Spirit. The goal is not to reap joy, peace, and prosperity merely in the body or in our human affairs. Our object is to arrive at spiritual peace and a spiritual prosperity.

Spiritual Liberation

Peace achieved through treaties does not bring permanent peace. The only genuine peace, which will come to earth, will come through those who are awake to spiritual reality and who no longer reach out for purely material demonstration. Those will then be able to set the pattern which, ultimately, will liberate human consciousness. We have been told that if there be but ten righteous men in a city, then that city can be saved. Although this remains to be demonstrated, it is reasonable to believe that as

[1] John 18:36.

53

little groups here and there center their attention on spiritual unfoldment and spiritual demonstration, then, ultimately, the vision of "my kingdom," the spiritual kingdom, will spread.

If a little book like *The Infinite Way* can attain a world wide circulation, with no advertising whatsoever, without even book or department store sales to any extent, but all this activity the fruit of the seed within itself, is it not just as possible that this seed of Christ, of spirituality, planted in our consciousness, can and will spread all over the world, if and when we go out carrying it to the world?

I do not believe that any teaching of itself can do this for the world, but the Spirit alive in our consciousness can do anything and everything for the world. No teaching, regardless of how noble it may be or what lofty sentiments it may propound, can lift the world. It is the consciousness behind the teaching which is power. There were sixteen years of healing consciousness behind the book, *The Infinite Way*, before it was loosed to the world. The healing consciousness in that book, regardless of the message in it, is power, but how much greater work could the Spirit of Christ Itself do when It is present as a reality in our consciousness—not another message about Christ, but Christ Itself manifest as the consciousness of the individual. Then the message would spread a thousand times faster, a million times faster, than it has spread through *The Infinite Way*, through the healing consciousness out of which that book was written. When Christ Itself is made manifest in individual consciousness, that Christ will spread like a flaming torch from one to the other, until everyone has been touched by its light, fired with the Spirit, through the study of spiritual wisdom or by contact with an illumined individual. Then as individual consciousness ignites, the flame spreads far and wide, from one to another throughout the world.

I am one of those teachers who expects miracles in the next few years along the line of spiritual development. My first inner illumination was in 1928, and it resulted in my going into the practice of spiritual healing. But when the second experience came there was an even greater degree of illumination. It was an inner initiation and a conscious at-one-ment with spiritual power. When that happened, the Voice within revealed that there would be a work of a spiritual nature in the world and in that work a part was to be given to me. About every six months since that time, there has been another illumination and unfoldment, and each time a message has come with it, and a part to play in this work.

The work that has unfolded within me has brought the realization that, as the mind and consciousness of men are awakened, all worldly evil will fade into nothingness. Up to the present time, all great civilizations have reached their zenith and have then disintegrated and been destroyed. This could happen again. If it is not to happen again, however, it can only be prevented by those who receive the spiritual seed in their consciousness, permit it to develop, and then carry that seed of spirituality out into the world.

There is nothing more now in the intellect or in the physicist's laboratory that will save the world. The saviour of the world is the Christ, spiritual consciousness, that divine Love which flows from within. In the developed spiritual consciousness, there is such a sense of infinite individuality that no one would want to be subject to another or make another subservient to him. One is subject only to God, the divinity of his being. That is the reason why in our religious work we do not have an organization. Each and every student is completely free, so that only the Christ of his own being is that which demands his loyalty. We should be willing to serve the Christ of each other, but should not be willing to cater to people. In this developed spiritual consciousness, we love our neighbor as ourselves; we cooperate, and yet we are not under any bondage, any yoke, or any debt one to another. All our allegiance is to the Father within, to the Christ of our individual being.

Spirit a Universal Force in the Consciousness of Men

Let us meditate on "Not by might, nor by power, but by my spirit."[1] We begin with a realization of the power of the Spirit. We have complete faith and reliance on the power of the Spirit: the power of the Spirit to express Itself universally; the power of the Spirit to manifest Itself as health, wholeness, bounty; the power of the Spirit to manifest Itself as joy, peace, dominion, harmony; the power of the Spirit to be a transforming power, changing this mortal scheme of existence and even eliminating it, if necessary.

[1] Zechariah 4:6.

We are familiar with the power of electricity and we know the power of dynamite. We know the power of the atom. Now let us realize the power of that which is invisible to human sense, that which human sense finds it difficult to accept. Let us come to an understanding of what is meant by the term the Christ or the Spirit. Let us really begin to feel the Spirit, and to know Its presence, Its power, Its government, and Its jurisdiction. The Spirit is a power in the consciousness of men—not just of one man or two or three. Spirit is a power in the consciousness of men. If knowing the truth will make us free, then let us know the truth and its universality. The time has passed for us to be thinking of the power of the Spirit only in terms of redeeming our own little human existence. Let us turn from undue concern for our life or our body and begin to see and realize the power of the Spirit as a universal force in the consciousness of men.

What difference can it make about the next ten, fifteen, twenty, or thirty years of our human span? What is so important about them that we should be devoting our time and study to the things of the Spirit solely for them?

Let us see if we cannot catch the vision of the Master which was of a universal salvation, a universal Presence and Power, that would set all men free from material sense—material limitation, false appetites, false desires. Let us see if we cannot begin to understand that this infinite invisible Spirit appears as the health and the harmony of the universe; that this infinite invisible Spirit, Substance, appears as divine grace throughout the world, to all receptive thought, to all those who are spiritually minded.

If, then, we see God, the divine Spirit of the universe, as a universal Presence and Power, that will include within it the good of every individual, even our own good. That was somewhat the experience of Job in his praying for his friends. This is giving up using the Spirit, or God, for our personal purposes or our personal advantage. This is praying for the world. I see inwardly that we are spiritually one throughout the world; I see that there is an invisible brotherhood, an invisible tie, an invisible thread, reaching from individual to individual throughout the world, having its source and foundation in God. The Spirit, Itself, carries that message to all those who are receptive.

This message is the message the Master gave us. Undoubtedly for several hundred years that message bore great fruit: There were spiritual healings; there was great advancement; and no one can deny that to some extent the light of that message has seeped down through the ages to men and women of receptive minds. The message of the Christ has born rich fruitage in the literature, music, and art of the world. Christianity is exemplified in the more enlightened forms of government, and its spirit impregnates the great historical documents such as the Magna Carta, The Declaration of Independence, the Bill of Rights, and The Constitution of the United States. There is no question but that the message of the Christ has been leavening human consciousness throughout the ages, reaching and transforming the receptive thought.

It would appear that in this age the time has come, and the possibility is here, for a greater awareness of this universal Power, which up to now has been used too often for personal gain. Even in days of old, this spiritual message was hidden from the world in monasteries and in convents, where the priesthood could have it and utilize it, but it was given out to laymen very sparingly.

This age seems to be the age in which great segments of the population have reached a state of consciousness which is receptive and responsive to this message. It is penetrating and permeating consciousness and showing forth in fruitage. Throughout the world there is a spiritual awakening; there is a spiritual gathering; there is a spiritual rising. I can see that what is known to any one of us today is likewise known throughout the world to others of receptive and responsive thought. When I meditate, I often become receptive and responsive to spiritual ideas that are being entertained in consciousness elsewhere. We do not know but what the very things we are writing are being received out of the infinite divine Consciousness, because somewhere else other consecrated people are sitting in meditation, in conscious oneness with God, realizing the very message that we may be voicing through the words in this book.

Where do these ideas come from that are finding their way into these writings? Do they come out of the author's brain; do they come out of some personal contact with God? I should hesitate to think that that is true. No. It is because in heaven and on earth there are those who are devoting themselves to the message and the mission of the Christ. Wherever and whenever consecrated followers of the Christ meet, wherever and whenever they contemplate truth, wherever and whenever they realize truth, that Word becomes the instantaneous Word unto us—the omnipresent Word unto us.

There is no such thing in Spirit as time or space. Neither is there such a thing as minds many. There is only one mind. So this message, as it takes place in my consciousness this moment, will automatically be taking place in the consciousness of everyone tuned in to the realization of the Christ. In the same way, I am sure that much of what comes to me is really the conscious realization in the minds of consecrated souls in heaven and on earth; and it is my desire to be so in tune with the Infinite Invisible, or with the divine ideas that flow through all spiritual being, that I am merely a point of receptivity for them.

We, of one mind, are brought together for this message through our reading of this book. Does that mean that we are the only ones on earth? No. It means that throughout the world there are individuals and there are groups of two or three meditating and communing together. These groups are opening their consciousness to the Christ, seeking guidance and direction. And who can give it to them? Only the spiritually illumined can do that, those who themselves sit in meditation singly, individually, or collectively, realizing Spirit—Spirit expressing Its integrity, Its strength, Its power, Its protection. We can make that Spirit available to all those who lift their thought to It. We can make the power of God available to people throughout the world who reach up and say, "Oh, God, help me! Oh, Christ, where are you?"

Every such thought can find the spirit and power of God present through our realization, just as we are expressing it through the realization of others, either in heaven or on earth. So let us who have in some measure ceased being concerned so much about our own demonstration, let us devote some part of every day throughout all time, to the realization of the presence of God universally, wherever an individual opens his thought to any concept of God.

CHAPTER FOUR

ERROR

OUR conscious oneness with God constitutes our oneness with all spiritual being and idea. Meditation should result in the consciousness of the presence of God. This conscious awareness of the presence of God is the foundation of our entire experience.

Since God is infinite good, our being consciously one with God means that we are consciously one with infinite good. Then we do not have to try to get at-one with a good home, a good automobile, a good wife, a good friend, a good book, or a good teacher; we only have to realize at-one-ment with God, and God appears to us: God becomes visible and manifest to us as the good home, the good wife, the good automobile, or the good anything else that may be our need at the moment.

When we try to help ourselves or others through spiritual realization, it is the Christ that does the work; it is the Christ that dispels the illusion; it is the Christ that operates as healer, reformer, supplier. But what is the Christ? The Christ is our individual consciousness when that consciousness has been released from its fear, hate, or love of error.

Now let us put that into practical, usable form. Let us assume that there is a shadow on the wall. As we look at it, we can see that it is a shadow, and of course we do not hate it, or fear it, or love it. If I thought that that shadow were some kind of an evil presence, I might very well hate it or fear it; and if I thought it was a person, I might love it. Knowing it as shadow, however, I can neither hate, nor fear, nor love it: I look on it with complete indifference, knowing that its only existence is as shadow—virtually nothingness, without substance.

When I am called upon for help and recognize that the problem, whether physical, mental, moral, or financial, has no more substance than that shadow—that it is not power, it is not presence, it is not reality—that attitude is what determines my healing ability. That constitutes my degree of Christhood. When I can face any form of disease, sin, lack, limitation, or death and take the same attitude toward it that I do toward that shadow; with no desire to erase it, no desire to wipe it out, no desire to get rid of it or overcome it or rise above it, no desire to deny it; but merely with the ability to look at it and say, "You are a shadow, so what?" —then harmony is revealed.

We have nothing to offer the world except our spiritual integrity, and this spiritual integrity is our ability to recognize the nothingness of error. Spiritual integrity cannot be measured by the number of books we read or the number of human virtues we may possess. In ordinary metaphysical practice, it is the habit immediately to deny the error—if not in words, in thought; if not in thought, in attitude. A mental wall is built against it. In this work we reverse that. We do not put up any mental wall against a shadow; we are utterly indifferent to it;

divinely indifferent to it, if you will. We do not have to hate it, fear it, or love it, knowing that it exists only as the shadow of a belief, a mortal belief, a material belief, but having no more externalization or reality than that shadow. The shadow cannot be externalized into a reality; it can never be anything more than substanceless shadow. We cannot externalize an error. In our mesmerized state, we may *think* that we see a white poodle; we may *think* that we see a sin or a disease, or even that we *feel* one, but none of these errors has any existence as an externalized object; it has no existence as thing: it has existence only as a substanceless belief, shadow, or appearance in thought.

The degree to which we can look at that shadow, and not be disturbed by it, and not immediately have to say, "There is no such thing. It does not exist in reality," constitutes our degree of unfolded Christhood. There must be no resistance to error, since error is to be recognized as nothingness. Spiritual integrity, in a metaphysician who thinks of a sin or disease as something which must be removed, would consist in sitting up all night battling it, fighting it, declaring against it. If he did not do that, there would be no spiritual integrity in him, since in his thought is the belief that it really and truly exists. But spiritual integrity for us consists in the ability to say, "I am with you; I will be with you." The *I* is God. And this truth of the nothingness of error is omnipresent where I am and where you are. It is effective if we are consciously aware of the nothingness and the no-substance of error.

On the positive side, we could call this knowing the allness of God; yet the danger of just saying, "God is all," is that you have not yet accounted for the appearance, called sin, disease, death, lack, or limitation. Any church in the world, regardless of how orthodox it is, will agree that God is all; but in agreeing that God is all, it also agrees that there is something besides God. In the metaphysical approach, people are even more ready to agree that God is all; but they also have something besides God, and that something is a claim or a belief. Both see something other than the allness of God: the orthodox Christian with his allness of God is getting rid of a sin or disease; the metaphysician with his allness of God is getting rid of a belief or a claim. The name has been changed, and perhaps the changing of the name has helped to lessen our fear of it. It seems to be much easier to handle a problem by knowing: "Well, this does not exist as a condition; it is merely a belief, suggestion, or appearance." But you see that even in that recognition there is still the allness of God *and something*. Now let us go one step further and come to the allness of God *and nothing*. We achieve that state of consciousness not by declaring the allness of God, but by understanding the nothingness of that which we are calling nothing. So our spiritual integrity, then, is made manifest in our ability not to resist error, not to declare against it, not to put up a mental wall against it, but in our ability to respond with an unconcerned "So what?" in some form or other. Others may find more elegant language in which to say it; but it will still mean, "*So what?*"

No Resistance to Error

"Agree with thine adversary;[1] . . . resist not evil."[2] Although there are statements in Scripture that contradict that, those two statements represent the very highest Scripture. "Agree with thine adversary" and "Resist not evil" are used in the same sense in which we would say, when confronted with error: "Do not set up a mental wall against it; do not set up a mental rebellion against it; do not set up a mental denial against it; but learn to wait in silence."

Our love for each other is very great. The deeper we go in this work, the more we learn to love our patients and students because, as we come to know them better, we know the fine qualities they really have underneath their exterior. But that love does not manifest itself in pitying them because of their ills; it manifests itself in the realization of the unreality of these ills. We prove our awareness of this unreality in the degree of our lack of resistance to them, our lack of opposition to them, our lack of fighting them.

> The battle is not yours.[3]
> Stand still, and see the salvation of the Lord.[4]
> Open his eyes, that he may see . . . and, behold, the mountain was full of horses and chariots of fire.[5]

In other words, open our eyes that we may see that there is no enemy; there is no opposition. Those who

[1] Matthew 5:25. [2] Matthew 5:39.
[3] II Chronicles 20:15. [4] Exodus 14:13.
[5] II Kings 6:17.

66

are for us are more than those who are against us.

As a matter of fact, we have to go the full distance and see that there are none against us; but that what appears to us as an enemy, in the form of sin, disease, lack, or limitation, represents the universal sense which is always around us. The secret of healing work is found in this particular unfoldment, in this particular lesson. If error exists as a reality, every metaphysician is a criminal, because no metaphysician does anything to or for or about error— no matter what his form of practice. He does not give medicine; he does not manipulate; he does not massage; he does not operate; and therefore, actually he would be *letting* error alone to develop and grow and multiply, *if* it were true.

Our spiritual integrity lies in the degree of our awareness of the nothingness of what appears to be sin, disease, lack, limitation, and all the rest of the discords of human experience. We, however, must practice; we must develop the ability to look error of any form right in the face, and not get this thinking process of ours working, not permit it to engage in a campaign against error. Spiritual integrity demands that we develop the ability to sit back and agree with our patient and give the assurance: "Yes, I will be with you; I will be taking care of you." And certainly we will, and in no finer way than by not fighting the error.

While infection and contagion are not in and of themselves a danger, the belief that they are dangerous is power and makes people the victims of them. The person of realized Christ consciousness removes the visible evidence of infection and contagion through his spiritual integrity, which consists of his awareness that God alone is power, Soul, life, and that these other things, called infection or contagion, are not power. In the same way, the world has given power to bullets and to bombs, and in the world, they have the same power that infection and contagion have in the world which is unaware of its true identity.

Our understanding should include, above all things, the conscious awareness of God as the only power. That is the ability to say to Pilate, "Thou couldest have no power at all against me, except it were given thee from above";[1] the ability to say to the atomic bomb, "Thou couldest have no power"; the ability to say to those who would utilize or throw the atomic bomb, "Even your evil *thought* has no power."

Malpractice Is Not a Power

We know that malpractice is not a power, but we have all seen people made sick and die through malpractice. Now, what really did that? The malpractice, in and of itself, had no such power. Malpractice is wrong thinking or evil thinking. In and of itself, it has no power, since we could sit here all day long and say, "He is dead and he knows it; he is dead and he knows it"; but it would not change life. We could say, "He is sick; he is sick; he is sick"; but we could not produce a sickness with that erroneous thinking. If, however, we could induce a person to *fear* the malpractice, we could kill him with it. It has

[1] John 19:11.

68

been done over and over again. If we can make a person *fear* malpractice, we can destroy him with it.

That was part of the old Hawaiian kahuna teaching. They sent abroad the belief that some of the kahunas could malpractice and kill. The result was that if a person went to a kahuna for help, the kahuna would probably ask, "Well, now, is there anyone who hates you or envies you? Is there anyone who wants your wife or your husband or your money?"

"Oh, yes; yes, there is."

"Well, we shall have to get rid of him first, and then you will be free."

The person who was to be removed knew that his enemy had gone to the kahuna, and his belief in the power of the kahuna was so great that he began to tremble and fear, and in a few days was dead.

The evil thoughts of individuals or groups are without power, unless we, individually and collectively, give them power. It is an impossibility to give power to something without suffering from the belief that you, yourself, have accepted. Therefore, it is always your own belief that is malpracticing you, not somebody's thoughts about you.

The world is entertaining false beliefs which are so universal that they constitute a universal malpractice. From the moment of conception, everyone comes under the universal theological belief that the life span is three score years and ten. At the same time, he also comes under the medical belief of a life expectancy of only sixty or sixty-five years. Now, those beliefs operate, and they act upon us, unless we ourselves consciously realize:

69

All power is in divine Intelligence, divine Love, the divine Consciousness of my being. The place whereon I stand is holy ground, since God is the very mind and life of me. Therefore, no law acts upon me but my consciousness, which is the law unto all creation. Nothing can affect me, except in the degree of my reaction to it. It is not *it* which has power; it is my reaction *to it* that has power.

It is our *reaction* to every person, circumstance, or condition that is power. It is like that word "temptation." So many people have found themselves in trouble through temptation. They have been tempted with money; they have been tempted by power; or they have been tempted by something else. But temptation in and of itself is not power. It is our reaction to it that gives it power. There is where the power lies—in our reaction to it. If a person can learn to be governed by the divine Consciousness of his being, he will not react to anything in the external. Therefore, he will not react to universal fears.

To fear infection or contagion is to react to the belief about them. To fear human thought, whether individual or collective human thought, is merely to react to a belief about it. But to establish ourselves in Christ, to establish ourselves in Truth, means to come to the realization:

I am centered in God. Nothing can enter, that can in any wise defile or make a lie. I and my Father are one. There is no power reaching me from outside my consciousness—no good power and no evil power. All power is flowing through from within my own being. And it cannot be an evil power, since God is the life and Soul and consciousness of my being. Even if there were an evil human thought in me, or flowing out from me, it would not harm anyone, because it would not be power unless the person toward whom it was directed gave it power by reacting to it.

Any type of error represents individual or collective human thought or belief, and our harmony is dependent on our own reactions to these beliefs—regardless of whether or not we are dealing with depressions, disease, or periods of national unemployment. If we see that disease is not a power acting upon us, but that it is a belief to be disregarded like the shadow on the wall, then we become the law unto the shadow, and it can do nothing to us. And it could not anyhow, unless some of us mistake the shadow for a ghost, and have a convulsion.

Most of the major books of The Infinite Way contain chapters on "The Nature of Error." There are people who object to this emphasis on the nature of error. Most truth students like to say, "Well, it is not real; why bother about it?" Years of practice, however, have revealed that if we do not bother about it, it will be bothering us. It is only in the degree, not of our *neglect* of it, but of our *understanding of it as nothingness*, that we are freed from it. To look out of the corner of the eye and neglect the shadow leaves us at the mercy of the belief about it; but to look it squarely in the eye and say, "I know you; *you are shadow*," is awareness; that is understanding; that is facing the situation. That is why so many denials in

71

metaphysics are so useless. We get into the habit of saying, "There is no disease; there is no sin; oh, it is not real!" That does not do anything for us.

The Secret of Healing Is Reaction

The thing that helps is to come into an actual awareness of the unreality of error and to realize *why* it is unreal, what makes it unreal—that it is unreal because in and of itself it never was anything. Our reaction to it is where the training comes in— not in doing something to error, but in developing our reaction to it to the place where we can actually look at it and say, "Thank you, Shadow!" All of this leads us to that point in which there is no mental resistance to error. That is wherein this work differs entirely from much metaphysical teaching. We are developing ourselves to a point of non-resistance to error.

We do not look to a person for fairness, for fair play, or for justice. There again is the evil or the error in a great deal of the present day teaching, especially when people have legal cases. It is the practice to see the judge or the jury as having the mind of God; but that is an impossibility, because it is an attempt to put spiritual qualities into human beings, and it cannot succeed. An entirely different result is achieved when a person enters a courtroom knowing that there is no judge and there is no jury; there is only God, manifesting Its own individuality, God expressing Its own presence and not a person or persons displaying God qualities. So often metaphysical practice comes down to the human level and tries to see a human being as if he were spiritual. A human being will never be spiritual. A human being will always be a human being, until the spiritual nature of his being wipes out the human aspect, and divinity, itself, becomes apparent.

Again I am repeating: Watch that you do not immediately react and try to deny or overcome or resist error, but in the presence of any phase of error, be quiet, and listen for the unfoldment or revelation of Truth to come through to replace the erroneous appearance. "I can of mine own self do nothing. . . .[1] For my thoughts are not your thoughts, neither are your ways my ways."[2] Human thought is not power, even when it is good. In the presence of any erroneous situation, try to do no thinking, but do a great deal of listening. Take the listening, receptive attitude.

When we come to this place in thought where we do not start denying the shadow, but where we know the unreality of all forms of sin, disease, and death and know that they, in and of themselves, have no power and can do nothing to anybody, except in the degree of our response to them; we have come to the Christ.

Regardless of what my needs may be in life— whether that need be for a dollar bill, a taxi, an automobile, a home, a wife, companionship, opportunity, business, or an employer or employee—it is the Christ that will produce it. The Christ is omnipresent; but it is the degree of my *conscious awareness of the Christ* that will provide for the need. The degree of my consciousness of the presence of God

[1] John 5:30.   [2] Isaiah 55:8.

73

will appear as whatever thing or person is necessary in my experience.

Remember that God is omnipresent. "Whither shall I go from thy spirit? . . . if I make my bed in hell, behold thou art there."[1] There is no place to flee. Here and now, God is. Where I am, God is. All that God hath is mine. But none of that knowledge is of benefit to anyone in the world, except in proportion to his conscious awareness of that truth. We can have a million dollars in our pockets and not be able to buy lunch with it, if we do not have the consciousness of the presence of that money in our pocket—if we do not have the awareness of its presence, and what it can do. In the same way it is possible to have all the God there is in the world, and yet get sick and die, unless we have the absolute conscious awareness of the presence of the Spirit.

Ever since our beginning as human beings, we have not had that conscious awareness of the Presence. Even if we have been voicing it—even though we have been saying, "Oh, God is everywhere! God fills all space! God is everywhere!"—yet we have had sin, disease, lack, and limitation, all the while we have been making those statements, showing that the statements are mere statements, and not a matter of conscious awareness at all. As statements, they are of absolutely no value.

But to have the conscious awareness of those statements, makes it a different story. In that awareness, I do not have to fear sin or disease or anyone's calculations or miscalculations. As I learn to cultivate the listening, receptive ear; as I develop this

[1] Psalms 139:8.

74

ability, this power of silence; as I maintain the mood of expectancy within my silence and my stillness and receptivity; all of a sudden I feel something which is like a deep breath, or a sigh; or it may come in some other form, because to each one God appears in an individual way.

Sometimes the Spirit draws a picture, but ninety-nine times out of a hundred it appears to me only as this little gasp, almost a deep sigh; and when that happens it is as if my whole body and arms were just being filled with a soothing warmth flowing through, or a warm stream of water coursing all through my body. It is the conscious awareness, or feeling, of the presence of God. It may be a light, tingling sensation, but more often it is just this little sigh. Now, that, to me, is conscious awareness of the presence of God. That is God announcing Itself, declaring Its presence, or making me aware of Its presence. That is God's way of telling me that I am on the beam, and all is well.

Then watch the miracle. Watch Spirit perform all the functions of my existence and yours. It is the Spirit that performs all healing work. It is not my reaching out to your thought. It is not my pumping thoughts or statements of truth into you; it is merely my ability to sit and become one with the Father, and then let the infinite invisible Spirit appear as whatever healing or corrective influence may seem to be necessary.

Once this Spirit is made manifest, it will appear as whatever the need of the moment may be: It may be dollars; it may be a home; it may be a book to write or to purchase; it may be a teacher to find.

Whatever need appears, the fulfillment appears soon after the realization, recognition, or feeling of the Presence has been made manifest. The Spirit of God appears tangibly as form; or rather, let me put it this way: The consciousness of the presence of Spirit appears tangibly as form. The Spirit was there all the time, but it did not do anything: It was the conscious awareness of It that brought the results.

Establishing the Consciousness of the Presence

Consciousness, or the conscious awareness of the presence of the Spirit, appears in tangible form. The consciousness of the presence and the power of God appears as fulfillment—as the fulfillment of everything that can ever be needed in my experience and yours.

In the morning, therefore, before you leave your home, wait until you have felt that little answering "click" that says to you, "*I* am on the field; *I* go before you." It does not have to say those words to you, but it means exactly that: "*I* will go before thee, and make the crooked places straight. *I* will take care of all the problems of the day. *I* will be out on the road seeing that the lanes are kept open." That conscious awareness of the presence of God appears as every phase of harmonious experience throughout the day. However, because of the hypnotic influence of universal thought and belief, it is necessary that we establish and re-establish our conscious awareness of the Presence over and over again.

When once we feel the conscious presence of God, let us not think, "Oh, now I am all right forever and forever." You are not. Go back and get the feeling again in the afternoon, if you can, and do not retire without it at night. Never retire without it at night, and for this reason: Sleep is the next stage to death. When you sleep at night, you virtually die, except that the depth of your dying is not quite so deep as death itself, and so you do come back from it in the morning. The interval of sleep is really only a light form of total unconsciousness, which is death. The word "death" means totality of unconsciousness, and, therefore, sleep is the next thing to death itself.

No one on this path should ever go to sleep in total unconsciousness or death. Before going to sleep first establish a conscious awareness of the presence of God. Then you can let your body go to sleep or rest, or stay awake all night; but it will never disturb you whatever it does. The body does not sleep. It is just as dead when it is awake as when it is asleep. It is our sense of things that really sleeps. If we were to stay awake twenty-four hours a day in the conscious awareness of the presence of God, the body would go on functioning with the same regularity and ease.

When you attain the sense of God's presence, this "click," before you retire, you may sleep, or you may not sleep. It does not make any difference, but if you sleep it will not be an unconscious sleep. It will be a lying back in bed and a resting of the body, but the consciousness will be functioning even though to appearances you are asleep. You will find that, sometimes, you receive your greatest spiritual illuminations during your sleep, since your con- sciousness is not asleep: it is only your body that is at rest.

CHAPTER FIVE

THE I THAT I AM

ON the spiritual Path you will be tempted, not a hundred times, but a thousand times, to believe in a selfhood apart from the *I* that I am; you will be tempted to believe that you are that selfhood, or that your son or your daughter is a selfhood separate and apart from God. Each time it will be an effort to remember: *I* is God; *I* is infinite being: *I* is infinite individuality. Then when you have achieved that realization you can rest—but only for a few minutes, until the next temptation comes along. You will not solve all your problems by an intellectual agreement that *I* is God, that *I* is infinite, and therefore, that *I* is infinite wealth and infinite health. Ultimately, that truth will solve all your problems, but not until it has been rooted and grounded in your individual consciousness.

As inspiration pours through, as the light comes in, we are lifted into a realm beyond this world; it is almost like living in a dream. But it is not a dream; it is living in reality. However, the difficulty is that every once in a while we come down to earth—we come down to earth, either because our own body starts to make a noise, or someone else's body or pocketbook does. Then it is that we become

79

responsible for the re-establishment in our own thought of our true identity.

The secret of discord and the secret of harmony lie in understanding true identity. Regardless of how many books we may write about it, or how many different ways it is presented, the secret is: *I* is God, and not man. *I* is consciousness, and not body. *I* is life eternal: It was never born; It will never die. This truth must be established in your consciousness. Each time error hits up against your thought, in one form or another, it must be rejected with that ultimate realization: *I is God consciousness*. That *I* is infinite, eternal, and all-inclusive; It includes within Itself every idea of rightness. But remember, It contains no thought, no feeling, no trace of anything less than ultimate perfection; and remember, also, all that God is, I am. "I and my Father are one."[1]

Every time a call comes—not only a call from patient to practitioner, but a call of the world, a claim of the world, a belief of the world, whether in the newspaper, on the radio, through the air, or through friends—work until the *I* has been consciously established as the reality of your being; and therefore, you know that nothing is true of you save that which is true of *I*.

See what happens then in the handling of problems. Problems disappear, since *I* can have no problems. My consciousness, which is God consciousness, can have no problems, and this truth eliminates from belief everything unlike itself. This means that there is work for us to do, as well as moments of sitting on a cloud. We really have work to do in the training of

[1] John 10:30.

80

our consciousness. And that entails something else.

All of us, as human beings, have traits of character built up by our environment, education, and experience, which do not fit in with the *I* that I am; therefore, it becomes necessary to take ourselves in hand and learn to govern and control ourselves so that we bring all things into alignment with the *I* that I am. If by nature we are fearful and doubtful, if by nature we are envious or jealous, we should not try humanly to make ourselves over; we are not going to be psychologists and say, "I have this evil trait and I must replace it with this good trait." I do not mean that. But I mean that in the constant realization of the *I* that I am, we recognize what seem to be our human weaknesses and we permit those traits to disappear and fade out of the picture.

We do not substitute a good human quality for a bad one; but in the realization of the *I* that I am, we learn to *let* the erroneous human traits drop away. Do not make an effort to get rid of them; but let your effort be to live in the *I* that I am. That will take care of everything. The moment you try to get rid of a negative human quality, you will find yourself with ten times more of such qualities than you had before.

This point is well illustrated in the story of the wealthy Hindu who was reaching the latter stages of human experience. He realized that he had lived a life of indulgence and that now he must get ready to meet his God. And so with all seriousness he went to visit a great master. With a serious face, he said, "Ho, Master! all my life I have wanted to know God;

I must know God. Will you teach me about God?"

Of course, the teacher could see that this man was not interested in God, but that he was trying to buy a little corner of heaven for himself. The master did not want to waste time with that kind of person; he would not cast his pearls before swine. So he replied, "You have the wrong impression. You think God is something difficult to find. You think that you require a Master to help you find God. That is not true at all. Finding God is very simple. Just go home and find a quiet corner of your room, and then do not think of blackbirds. Do not think of big flocks of blackbirds; do not think of little flocks of blackbirds; do not think of a dozen or six or four blackbirds. Do not even think of one blackbird—not even a single blackbird. Then, when you have succeeded in eliminating all thought of blackbirds from your consciousness, you will have found God—God will be right there." You know what happened, do you not? Instead of not thinking about blackbirds, the wealthy Hindu gave birth to blackbirds by the millions.

Many of us have had the same experience. In trying to overcome sensuality or false appetite or greed, in making an effort to get rid of erroneous human traits we have found that they multiplied themselves over and over and over. Do not try by an act of the will to eliminate these errors; do not condemn yourself for any false or negative traits you may have; do not plague yourself. Be satisfied to see them evaporate in your constant awareness of the *I* that I am. Do not try to get rid of negative qualities; do not try to get rid of evil human qualities or traits. Be satisfied to see them dissolve and disappear of their own nothingness, as you abide in the secret place of the most High, as you abide in the consciousness of the *I* that I am.

Human Goodness Is Not Spirituality

The more you learn to identify yourself with the *I* that I am, instead of with body and human experience, the more spiritual qualities will you show forth in your experience. If I were to try to be a very good human being, I would fail. But if I try to forget my humanness and abide in the *I* that I am, and realize that *I* is God, then It asserts Itself in the body, in the thoughts, and in the actions that flow forth.

That brings up a very important point—a very difficult one for most people to see. It takes the spiritual life to reveal to you that this is the truth. *Your good human qualities are no more spiritual than the evil ones.* Yes, humanly, your good qualities are better. It is better to have good human qualities than to have bad ones. But these qualities are not spiritual. Spirit transcends all human goodness. Spirit is something entirely different from human goodness.

A person may be a fine, high type of human being today and tomorrow succumb to some temptation and be evil. Human goodness can become evil. For instance, charity can become evil and so can security. Social security can be a hindrance to those on the spiritual path, although this need not necessarily be so.

The moment that a person knew that he had a

83

hundred dollars a week income for life, if he were not well-grounded in the spirit, he might place his dependence on that income rather than on the Infinite Invisible. People have said to me that practitioners ought never to have to earn their living in the practice; they should have an income outside of and independent of the practice. That is wrong. Nothing could be more harmful to some practitioners than to have a private income, because then they would not be relying on the Spirit; they would be relying on their income. It is just as incorrect to rely on an income for your support as it is to rely on your patients. And of course, you know that it is absolutely wrong to rely on your patients or your students for your support.

There is no genuine practitioner in the metaphysical or spiritual field, except the one who is dependent on God. The supply may seem to come from an income or it may seem to come from a patient or a student. It is perfectly legitimate for it to come in any of these ways. But *relying* on it is the evil. Many practitioners who have an independent income are apt to rely on that income and not on God. They may fool themselves into believing that they are relying on God, but most of them are placing their trust in their income. On the other hand, there are some practitioners and teachers with wealth, who have not succumbed to the temptation of believing that that wealth is their supply. They have the consciousness of the truth that God is their supply, and then, their wealth is no detriment to them. But ordinarily speaking, having an income or having wealth may lead, and often does lead, to a reliance on it instead of on God. So you see that, at times, human good may bring about evil in our experience. Therefore, for us, it becomes of paramount importance to realize that all power is in God. All power is in Spirit.

Sometimes the belief that evil is power, as, for example, belief in the power of evil thoughts, will lead to the opposite belief that good thoughts are also power: evil thoughts are a power for bad; and good thoughts are a power for good. Do not believe that. All the good thoughts that mothers have had for their children have not kept their children from experiencing illnesses and accidents and death. All of the good human thoughts that we think about our mothers can never save the mother from pain, discord, or disease. All the human love we could bestow upon each other, good as it is in its way, is not the spiritual ultimate, because it is not power. No matter how much you love your mother, your sister, your brother, or your child, that love, in and of itself, is not spiritual power; otherwise, it would be raising them from the dead, or raising them from the sick bed.

Spiritual Love versus Human Love

Spiritual power is something separate and apart from human love. Spiritual power is not something you possess, to give or withhold; it is the gift of God, and when realized by you, it operates in the experience of those with whom you come in contact. Do you not see that a practitioner does not have to love his patients humanly in order to help them?

Do you not see that a practitioner never should love his patients or his students merely on the human level of love? The love should be the love of God, and be universal, impersonal, and impartial; then when the patient or the student requires a lift, that divine Love is there to lift him; whereas human love could never do that.

Let us remember that human hate and human love are not power. Human hate is a quality that we all want to see disappear from the world, and be replaced with human love. We who are on the spiritual path, however, must learn to rise above human love to the divine Love—that Love which is impersonal, impartial, and universal. Almost every one in the world is saving money, so far as he is able, for his children, for his grandchildren, or for those who are to come after him. But how many of those people, except those few who are in the bracket of the multi-millionaire, are dividing a part of their wealth with the children who are not their own, or the grandchildren who are not their own? How many are taking even a thousand-dollar estate and dividing half of it in a universal sense of love? No; no; no. Usually the person with one or five or ten thousand dollars, leaves it to one, two, or three persons, and those one, two, or three, his own children or grandchildren. There is no sense of universality or divine love in that. That is the same as if we were taking our income and spending it on ourselves and our family. There is nothing spiritual about that, nothing loving about that. It indicates a degree of selfishness, not love.

We, at some time on our spiritual path, must

begin with some sum like five percent or ten percent of our income, and learn to spend it in a universal sense, to spend it on something that is of no benefit to ourselves or our family—something that is universal: for education or religion; or for the children of those who cannot afford things; or for orphans or for old people. It must be for some purpose that is impersonal and impartial. Sooner or later as we do that with five percent of our income, or ten percent, we shall find ourselves doing it with fifteen percent and with twenty percent. There are people who are giving eighty percent of their income to some impersonal, universal purpose and are still finding sufficient for themselves and their families.

Human love would force us to take all that we have and spend it on our own loved ones. Universal love permits us to begin, at least in a small degree, to be impersonal and impartial with our money, thereby saying that this wealth is not ours, it is of God; and because it is of God, it belongs to the world; it belongs to the world of God's children.

Spiritual love shows us how to be impersonal and impartial in our love. It shows us how God's rain falls on the just and the unjust. It shows us how the impersonality of God's Word is expressed. It shows us why we can heal sinners as well as saints; and that sometimes it is easier to heal sinners than it is to heal saints, because the saint, as a rule, represents a high degree of selfishness. Watch this. It is one of the most difficult points on the spiritual path. Spiritual love is very different from human love; spiritual love transcends human love; and yet spiritual love is made manifest in human love. It is a mystery and a paradox.

If every truth student in the world would begin to express spiritual love, we could raise the world in one generation. But we have to begin with ourselves, since the *I* is God. We are the ones who must express the love of God—not the love of man, but the love of God. We must express that love universally, impersonally, and impartially. When we express that kind of love then we shall know why human hate or human fear is not a power. How can it be a power over the *I* that I am, which is God? But how can I be claiming for myself *I*-hood, Christhood, when my entire experience is centered around demonstrating things for myself and my family?

In this work, we learn not to draw love *to* us but to let it flow *out from us*. We learn that God is not a power that is outside of ourselves, and yet God is universal power. God forbid that God should do anything exclusively for one person. God is universal law which must be manifested and expressed as you and as me individually, if we are to claim that *I* is God. We cannot say that of the personal I. We must not make such a statement and then later deny it in practice. Once we have made the statement that *I* is God, we have to bring our life into conformity with it. If we accept this teaching, we accept the fact that the *I* is God, and then, each of us has to begin living as if *I* were God. That means to stop living *to* me, or attempting to draw good *to* me; and instead, to begin living out *from me*, and to include the universe in my love—not just my wife, my children, or my grandchildren.

The *I* which is God never criticizes, never judges, never condemns; and when It does appear to do those things, it is not for the purpose of judging, criticizing, or condemning; but in order to bring to light the error of the situation, that it may be transformed. There still persists a teaching in some metaphysical movements that there is a mental cause for physical effects, such as that resentment causes rheumatism or that hate causes cancer. I do not say that in criticism, judgment, or condemnation, but only to point out the error of the teaching. Never criticize, judge, or condemn, merely in the sense of criticizing, judging, or condemning; but use your criticism, judgment, or condemnation as a constructive power for the purpose of exposing the error and correcting it.

The *I* which I am is the source and center of the world's good. The *I* which I am is that point at which all the infinity of God pours Itself into the world. Reverse yourself. Stop living as a human being, utilizing the things of God for your own benefit. See yourself as that place in consciousness through which God pours Itself forth to the world— to that world which is not yet aware of its true identity. Just as the lighthouse is established for the benefit of the ships that must pass by and have the benefit of its direction, so are we the light of the world, that those not yet aware of their true identity may be lighted on their way.

Spirit Reveals Itself in the Silence

I want, above everything else, to emphasize the fact that human evil is not evil and human good is not good; human evil is not power and human good is not power. Now, when we are called upon in any experience of our own or another's for help, please remember, first of all, that no amount of human power, no amount of good human thinking, is going to solve the problem. There is a Spirit in man that does the work, the Spirit Itself, that Spirit which is God. We may as well get used to the idea of sitting patiently with ourselves, silently with ourselves, until that power of the Spirit comes forth and does the work. No amount of human good-will, no amount of human love, is going to help us lift another's burden, spiritually. No amount of human good thinking, is going to help us heal another's diseases or infirmities. It is the Spirit of God made manifest as our individual consciousness that does the work, and we must become imbued with that Spirit. We do that in silence, in meditation, not through being good human beings or moral human beings or by taking pride in how good we are. There is a Spirit in man: That Spirit is in the good man and that same Spirit is in the sinner. "God is no respector of persons."[1] God is omnipotent and omnipresent; God is our very own consciousness awaiting our recognition. The moment we turn to It, whether we turn to It as a good human being or a bad human being, It begins to manifest Itself and, from that point on, It dispels all of our qualities of evil and many of our qualities of good.

I am receiving letters every day in the week from people I have never met, telling me what the reading of The Infinite Way literature is doing for them and

[1] Acts 10:34.

how it is affecting their experience. These letters tell me how things which had been wrong in the lives of the writers have been righted, and how things have smoothed out in their human affairs—in their physical and in their bodily affairs—since applying these truths. They are, evidently, among those people who took my words in the chapter on "Meditation" in *The Infinite Way* literally and who, therefore, began to acknowledge their oneness with God from morning to night. Probably, they were the people who glimpsed the meaning of the chapter on "Immortality," and saw that immortality does not mean longevity in the flesh. It means the eternality of consciousness shown forth as a physical experience. As they embodied these truths in consciousness, they found expression in their experience.

Let us now consider what is known as the law of karma. Many people are held in bondage, in their own thinking, to the beliefs of their past. That is one of the most difficult beliefs we have to eradicate— this belief that our past human experience, even here and now on this plane, is acting as a law to prevent our further development. In all our treatment work, let us handle that suggestion specifically. Let us know that no human experience can ever find expression in our spiritual life.

When you wish to help anyone, *meditate*. Try to realize the presence of God. You will soon be able to carry on all healing work through meditation, simply through getting quiet within. Then when a problem comes—mental, moral, physical, or financial—you will resist the temptation to think thoughts, to make affirmation or denials, or to believe that in any way your human thinking has power. Catch this vision that your human thoughts are not going to heal anyone of anything. No matter how good those thoughts are, no matter how powerful they seem to be, they are only human power.

If you can realize that in meditation, in quiet, and in confidence, there is peace; in the stillness, in the joy of the silence, there is the presence of God to be realized; then you will have learned the whole secret of the seers, the saints, and the saviours. The greatest secret in the world lies in the word *silence*. That silence means the ability to sit in peace and let the divine realities unfold, to let God speak, to let the Spirit voice Itself, to let Truth express Itself. This does not mean destroying the human senses or the human intellect. It means utilizing them, using them, letting them be an avenue or a means through which you become aware of the presence of God. In meditation, in a peaceful and serene stillness, God makes Itself manifest as power, as presence, as healing, and as supply; but you see it is God that has to do the work. It is God, the divine Reality of our being, showing Itself forth in the glories of what appear as wonderful human experiences.

Learn the meaning of "Peace, be still." Learn to let this act as a treatment, and not be merely "Peace, be still" coming through the lips, but peace in the body and in the mind. The more you attain this reflective state of thought—this inner calm, peace, and poise—the greater the power of the Spirit that comes forth to transform your world.

Knowest thou not that *I* am with you? Know, also, that all that *I* have is thine. To repeat those words merely as statements, is not power; and we learn one day that they are not even true. That has been the tragedy of organized religion: it accepts such statements as truth, when they have not been proved in experience. The only true statements voice themselves to you in the silence. In that silence Truth, Itself, speaks and manifests Itself.

For a minister to preach these words or for a practitioner to tell them to you does not make them true. It is when the Word is with you and within you that it is power. Those who recorded the Word in Scripture received it within their own being, and that is why it became living water; but when we repeat the word of God through the lips it is only a quotation. Let us remember that. If you can hear within your own silent being those promises that are in Scripture, they will be a law unto your being, as they were to Elijah, and Elisha, and Paul, and all the other spiritual leaders.

You cannot find God in the intellect. God is found in the still small voice. And so, let the still small voice utter Itself to you, and then you will find that you have all the Power and all the Presence that any saint or seer has ever had. It is not your power; it is the power of God. We want to be glorified with God's glory. What we need is the power of God, expressing Itself *through* us and *as* us.

CHAPTER SIX

THE DIVINE CONSCIOUSNESS

"Lo, I am with you alway, even unto the end of the world."[1] "I am with you alway." That *I* is God. *I*, God, the divine Consciousness of my individual being, is ever with me. It could not be any other place and still be the consciousness of my own being; nor could I be separate or apart from consciousness, since without consciousness there would be no being; there would be no "I" or "me." *I*, divine Consciousness, will be with me, as long as I exist as an individual. As long as there is continuity to my own being, God, divine Consciousness, will be with me. In fact, *I* is all there is to me, manifesting Itself, Its glory, as my individual being. There is no It *and* "me." There is only It, manifesting Itself, expressing Itself *as* me. The Word, divine Consciousness, becomes flesh as individual me.

This oneness is the secret of immortality, of eternal life; probably, it is the reason for the word "alway": "Lo, I am with you alway"; *I* will be with you "unto the end of the world"—the world which Jesus overcame. "I have overcome the world."[2] There is an end to the world: the world is not immortal; the world is not eternal; the world will not last forever. What is this world that comes to an end? It is really

[1] Matthew 28:20.   [2] John 16:33.

not a world at all. The things that are of God are eternal and immortal, this world that "I have overcome" is not a world, but a false sense of the world, a false image, a belief about the world. Jesus, not even as the Christ, ever overcame anything that actually existed. He could only overcome a false sense about reality, a false belief about it. Therefore, until all false beliefs are eradicated, until the world has been overcome within ourselves, this Christ will be present to overcome it. When the world has been overcome, then it will be discovered, not that there was a Christ present to overcome it, but that *I am* that Christ.

Wherever we go, under all circumstances and conditions, remember that "I am with you alway." *I*, your consciousness of your own identity, have always been with you. You perhaps remember yourself as you were in kindergarten, primary school, grammar school, and high school. Always there was that which you called *I* looking out upon this world of experience. You were always there, observing and experiencing. If there had been no *you* there, there would have been no observation; there would have been no experience. You watched yourself in illness and in health; you watched yourself in childhood and in maturity; you watched yourself get married; you watched yourself in business and in the home. *I*, my identity, the realization of my true being, have always been there, watching everything I do, throughout the day. *I* even know when I lay myself down to rest at night. *I* am also there to put myself to sleep; to let myself rest. *I* am always present. *I* am always there.

Even people who to sense are dying, or passing on, have been known to say, "I am dying! I am going! I am going home. I am going to the Father." Always this *I* was there as conscious identity and as a witness even to one's own passing, showing that there must have been a part of "I" or "me" which survived even the experience of passing, since it was consciously aware of the activity of passing. Therefore, it was not dying, or death as we understand it, but merely a conscious passing from one form of experience to another. Follow this carefully, because this is the revelation of the conscious continuity of experience, and in this conscious awareness of conscious continuity, lies your ability to demonstrate eternality and immortality. This *I*—and It is really God, or the Son of God, called the Christ—is ever with you. And though you walk through waters, It will be with you; the waters will not cause you to drown. Though you walk through the fire, the flames will not kindle upon you. *I* will always be there as a witness to all that is going on; and if you accept It as such, *I* will be the Saviour, the Christ, or healing influence, to any and every experience. When you take *I* into your meditation, take it in this light of conscious identity, conscious continuity of identity, and watch the unfolding of the divine Idea as immortality, eternality, harmony, and perfection.

The Letter of Truth Does Not Heal

There must be such a degree of spiritual unfoldment that when a call for help comes, the realization of peace comes at the same moment, and comes without conscious effort. When it is necessary to resort to the process of remembering the letter of truth, even though release comes, the permanent healing may not always come with it. Here is the proof of the message of The Infinite Way: the letter of truth does not heal. You may go through the process of knowing truth as much as you like, and you may bring relief to people; but actual healing, especially healing of that which the world calls a serious condition, is brought about through a spontaneous and instantaneous realization of peace the moment the call comes, and sometimes even before the call comes.

This raises the question: How do we attain this state of peace when a call comes to us? It means actually living, moving, and having our being in that consciousness which is a state of peace. It means that, from rising in the morning until retiring at night, we are training ourselves not to accept suggestions coming from universal mortal belief. It means taking the statements of the Master and making them practical, even when they are are as nonsensical to world sense as not to sue your neighbor; or if he wants your cloak, to give him your whole outfit. All of these sayings of the Master— "Resist not evil"[1] or "They that take the sword shall perish with the sword"[2]—are to be embodied in our consciousness. We are to learn that, in our innermost being, we are not to oppose, not to fight, and not to wrestle; but we are to stand fast in the realization of Christ, of Omnipresence, of divine Love, as the healing principle of the universe. This Christ consciousness

[1] Matthew 5:39.   [2] Matthew 26:52.

97

can be attained, but usually it is possible only by learning the correct letter of truth as the basis for this state of consciousness.

Two letters written to students illustrate the importance of the correct letter of truth together with its limitations:

It was evident to me on the first reading of your letter that there is yet one thing lacking. So far as knowing truth is concerned, you know the truth. You have known all of the truth there is to be known when you have said, *"I am."* When you can realize that your body is a manifestation of all that *I am,* you are knowing the truth. However, you have included in your statement of truth the old erroneous belief that your body manifests your thinking. That is not true.

Since God made all that was made, and all that God made is good, does that not make it clear to you that your body is a God-made body, and is therefore perfect? You could not change that perfection, even with your thinking. What you have been speaking of as your body is not your body at all, but the mortal concept of body. It is a universal belief, not belonging to you.

Now, let us come to the heart of the situation. It is necessary that you experience the actual feeling of the presence of God, that you feel the "click," the answering response, or that you hear the still small voice. This should be your work from now on. Read a little, but read merely to give an impulse to your thought, and then meditate. Be still. Practice this only for short periods—

five, or six, or seven minutes—but return to it several times during the day. Turn within, and ask the Father to reveal Itself to you. Say to the great Within, "Speak, Father, thy servant heareth."

This second letter is to a practitioner who has found a response in her own inner being to *The Infinite Way* and my other writings; but she has been so trained in the mental processes of knowing the truth and repeating statements, that it is difficult for her to make the transition to that place where the student does not think thoughts in order to heal—*he merely becomes still and feels!*

I am working with you. This means that every day I take you into my work, not only as I meditate, but as the lecture and class work unfold. It is natural that the truth unfolding as my consciousness will, at the same time, unfold to you who are receptive and responsive to this work. That, you see, is the process that goes on when you treat others, and they receive a healing. You do not actually treat them in the sense of sending thoughts to them. This work is not a transference of thought. You do not transfer your thoughts to any one—send out good thoughts to them or send out thoughts of truth. But as you are receptive, and God, Consciousness, unfolds Itself to you as truth, those who have reached out to you for help receive that truth. Sometimes they receive it in a message or a word: sometimes they actually receive the same idea you are thinking; and at other times they merely see health restored. But

99

whether they catch an idea from you or from God or whether truth merely manifests itself as a healthy body, that is what has taken place. *Truth unfolding in and as your consciousness has become manifest as the consciousness of your so-called patient.*

Therefore, it is natural that the truth unfolding as my consciousness will at the same time unfold to you who are receptive and responsive to this work. This, of course, will bring to you that "peace of God, which passeth all understanding,"[1] and a wonderful sense of quiet, happiness, and confidence.

Problems all dissolve as this consciousness unfolds. Problems cannot disappear except as consciousness unfolds. Scripture says: "There shall no sign be given,"[2] and then it says, "These signs shall follow."[3] This means that we do not play the piano before we have taken piano lessons; but if we are faithful in our study of the piano, the ability to play follows. This is true of the demonstration of harmonious existence. In proportion to our spiritual discernment of the laws of life and Spirit, we are enabled to bring forth harmonious daily living.

You are recognizing problems, regardless of their nature, as universal beliefs. You are refusing to handle them in any other way, and of course, you are turning to God to realize the peace that comes from within. This is all correct. In your work, regardless of the nature of the work, or the

---

[1] Philippians 4:7.   [2] Matthew 12:39.
[3] Mark 16:17.

nature of the problem, when you go into your meditation, or what you may call treatment, be sure that you make the contact within you. Be still until you feel the response within. It comes sometimes as a still small voice, and at other times as the realization of God's presence, a recognition that God is on the field. Always remember that it is not that which takes place as the activity of the human mind that is the healing power, but the actual contact or realization of God. *It is the contact itself, the very realization of God's presence that heals.* It makes no difference what problem we take into the silence, as long as we receive the answering "click" or awareness of God's presence.

Does not this again show you what I mean by the fact that truth must be established in your consciousness as a principle? Otherwise, regardless of what word you may say to a patient or a student, it will not register. It must be an established state of awareness within you. Then it imparts itself to your patients or students, and, surprisingly enough, even if you do not voice it, even if you say nothing about it, they catch it. The mere fact that it is an established state of your consciousness makes it evident to them.

No Transference of Thought in Spiritual Healing

This work is not the transference of thought. Therefore, never in your treatment, never in trying to help someone, try to get your thoughts over to him. Never try to impress him with the truth. Never use the word "you" in a treatment. Never say "You are spiritual," or "God is with you." Never in any way do anything that would tend to act as a treatment which is transferred from one individual to another. When you fall into that habit, you are in the realm of mental treatment; you are in the realm of mind over mind, or mind over matter. That is not spiritual healing.

All of this truth, as we know it today, had its beginning in thought transference and in mental suggestion—one mind conveying ideas or thoughts to another mind. In the early days, as a help in the transference of thought, the body was also manipulated. The practitioner rubbed the top of the patient's head or sat knee to knee with the patient, or spinal cord to spinal cord. Students and workers, during this experimental stage, believed that through the magnetic channel of the spinal cord or through some physical contact, the thoughts of the practitioner would be transferred to the mind and then to the body of the patient.

Much metaphysical practice had its beginning in this type of treatment. It served a purpose as a first step leading up to the secret of Jesus' demonstration of *spiritual* healing. It was a bridge, possibly a necessary bridge, enabling us to go from the kingdom of the mind to the realm of the Soul. It served as a stepping stone, but ultimately, it was found that there is a higher realm than that of mind—the realm of Soul, Spirit, or God—which leads us back to the kingdom within. In that realm we find that it is not necessary to transfer thought from the practitioner to the patient, because there is only one consciousness. Everything that is taking place in my consciousness as truth must be taking place in your consciousness as truth, since there is only one consciousness and one activity. You might ask, "Would it not be true then, that any evil thought in my mind could transfer itself to your mind?" The answer is, "No, since evil or error is not a power and cannot transmit itself or move itself from where it is."

For instance, suppose I actually believe that two times two are five. Such a false belief actually has no reality, no substance, and no power. Your *knowledge* that two times two are four would be your protection against *my belief* that two times two are five, and that in itself, would bar any such erroneous belief from your consciousness.

In the same way, then, your understanding that life is eternal, that life is perfect and spiritual, would be your protection against any individual or collective malpractice which would try to impress itself on you with the belief that you are sick or that you are poor. Is it not clear that a knowledge of truth is itself the protection against any belief of error? For example, the child who does not know that two times two are four might for a while be deceived into accepting the belief that two times two are five; but the minute he began playing with blocks, or other objects, he would quickly discover that two times two are four, and through experience, that erroneous belief would be cast out. Actually the first realization that comes to us of God as individual life, is thereafter a protection to us against any belief to the contrary, whether individual or collective.

In treatment, in prayer, and in meditation—regardless of the nature of the claim, regardless of the person for whom you may be working—please remember to keep your thoughts between you and God and do not try to convey them to your patient or to some other person. You will soon prove that if you will maintain the contact between your outer self and your inner Being, that is, between yourself and God, that it is not necessary to project your thought, but that you will not have to know who is sick, or when, or where. Healing will be brought about merely by the patient's thinking of you, merely by his reaching out to your consciousness. Contact with you will be the healing agency, since you will always be living, and moving, and having your being as divine Consciousness. You will not accept any suggestion of a selfhood apart from God, but you will maintain at all times your constant and conscious oneness with God. Then you will have such experiences as the Master had with the woman who touched the hem of his robe. Even though he did not consciously know that she was there seeking help, she received help.

The centurion's servant certainly did not know that any treatment was being sought for him; yet even though he was miles away he received his help. You and I know that he was not expecting help or waiting for it; nor was he expecting to receive any good thoughts from the Master; nor did the Master send any good thoughts to him. More than likely Jesus said something like this to the centurion: "Your faith has healed your servant. You had your servant in your consciousness; you brought yourself and your servant to this Christ consciousness; and in accordance with your faith or understanding, so be it unto you and your servant."

Some one may come to you and ask: "Will you help me, or my child, or my aunt, or my uncle, or my grandmother?" These people may not be aware of the fact that help has been requested; they may not know anything about prayer or treatment. Yet that one person in coming to you, to your consciousness, will find help for the members of his family. When you are asked by anyone for help, that person is in your consciousness, as you are realizing yourself as the consciousness of the Christ; therefore, the whole activity takes place, not from practitioner to patient to patient's relative, but as the activity of the Christ as individual consciousness. Christ is individual consciousness; Truth is individual consciousness. This Truth, expressing itself as my consciousness, becomes your consciousness and the consciousness of all those who turn to you.

Find your peace, the quietness and stillness of your inner being, and let *that* do the healing work for you. Do not try to help by attempting to reach your patients' thought. Do not try to get them to understand some truth, or even wish that they would understand some truth because if they could understand all the truth you could give them, they still might not be healed. *It is not understanding truth that heals: it is the divine state of spiritual consciousness that heals*; and the one who has that state of consciousness is a practitioner.

When the practitioner feels an uplift, a sense of freedom, the patient will respond. It is true that there are still some cases which are not healed or met. There should be fewer and fewer of these cases as time goes on; however, there still seem to be a few, and I, for one, have not solved that riddle. I do know that whenever healing does take place, it is because the practitioner has felt this sense of peace, of oneness, of divine Being. When we understand that we do not have to reach our patients, that their healing has nothing to do with transferring thoughts to them or thinking about them, we then realize that healing has to do only with our own relationship to God. You may think I am stressing and repeating this too much; but I cannot stress it too much, or repeat it too often, because, from now until the end of time, you will be tempted to reach out to some patient. You will be tempted to say, "Oh, if he were only here so that I could explain this to him." You will be tempted to think of time and space as having something to do with the healing; they have nothing to do with healing. Healing has to do only with your degree of conscious oneness with God.

Teaching Spiritual Healing

In teaching the subject of spiritual healing, the first step that must be emphasized is attaining the conscious awareness of the presence of God—the study, and finally, the embodiment of such ideas as are expressed in *The Infinite Way* in the chapter on "Meditation." To live in the conscious awareness of the presence of God is the healing consciousness. This requires conscious effort. In the beginning it is necessary for each one of us to realize consciously our oneness, to realize consciously the nothingness of anything separate or apart from the oneness which I am. Through grace, through gratitude, through acknowledgment of God as the source, the presence, and the power; through conscious recognition of God as the divine law, power, and being unto our experience, we take the first step leading to the attainment of the consciousness of oneness. This also is the first step which must be given to our patients and to our students. We must help them to attain conscious oneness with God: give them a program similar to the one outlined in *The Infinite Way*, or such as is shown forth in all of the other writings, and help them to develop the ability to recognize God as the omnipresent source.

Then, of course, the second step students must be taught is the need for meditation, for quiet introspection, reflection, cogitation. In doing that, it is necessary that they begin as we have, with some subject, some idea, and then ponder it—think it through. Even if there is no opportunity or occasion for sitting in the silence at first, if the student forms the habit of taking a spiritual statement into consciousness and pondering it for five, six, or seven minutes, it will develop in him the ability to concentrate on one thought or one idea. That leads naturally to the next step, which is meditation, or the ability to listen and hear that "still small voice."

The third step is teaching the student the nature of error. Spiritual healing cannot be realized while there is the belief in thought that there is a power to be overcome. As long as the student or practitioner believes that there is a sin or a disease to be healed or overcome, he cannot realize Christ-power. Christ-power is the realization of oneness. It is the realization of the truth that *I am He*, and that there is no sin or disease to be overcome. Christ-power is not truth over error; it is not good over evil. Christ-power is individual awareness of one Presence and one Power. That is another reason why there is no need to convey thoughts from practitioner to patient, since there is nothing in the patient's thought that has to be corrected or overcome or healed. The practitioner who entertains the belief that there is a thought or condition in the patient to be overcome or healed is not practicing Christ healing. Christ healing is: "What hinders you? Rise, take up your bed and walk." In other words, there is no power to stop the harmony of your being from being made manifest.

Christ-power is the recognition that even Pilate had no power except that which was derived from God. It is the recognition of infinite, instant perfection here and now; and therefore, to understand the nature of error is to know the absolute nothingness of that which appears as error.

As a descriptive term we use such words as "hypnotism" or "suggestion" or "appearance"—any term that will show us that that which is appearing to us as an error is not an error and must not be fought. If we merely say error is hypnotism, and then try to overcome hypnotism, we may as well have tried to overcome the cancer or the consumption. No, the reason for changing the name of a disease into the word "hypnotism" or "mesmerism" or "suggestion" is to convey to our thought the fact that we do not have to battle it, because it is nothing more than nothingness. Therefore, the nature of error is to us of supreme importance, since the nature of error reveals to us that there is no error. Knowing the nature of error is not finding out what caused the disease, I assure you!

Our fourth step, in bringing to light this truth and teaching it to students, is the all-important point that the visible world is the result or the product of the invisible world. God, the divine consciousness of Being, is the causative principle and substance of all creation, including our daily experience. God, our divine Consciousness, appears to us as the money we need, the transportation we need, the job we need, the sale we need, the purchase we need, or the parking space we need. We do not attempt to demonstrate these things. Our only demonstration consists of the realization of God, our own consciousness, as the cause, substance, and law, of all form; and then we let those things be added unto us, knowing that the heavenly Father, the divine Consciousness within supplies our need.

CHAPTER SEVEN

GOD

WHEN we say, "*I* am God," or "*I* am a law unto my universe," we are not saying that a human being is God, or that a mortal is spiritual. Never forget that it would be nonsense to try to spiritualize mortal man, or to make God out of a human being. That has been one of the mistakes of religion throughout the ages—setting apart some individual and making him God, taking some person, some human being, and making of him a God. The truth is that only God is God; but God is the individuality and the identity, and the reality of each one of us when we have overcome our sense of humanhood. Often when you see people who work from the standpoint of "I am," you will find them confused, walking around saying, "I am God." They are the very people who are apt to be walking around with an empty purse, a diseased body, or a pair of eyeglasses, and yet they continue to say, "I am God." You can see how ridiculous that is, because that is not God at all. *I am God.*

That *I* is a universal, infinite, omnipresent Being, and It is the reality of your being and of mine when the human sense of self has been overcome. You do not lift the human sense up and make it immortal or spiritual. That is the reason treatments that say, "You are spiritual," or "You are perfect," or "You are rich," are of so little value. Such statements are not true at all. If they were true, you would not find it necessary to repeat them. Can you imagine Rockefeller or a Carnegie or any man of recognized wealth, walking around saying, "I am rich?" And you almost never hear a healthy person say, "I am healthy." When you make these affirmations, it is because you believe you are the opposite; you are trying to fool yourself into believing that you are something that you really are not. When you simply repeat the words, "I am God," that is not true; but when you *hear* those words *within* you, that is Truth. That is God announcing Itself as the reality of your being. When you hear a voice saying, "Know ye not that I am God?" you have heard Truth; and in hearing that Truth, all that is human, all that is mortal, disappears. At least it disappears in a measure; and as, more and more, you hear the still small voice there will be less and less of the human or humanhood to be dispelled.

This is confirmed in the statement of the Master, "I have overcome the world."[1] He did not say, "I have improved myself in this world's goods," or "I have improved the health of this world or the wealth of this world." He said, "I have overcome the world." And again you will find that same idea in his statement, "My kingdom is not of this world."[2] "My kingdom"—the Christ kingdom, the spiritual kingdom—is not of the human world. You cannot bring the Christ into the human world, but you can

---

[1] John 16:33.   [2] John 18:36.

overcome the human world, and find that kingdom within where the Christ is king.

In our favorite passage in Luke, you will find: "For all these things do the nations of the world seek after"[1]—things to eat, things to wear, and things to possess. What are the nations of the world? Who are the people of the world? Are they not those whose consciousness is centered on things, the people who dwell in an atmosphere of things, acquiring things or needing things—*things*, *things*, always *things*. The nations of the world are seeking things; but not you—not "ye, my disciples," ye of spiritual consciousness. You are not seeking things; you are seeking the conscious awareness of God as the reality of your being. That is all you can ever seek in this work, and that attitude reaches its ultimate in Paul's declaration: "I live; yet not I, but Christ liveth in me." When you say, "Christ liveth in me," that is not a mortal speaking. The mortal, the human being, the planner, has faded out of existence, and you have become the witness to the activity of the Christ—to the life of the Christ. You are now watching the Christ work *in* you and *through* you and *as* you.

You are setting aside humanhood and living in your Christhood, when you are not thinking, planning, worrying, fearing, doubting—in other words, when the human mind is less active as a thinking apparatus and more active as a state of awareness. When your thinking is the witnessing of God in action, watching God unfold, then you are living more of the Christ life and less of the human life. The more you find it necessary to plan your days,

[1] Luke 12:30.

112

weeks, months, and years—the more you have to take thought for your life—the more of humanhood is in evidence and the less of spirituality. On the other hand, you are living your Christhood in the degree in which you find your work given to you to do each day, your supply provided, and all your activity unfolding in a normal, natural way; and when this happens you can then say, "I, God, is the reality of my being." You have reached a place in consciousness where you understand the meaning of "*I am God.*" This *I*, which becomes the law unto your being, is not the conscious thinking you or I. It is the divine Consciousness of our being, revealed in the degree in which conscious thinking, in the sense of planning and struggling, fades out of existence.

God Is Infinite Individuality

We do not annihilate ourselves or destroy our individuality in this way; we increase it. But at this point, we must understand that God is infinite in Its individuality, and that, therefore, God is expressing that individuality as individual you or me. It is still God, but it is God appearing as you or as me. Because that is true, you can say, "I have overcome the world," or "I and my Father are one," or "I live; yet not I, but Christ liveth in me," or "I am the way"—anything that will give you this sense of *I*, and that will, at the same time, subordinate human selfhood, not glorify it:

"Glorify thou me . . . with the glory which I had with thee."[1] Glorify thou me with all *Thy* glory.

[1] John 17:5.

113

Let everything I am, or do, be God in manifestation—not the glorification of my personal knowledge, or awareness, or achievement.

To be glorified with God's glory leaves no room for us to glorify humanhood and to call that humanhood God, or even to call it spiritual. Humanhood is not to be spiritualized; humanhood is to be overcome. It will never be necessary to overcome anything of a spiritual nature. But you must overcome this world; you must overcome personal selfhood. You must understand the Master when he says, "I can of mine own self do nothing."[1] He was turning away from his own personal powers, or conscious thinking, and recognizing, "The Father that dwelleth in me, he doeth the works."[2] That Father within is the *I* or *I am* or *reality* of being.

Only *God* is *God*. This is the teaching of The Infinite Way: Only God is God; man is not God. The Infinite Way never teaches that man is God. But God being infinite, God appears as infinite individuality—God appears as the allness of you and of me *when we have overcome the world*. When we have overcome the temptation to be concerned about that little "I", when we are no longer taking thought for that little self, then we can say, "*I* am God," because then it is actually true.

Heretofore, our attention in the world has been centered on persons and things. It did not make any difference in what form the things appeared. The emphasis has always been on health, wealth, harmony, home, or companionship. The transformation

[1] John 5:30.   [2] John 14:10.

that is necessary now is a complete about-face to where thought is focussed on our *consciousness*, and the ability to let that consciousness flow forth in whatever form is necessary to our unfoldment.

We do not take thought for any thing, for any person, or any demonstration. Nothing that appears in the world of form is our concern. That does not mean that we are eliminating persons or things from our experience. On the contrary, as concern for the people and things of this world lessens, we usually find ourselves with more of them; only now we utilize them in their right sense. For example, if a ring comes to me, I wear it and enjoy it, but there is no sense of possession, no sense of its being mine or no sense of desiring it. It just comes; I put it on, and I enjoy it. Now, the same thing can be true of clothing or of friends or relatives. It can be true of marriage. Whatever consciousness brings to me, I use and enjoy. But there is no sense of possession, no sense of needing anything, requiring anything, or desiring anything. There is only the realization that God, as my consciousness, is appearing to me at all times in every form necessary to my experience, watching as it unfolds from day to day. In this way, all power is placed in consciousness rather than in things.

We take the first commandment and realize that all power is in God—the Consciousness of my being—and because the nature of God or Consciousness is infinite intelligence and divine love, It not only knows our need before we do, but It has the love necessary to provide whatever is needed for our unfoldment. Therefore, when we are centered in the truth that "I and my Father are one,"[1] the Father is revealed as the infinite, divine, spiritual consciousness of individual being. Its nature is infinite wisdom, divine love; and It is, therefore, forever pouring Itself forth as my harmonious daily experience. God, my consciousness, is appearing to me each day in the form necessary for the fulfillment of that day.

God Is Fulfillment

The word "fulfillment"—filled full—is an important one for us. We are always filled full; we are always a state of fulfillment, since it is God fulfilling Itself as our individual being. It is God fulfilling Its glory, Its grace, Its power and dominion as our individual experience. We must come to that place where God pours Itself forth as us, through us, in us, and for us; and God must become a living reality.

There is a teaching which states that God is divine mind, a formless substance, and that we impress our desires upon this mind, and then our desires come forth into form. This teaching makes of God a vehicle through which we can get what we want. The Infinite Way approach is a reversal of that. In our work, we have no desires, no wants, no wishes; we have nothing to impress upon the divine Mind. We are not taking thought for what we need, because we do not know what we need. We do not know where we should be tomorrow. We have no idea, furthermore, of what place we are

[1] John 10:30.

116

destined to fill in the spiritual scheme of existence. Therefore, our attitude is the reverse of any such teaching which would *use* God. The divine Intelligence or Consciousness, being infinite wisdom and divine love, knows our need, and because the nature of God is to fulfill Itself as our individual unfoldment, It does all things needful without our even being aware of what we need, want, or desire, or where we should be.

This is not an attitude of "let God do it," since that would involve a sense of separation from God. It is rather the understanding that since God is my very intelligence, I am always intelligently governed. Since God is the divine law of my being, then my experience is always expressing divine love, perfection, harmony, or good. Since God is infinite good, and all that the Father hath is mine, this infinitude of good is pouring itself through into expression as my experience.

This teaching is not fatalism; it is not a resigned acceptance that "Whatever happens God did it"; or "I will take whatever God sends me." Such an attitude is duality or two-ness. *This* way is the affirmation and reaffirmation of the great truths:

I and my Father are one.[1]
All that I have is thine.[2]
The place whereon thou standest is holy ground.[3]

God is forever fulfilling Itself as our individual experience. Then, in that consciousness, we can say: "Let Truth manifest Itself as It will, since Its will is

[1] John 10:30.   [2] Luke 15:31.   [3] Exodus 3:5.

117

only in the nature of infinite wisdom and divine love." Do you see the difference? There *is* a God. God *is*. Harmony *is*. We cannot create that harmony with our thinking, but through thought we can become aware of the fact that God is infinite law, that God is infinite, divine principle, forever expressing Itself as the harmony, wisdom, intelligence, and love of our experience.

That is knowing the truth, and the truth, then, makes us free. *Know the truth.* Do not be concerned with the things of the world—whether they be a home, money, a job, or opportunity. Be concerned only with the realization that God is fulfilling Itself as your individual experience; that God, the consciousness of your being, is always appearing as the form necessary to your unfoldment. Keep thought steadfastly on God; keep thought continuously on the Source and Substance, and not on the *effect in* which or *as* which God is to appear.

Omnipresence, Omnipotence, and Ever-Availability of God

The secret of this principle with which we are working—called the Christ Principle—is the omnipresence, omnipotence, and ever-availability of God. The entire message of The Infinite Way can be summed up in the words: *The omnipotence, omnipresence,* and *ever-availability of God.* That is the whole of it. Once you have attained the consciousness of the presence of God, you can take all The Infinite Way writings and throw them away, or give them away. You will no longer need them, because you will have the essence of their teaching: the understanding of the infinite nature of God, Its omnipotence and ever-availability.

This sense of God's presence and power is the principle that you will want to give your children, or that your patient or student will want to give his children. It must be built into the fiber of the child's consciousness from morning to night, and from night to morning. A child should never be permitted to go to sleep without a conscious remembrance of God as omnipresent in one form or another. Those who want their children to grow into a better sense of manhood and womanhood than these last few generations have experienced will have to do this by some means other than by human teaching, or through a purely human code of conduct. I do not believe children can be taught morals or ethics merely through human codes. But the person who once catches the consciousness of the presence of God never again has any excuse to violate any moral or ethical principle of life.

The real principle of life is this: your own will come to you. Your own state of consciousness will always be made manifest as your experience, and no man can take that away from you. No man can take your consciousness from you any more than he can take your knowledge of mathematics or music from you.

The greater the awareness of God which you attain, the greater degree of desirable things and persons will appear in your outer world. These things and persons will be your own consciousness appearing to you. Looking at your present state of affairs, you might say, "Then I have a very poor state of consciousness." That may be so. In that event, it is up to you to acknowledge that, and change it. It is up to *you* to change it. "Seek ye first the kingdom of God"[1]— the conscious awareness of God. Seek this consciousness of God and make it an ever-increasing awareness. God is here in Its infinity, but we attain that consciousness only in a measure. What the measure is, is up to us.

Everyone on earth has, potentially, the same consciousness as Jesus Christ. It is infinite; it is here; and it is awaiting us. The question is: are we willing to put in the hours of devotion; are we willing to make the effort required to train ourselves to be conscious of the presence of God, instead of seeking some *form* in which God is to appear. There is the whole secret. *It is up to us!* If we can rely wholly on the Principle, on Consciousness, we can attain the consciousness of the Christ.

No man could ever steal after he has caught the consciousness of God as his supply. No man would ever murder, if once he caught the consciousness of God as eternal life, as the life of individual being. It is only the belief that someone has a life of his own that causes a person to kill, even in self-defence. Even to kill in self-defence is an acknowledgment that we have a life of our own which is in danger. Such a thing would not be possible if the truth that God is life eternal were realized. You cannot destroy life eternal; no bullet or bomb can destroy that. The consciousness that God is the reality of our being dispels every condition leading to sin, disease, and

[1] Matthew 6:33.

death. The cause of the world's troubles is the sense of separation from God. The antidote for the world's troubles is the conscious awareness of God as omnipresent, omnipotent, omniscient—the reality of being.

When we worship persons and personalities—whether we do so in the form of a religious character, national or international characters—we are laying the foundation for our own destruction. Only in the degree that we can realize God as a universal presence, as an impersonal and impartial presence, as the life of *all*, as the mind and Soul of *all*, as the consciousness of *all being*, can we overcome the conditions of this world.

Is not the teaching of one God, and that God omnipotent and omnipresent, the only religious teaching that can end the quarrels among churches, end not only religious warfare, but all other warfare? The antidote for war is the realization of God as individual presence and power, God as our individual experience. This realization brings an awareness of spiritual power. Once we, as individuals, have proved that there is a spiritual power which heals our personal ills, lacks, and limitations, we shall begin to see that there is a spiritual power which can overcome any evil in human society.

God Appears as Teacher, Healer, and Saviour
Consciousness is infinite. Consciousness manifests itself as individual being—your being and my being. If I tell you that consciousness has manifested itself as my particular being, and as my particular state of

consciousness, and that that consciousness through me or as me is imparting to you this truth, you will probably agree. If you can sit in your office or home and help someone else, you will agree that that consciousness imparting itself to you as truth, as spiritual power, was that which enabled you to help your patient, neighbor, friend, or relative.

Now, let me carry this one step further, and show you that Consciousness is manifesting Itself as individual being within my consciousness and yours. Therefore, every moment of the day and every moment of the night, God is imparting Itself to you, within you, in an individual way, in some individual sense of person or power, as guidance and direction, and as a healing agency, as well as a supporting and supplying agency. At no time are you without your teacher and healer. God is manifesting Itself in your consciousness as teacher and as healer. Wherever you go, with or without a human being, with or without a book, you are carrying in your consciousness God's manifestation of Its own being as teacher, healer, supplier, protector, saviour.

Whether It appears within you as the idea of some personality in the past, present, or future; whether It appears to you as an externalized teacher or teaching; whether It appears to you as a position or as an investment, please remember this: God is omnipresent in your consciousness *as individual form*, as individual individuality. At all times and in all places, God is present within you as your teacher, as your teaching, as your companion, as your *everything of this existence*.

At this moment, I am thinking more particularly

in terms of teacher and healer, since what appears outwardly to you as teacher or teaching is not that at all. Teacher and teaching are *God manifesting in your own consciousness as divine idea.* It has always been present in your consciousness awaiting your recognition, and It will always be there *manifesting in whatever form is necessary,* to the extent in which you are willing to recognize God manifest as divine idea within you, and are not afraid if that divine Idea appears to you in some form which you have not heretofore experienced.

Consciousness never dies. The consciousness of any and every individual never dies. Individual consciousness never disappears from the face of the globe. Therefore, that consciousness which is known as Jesus Christ or Krishna or Buddha—that consciousness which is known as any great religious spiritual light or character—is omnipresent within *you,* and may appear to you at any moment that you open your consciousness. It may take the form of words or thoughts. But do not be surprised if it appears to you as a person, as the very image and likeness of some spiritual being.

Consciousness may appear to you as the form of what you conceive to be Jesus Christ or any other great spiritual leader, but it will not be the form of any of them, as their forms were known on earth. It will be their form as God made their form, and it will be visible to you in proportion to your interpretation of it. If you have been a Christian from birth, it may well appear to you as the form you have seen in pictures or paintings of the Master, Christ Jesus. On the other hand, if you have been reared in the

Hindu teaching, it may become visible to you as Krishna or Buddha. If you have come by way of Judaism, it may appear as what the world called Moses.

Whatever the form, it would merely be your *interpretation* of the Christ—of Christ consciousness. It may come to you as someone you have never known or never heard of—some ancient or modern teacher. And on the other hand, it may not come in the form of a person: it may come as ideas, words, or statements. But in your own thought do not limit the forms of expression; and do not rule out anything as impossible, because God is infinite, and God has a way of appearing infinitely. The Bible is full of references to God as *light*, but it also emphasizes the fact that God is *truth*. Therefore, God can just as well appear as a sense or statement of truth as a sense of light. But do not forget that God, or Truth, has always appeared on earth as an individual. God can appear to us in *any* form.

God is infinite individual being: God is omnipresent as your individual consciousness. This omnipresence may appear to you in any form which your consciousness can accept. Do not limit the form in which truth, guidance, health, healing, can come to you, because God is *infinite* in Its activity; God is infinite in form and appearance.

Accept the truth that God can appear to you individually: God can appear to you within your own consciousness; God can appear as teacher, healer, saviour; God can appear as direction, wisdom, guidance. Accept God in any form in which He may appear to you in your consciousness when you are in the silence. Do not be afraid of any inner visitation. The greater degree of unfoldment that you receive in this work, the greater will be the *inner* revelation of an individual nature coming to you. You will receive your individual unfoldment from God, and God will appear to you in an individual way.

So far as I am concerned, the healing of disease, the healing of sin, and the healing of poverty, are only the proof that the message of Omnipresence is true. The healing of the body is not the main function of this teaching; the purpose of this teaching is to make God evident and real to you individually as a living experience. God *is* a living experience. God is a living person and power—not "person" in our sense of person—but God is an infinite individuality to be realized by each one of us.

We can live and move and have our being twenty-four hours a day in God consciousness. That is the purpose of this work. The health, the wealth, the harmony, the peace, and the joy always accompany the consciousness of the presence of God.

Abraham called God "Friend." And Jesus called God "Father." Ramakrishna called God "Mother Kali"; the Quakers call God "Father-Mother." In whatever form these people have realized God, they realized It not as a name, but as an *actual experience* to which they gave the name "Father," "Friend," "Father-Mother," or "Mother." It was an actual experience which took place in their consciousness, like the descent of the Holy Ghost at Pentecost, an experience to which they then gave the name "God," or "Father-Mother."

What we have been doing in our religious life has been merely to *say* the names "Father," "Mother," "God," and "Christ"—without actually having had the experience of God in our inner being—all of which is but a hollow shell. The purpose and message of The Infinite Way is to make God a living reality, so that whether you close your eyes or open your eyes, you will always have the sense and feeling of this divine Presence, guiding, leading, directing, and instructing you.

CHAPTER EIGHT

THE HEALING MINISTRY

My oneness with God is my oneness with spiritual wholeness. The only place where disease has no reality and where it disappears, is in one's spiritual sense of life—in this intuitive spiritual sense of life that you feel when you are in the silence, when you are touching Reality. In this life, there is no sin, no disease, no lack, no limitation, no war. There is nothing going on in this spiritual sense of life but spiritual good. That is the reason I say that most of our work should be done silently and not audibly. Giving a person who has asked for help a barrage of metaphysical truths, to me, is nothing but nonsense. To me, the only way to respond to a call for help is to say, "I will help you right away." Just as fast as is possible, get back into that silence, where you can *feel* the very presence of God, where you can discern Reality. Then the patient will be free. When I have a headache, if a practitioner were to say to me, "Now, you know it is not real; of course you have not got a headache"; I would be inclined to reply, "Oh, go jump in the lake! I want freedom! I do not want a lot of conversation!" If the practitioner really and truly believed that the headache was not real, I would be healed long before he could assure me of its unreality. It is not how glib we are at blurting out these metaphysical truths that is going to help anybody. It is the recognition within of spiritual Reality. This you touch somewhere within your own being, and when you do, the whole human picture fades out and you begin to see divine Reality.

We should get out of the habit of telling and repeating testimonies. Testimonies are legitimate when they are used to exemplify some point of spiritual practice. You may want to illustrate a certain principle and use a testimony of healing as an example, but aside from that, give up the habit of testifying, either to your own healings or to those for which you may have been responsible, or to others of which you may have heard.

There is another important point to be considered in the healing work: this ministry is probably the most sacred of all human relations. The full explanation of that statement will unfold as you continue the work. It is a sacred relationship, and for that reason, confidences should never be breached. In the first place, we should neither mention the names of our patients or students, nor disclose who they are except as such information becomes known of its own accord. Never discuss one patient's problems with another, even when they are those of husband and wife, or when the problem concerns mother and child. Never be tempted to discuss one person with another. It is not good, and it might prove harmful.

The Healing Ministry Requires a Dedicated Life

In this work where patients rely so greatly on the help of practitioners, especially in cases involving pain or fear, it is necessary that the practitioner accept the full responsibility and be at the service of his patients. For that reason, two things are important in the conduct of a practitioner's office. One is never to let the telephone be occupied for more than two or three minutes, and if possible not more than one minute. A practitioner's telephone line should be kept open. A patient should not telephone a practitioner and find a busy signal once, twice, three times. Such delay sets up a human sense of irritation or fear that is not conducive to healing. Certainly, it is impossible for a busy practitioner to keep his telephone line open all the time. But if there are too many calls for one telephone, he should have two. A practitioner's home is his office—just a branch office, that is all. A practitioner no longer has a home in the old sense of the word. In many ways, in entering this work, one gives up one's personal life.

The second point to be emphasized is the importance of a practitioner's being within reach of his telephone. A practitioner should not be away from his home for social engagements; and if he finds it necessary to be away, there should be some provision made for leaving a message as to where he is and where he can be reached. In other words, this is a ministry; and when one enters it, one must be willing to give up one's personal life.

As far as possible, this dedication must become the practitioner's rule of life in order to maintain his own consciousness on a high level. The only thing that heals is the ability to maintain that consciousness, and that is not done if one is indulging overly much in social activities—making social calls and entertaining friends and acquaintances. The teaching of the Master on this point is very clear. In entering the healing ministry, one gives up all for Christ—even father, mother, sister, brother, husband, wife. This does not mean that they are given up in the sense of putting them out of one's life, but they are relegated to a secondary place, which is their rightful one. The *practice* must come first, and then, if there is any time left over for husband or wife, he or she can have it, but you may be sure that it will not be much.

That sounds hard, does it not? It sounds difficult. But actually, that is the way a healing ministry is carried on. It is the way a person must live if he looks upon this as a ministry and not just as a pastime.

In working with patients, especially during periods of pain and fear, I encourage patients to call me frequently: Call me in an hour; call me back in twenty minutes; call me back in two hours. When I first work with a person, particularly a person who comes to me with any claim of a painful or fearful nature, I encourage frequent calls, especially during the night. I have done some work where I have had the telephone ring every twenty minutes all night long. I have seen the crisis passed in many cases —actually healings brought about—through that persistent reaching out for help.

Another aspect of this work is the handling of the mail. From the very day that air-mail was inaugurated, I have used air-mail for all letters that have had to go over two hundred miles. When a patient or any person writes to a practitioner, he is really waiting for an answer. It is an incomplete job until he receives that answer. He may get his healing long before he gets the answer. It is not a question of healing; it is a question of courtesy and consideration. For that reason, our part is to get our answers off as quickly as possible, and to take whatever steps are necessary to have them delivered as quickly as possible. If it seems wise not to wait for an air-mail letter to be delivered, send a telegram, or make a telephone call. Let your patient know as quickly as possible that he is being taken care of, that the work is under way. That is all a part of the healing ministry —part of its service. It is the kind of service which is demanded of every person who expects to work in this field. I say this, primarily, for the benefit of those who will come to you for help, but I say it also, for your own sake. If you hope to be successful in this work, follow these suggestions. No one is ever going to be successful in this work if his heart and soul are not in it; and if one's heart and soul are in it, then he will want to seek the highest form of service there is.

Spiritual Maturity a Necessity

Will you be surprised if I tell you that one of the great sources of our trouble as individuals—even as students on this path—is the fact that we refuse to grow up spiritually and become spiritual adults? For that matter, men and women even refuse to grow up humanly and act like adults. An adult is a person who has arrived at the state of consciousness where he is an individual in his own right, where he is no longer dependent on mother and father, sister and brother, and where he does not transfer that dependence even to his children. An adult is one who, even humanly, should be able to stand on his own feet, and not be a mental parasite, fastening on to his elders or on to his children. How many people there are, even in this work, who are still leaners or parasites, leaning on mama or papa, on sons or daughters, or on sisters or brothers, and then wondering why they do not attain their freedom.

Spiritually, this is even more important. All demonstration in this work is based on the degree of realization of the truth that I and my Father are one. Now, ask yourself this question: "Just how seriously do I believe—to what extent do I believe—that I and the Father are one? To what extent am I completely leaning, depending, or relying on this truth or to what extent am I expecting something, some understanding, some support, some companionship from mother, father, husband, wife, child? I am not talking about *enjoying* our relationships with our relatives and families; I am talking about the degree in which we are bound by them and to them. We either make them subservient to us and do not give them their freedom from us, or on the other hand, we do not accept our freedom from them.

Many of our individual troubles in the world come from our failure to maintain our spiritual integrity. Out in the world of men and women, people do not even maintain their human integrity. Parents will not free themselves from their children, or children will not free themselves from their parents. There is much too much of a clinging to relationships which have long since served their purpose, instead of breaking loose from them. The birds are better off than we are; they push their young out of the nest and set them free to fly. We do not give our children their freedom if we can avoid it; we rarely ever set them free. And it is seldom that a husband or wife is given the freedom and independence to which he or she is entitled. There is too much of a clinging to human attachments, a holding on, perhaps because of jealousy or fear—for the most part, I think it is fear.

On the spiritual path, there is nothing more satisfying in the world than the relationships between friends, companions, students, or patients; nor is there anything more comforting than the understanding that can come between a man and wife in this work. But this understanding must be based primarily on our recognition of our oneness with God as the chief relationship. When we have established in consciousness our oneness with God, we become one with everybody and we can have the most satisfying relationships—and yet there will not be a dependence on any person as such.

We can take the work of a practitioner as an example. A practitioner who becomes dependent upon a patient for support, or supply, would soon lose his whole healing gift. If a practitioner became dependent on his practice for his living, he would lose his healing gift. It does not mean that practitioners may not derive their living from that source; they very well may; but their *dependence* on it would destroy their effectiveness as practitioners. Unless a practitioner can establish in his consciousness daily that "I and my Father are one[1] and all that

[1] John 10:30.

133

I have is thine"[1] and, in this realization, set the patient free, there is again that clinging relationship, which is detrimental to both practitioner and patient.

The same principle applies to the relationship between teacher and student. The moment that a teacher becomes dependent on a student for anything in the world, they are both lost, since the only true relationship is their oneness in Christ—their oneness because of the divine relationship of oneness with God. My oneness with God constitutes my oneness with everybody who has ever been through class with me. But it is such a beautiful oneness that there is no dependence, and there is no interdependence— just a cordial, "Hello," and a friendly, "Goodbye."

Each of us must establish, within his own consciousness, his freedom. Freedom is not a human characteristic: It is a spiritual quality; it is an activity of God, a quality and a quantity of God; it is of the nature of God. Therefore, only in Soul, in Spirit, can we find our freedom.

We find that our health is also a spiritual quality. Health is not in the body, and that is why we are not healing conditions of the body, since health is not a quality or activity of body. Health is an activity of the Soul, which the body reflects. The moment we find our freedom of Soul, we find freedom of the body.

In the same way, economic freedom is not found in dollars, and it is not found in marriage; and we have discovered that it is not found in investments. Economic freedom is found in Soul. Economic

[1] Luke 15:31.

134

freedom is a quality and an activity of Soul. If you make a conscious contact with your Soul, within the depths of your inner being, you will have found your economic freedom. True, it may seem to come through a husband or wife or an investment. It may seem to come through the practice, through the healing ministry, but that will only be the seeming—the appearance. In reality it will be coming from the Soul.

Therefore, if our income should be cut off in one direction, there is nothing to fear because, since Soul is infinite, not only in its capacity, but also in its expression, new sources of income will immediately unfold from another direction. No person will ever find his economic freedom, any more than he will find his physical freedom, until he finds his freedom in Soul, in Spirit, God—in his conscious oneness with God.

Very few people are willing to grow up—to grow into emotional, mental, and spiritual maturity. Within themselves, actually they do not want to be free. For many years I have watched this parade of human life, and I know how many people cling to the very circumstances from which they could be set free, if they really desired freedom and were willing to pay the price of freedom.

First of all, we cling to a bodily sense of life. In other words, we are afraid of what is going to happen to the body. As a matter of fact, the Bible tells us that unless we lose our life, we shall not find it. In other words, unless we lose that physical sense of life—that sense of life in body—we shall not find our spiritual sense of life. We have to lose our material sense of existence, in order to find the incorporeal or spiritual. That does not separate us from our body but it separates us from the false concept of body.

You will never lose your body, since your body and you are one. Your body is merely your consciousness formed, and you cannot separate consciousness from its form. You will never lose your body. Even should you decide to die some day, you will find that you have not lost your body. It will still be right there with you—right where you are. You will not leave it behind. When we agree—even in a measure within ourselves—to be free from the corporeal sense of body, no longer to be afraid of what happens to the body, we begin to find some measure of freedom.

We have to agree, moreover, that we do not care what happens to our dollars, since dollars do not constitute supply. Dollars are merely the form as which supply appears. If there were not dollars, there would be carrots or green peas or chickens. But it really does not make any difference in what form supply appears. If you have the consciousness of supply, you will have abundance, no matter what form it may take. If you touch that place within your consciousness where you realize that your own consciousness itself is the essence and substance of all form, then you will not have to be concerned about a physical body or a material dollar; and in that consciousness will come freedom from human dependencies and interdependencies. We have fashioned ourselves from our beliefs. We have fastened ourselves to someone's life, feeling that life is empty unless we are near some human being. We expect to have mother close at hand, or father, son, daughter, husband, or wife; and we clutch them to us. But when you have found your oneness with God, what a wonderful sense of freedom comes! In finding that oneness with God, you find yourself at one with everybody in the world in a beautiful and satisfying relationship. Each one shares the best side of himself with you and keeps the worst side away from you. Your associates come to you with all that is best in themselves and share that best with you. Watch it, as you learn to find that sense of freedom.

Setting Your Patient Free

At this point we are going a step further in spiritual living than has been taken perhaps by any other teaching that we know. The reason that this is possible, is because we have no organization or anything to which we can belong; we have no rules, and therefore, each one of us can set the other completely free in Christ. If there is an organization, or if we belong to an organization, there is a limiting sense of obligation which says: "I must support this, or this is dependent on me. This church needs my support, or I need the church's support." But do you not see that only when you have come to some spiritual unfoldment in which there is no attachment to person or thing, no dependence on person or thing, are you set free to find your own complete spiritual freedom?

Every person who goes into the practice must understand the meaning of spiritual freedom. Never for a minute believe that any patient who has come to you for help is under any obligation to come back to you tomorrow or the next time he needs help. When a patient asks you for help today, set him free. If you never hear from him again, or if he never comes back to you again, he has violated nothing, because you have no ties on him. You have no right to have ties on a patient or a student. They are free; they are free in Christ: they are free to come; and they are free to go. Every patient should be set free the minute you have completed your treatment. He is free. No patient should have to report back to you if he does not want to; he does not have to telephone you if he is not coming back; he does not have to pay you; he does not have to do anything for you.

In this work it is very wise, in so far as possible, not to think of people as owing you for last week's work, or last month's work. Let nobody owe you anything. What anybody pays you today, is paid up to date. If to his sense there is an obligation, and he wants to pay something more next week or next month, that is his business. But in your thought, set him free. Do not keep a set of books showing that somebody owes you money from last week. Such accounting is very bad business in the healing ministry. Nobody should owe you anything except for today; and if he does not pay it, he does not owe it to you. You hold him in no mental bondage and no economic bondage. That means that whatever cash comes in today is your day's supply, and what did not come in has nothing to do with you. You are not going to depend on yesterday's manna. In your own consciousness, you are living on the manna that flows today.

Naturally, there will be many days when more will flow than you can use that day. That does not prevent your putting it in the bank and using it tomorrow or next week or next year. The important point is: do not have a tie on your patient. Do not hold him in bondage as "my patient" or "my student," and do not hold him in economic bondage, saying: "He still owes me eight dollars." He does not owe you eight dollars or eight hundred dollars. Each day's work is complete in itself: if it is paid, it is; and if it is not paid, it is not. Remember your supply is coming from the infinity of your own being.

If you can let go of that mental clamp which would try to fasten your patient to you, you will have more freedom. What a freeing experience it is just to know that everything good is of God, and that you do not have to worry about whether your patient is going to change practitioners, or whether your student is going to find a new teacher, or be concerned about any other kind of change.

My oneness with God constitutes my oneness with all spiritual being and ideas, and the more that I can realize my constant oneness with God, the more beautiful friendships will I have. Many people are not *free* to live their own lives. Somebody has a mental clamp on them. Now, break that bondage. Do not let anybody hold you in bondage and do not yourself hold anybody in bondage. Set everybody in your world free. If you cannot accept your freedom in Christ—if you cannot accept your freedom in your divine sonship with God, the relationship that exists between you and the infinite Being within—you are not going to go far on this spiritual path.

Find the Kingdom Within

We now come to a most important point in all spiritual teaching: Do not try to find spiritual good in the human scene, but as quickly as possible go into meditation; get into that silence, into that place where you can commune with God, and there behold Reality. In the belief of human living, you will not find God, or spirituality. True, human living is a belief and a dream, but merely to say that it is not real is not going to get rid of it. Something further has to be done, and that is the point that is overlooked by most metaphysicians. That something is *to find your spiritual base within yourself.* Find that center of your own being where you commune with God, with the divine Reality, and feel that warmth; feel that gentle Presence; and then any and every form of error will be dispelled. It does not make any difference whether the discord has been in the form of sin, disease, lack, limitation, unemployment, unhappiness, or anything else. It all disappears if, and when, you touch that center within you.

Why do you think I spend so much time on this idea of meditation? Certainly, it is not because I want to close my eyes and get away from the world. I am not afraid of facing the world, but I know that in the human world I have no power to do anything about a human situation. It does not make any difference how much I know. I know that some of you have heard me say, "There is not a word of Truth in all my books, or in all the other metaphysical writings that have ever been printed." The reason is that when it is sent out into the world it is not Truth. It is the truth about Truth. Truth is that which *I am*. Truth is something that I sense and feel and touch within my own being. It is where God and I become one. It is that point in consciousness where I disappear and God alone becomes real. That is where healing takes place, and that is the only place.

The reason we are spending time learning truth, and reading truth, is only because it is one way of leading us out of the human sense of things into the spiritual sense. But the real object of reading truth and hearing truth is to lead us back to the kingdom of God within ourselves, to where we *feel* the contact, to where we feel this gentle Whatever-It-Is —we call It God, or the Christ. "I live; yet not I, but Christ liveth in me."[1] But I could *say* that from now until doomsday; I could put it on a record and play it; but that would not make it effective. There has to come a *feeling*; there has to be something within that actually feels *Christ* living. Then, when you have that, the error dissolves; it disappears. Otherwise, there is nothing but psychological healing.

Now there is nothing wrong in being healed psychologically. That is perfectly all right. Neither is there anything wrong in being healed medically. But in *our* work, the aim is the attainment of spiritual being, of spiritual reality; and that is the

[1] Galatians 2:20.

reason we are not concerned with either medical or psychological healing. We are dealing with that healing which is brought about as we attain a conscious awareness, a realization, of actual spiritual being. This thing that we call "Spirit, or God" does not exist just as words or thoughts. There really *is* God. Let no one doubt it. There really is God, a God that you can meet and *feel* and commune with and be with. It is pouring forth into expression. And *that* heals.

Therefore, when I say to a person, "I will help you; I will be with you. Do not worry; I am on the job," I do not mean anything human, because there is not anything in a human way that I can do. I learned years ago that Jesus was right when he said, "I can of mine own self do nothing."[1] He knew it, and I know it. But there is this *thing* within; there is this point of contact, at which the human experience fades out; all human power fades out; and there is just a wonderful sense of nearness, closeness, and oneness. It is something which makes you smile. You may not even have a good reason for smiling, but it brings a smile to your face as if you were saying, "All right, Father, I know you are there." That is all there is to it. But *that* dissolves the error.

Now, knowing this, why do we *ever* have a failure? It is only because we do not have a sufficient realization of our oneness, and do not stay in that awareness. That is the only reason. If we could only get more into it, and stay in it, we would have many more healings.

As we touch this center of our being, we get a

[1] John 5:30.

142

response—the Life, the Fire—which goes forth and does the healing work; and that is the kind of healing work we are trying to do. It is not that which looks at a human being and says, "Well, you are sick, but I am going to get you well"; or "I am going to turn to God and see what God can do about it." It is a looking away from the human picture, a turning away entirely from the human picture, and touching the center of your being. Then the work is done.

CHAPTER NINE

A HIGH FORM OF TREATMENT

WE must come to the realization that we are adults, and that we should be able to stand on our own two feet without being dependent on some one or some thing. This spiritual independence is achieved through the realization of our oneness with God:

"I and my Father are one." This oneness with the Father constitutes my oneness with every spiritual being and idea. Therefore, I need not seek my good or be concerned about my good, because my oneness with God constitutes my good. It constitutes the law of attraction, bringing to me all that is necessary for my unfoldment, for the revelation of my true being, for my daily experience. Right where I am, God is. Right where I am, the allness of God is. This ever presence of God makes me independent of person, place, thing, circumstance, condition, or relationship. Wherever I am, the fullness of God is revealing Itself. The place whereon I stand is holy ground. Right here, right now, the allness of God is made manifest as my individual experience, and the awareness of this truth is the law unto that experience. I and the Father are one. In this oneness is my self-completeness. I am, therefore, Self-maintained; I am Self-sustained. The Self of me, the Reality of me, maintains and sustains me, supports and upholds me, teaches me, enlightens me, enriches me.

This truth is a light unto my path. This truth is my salvation. The awareness of this truth—the conscious awareness of this truth—sets me free from human dependence. I am in the world, but not of it. I enjoy all the experiences, all the relationships, all the joys, all the companionships, that are a part of God's spiritual creation. And yet I am free. All those with whom I come in contact are free—free to enjoy each other, but not to hold each other in any sense of bondage, physical, mental, moral, or economic, Each one is free in Christ. I find my freedom in Christ. I find my economic freedom, my political freedom, my physical freedom, my moral freedom, in Christ, in Spirit, in Soul—not in any outside dependence.

God has supplied me in the beginning with everything and everybody necessary to my unfoldment, and this is a universal truth. It is true about everybody in proportion to his awareness of his spiritual identity and his oneness with God. "I will never leave thee, nor forsake thee."[1] How true it is that I cannot escape from my Self. *I* will always be with me. I might travel the world around, but I can never escape from myself because I take myself with me wherever I go. "I will never leave thee, nor forsake thee." The *I* of me, the Self of me, which is God, is always where I am.

[1] Hebrews 13:5.

Consciously bring these truths to mind from time to time, especially if you find yourself becoming ensnared in the human belief that you are dependent on mother, father, sister, brother, husband, or wife; or if you should forget your oneness with God and believe that you are dependent on your job, your position, your patient, or your student. Never let these human ties fasten themselves upon you. Remind yourself that I and the Father are one. In this oneness is your completeness and your allness:

Leave all for *My* sake. Leave mother, sister, brother, father; leave every human dependence and find your allness in *Me*, in Christ, in Life; find that *I* am all things unto you. *I* am your teacher, your healer. *I*, the divine Consciousness of your being, will never leave you nor forsake you.

All Healing Is Instantaneous Healing

Healings are dependent upon your reaction to the call for help. This is the law in every case. There is no evil in this world; there is no sin, no disease. There is no power in the world that can do anything or cause anything or be anything. The only cause is God, your divine Consciousness. That is the only creative Principle there is in the universe and all It can create is good. Your sufferings are caused, not by anything that is in the world, but by your reaction to erroneous claims. This is the principle of scientific healing. Regardless of the call that comes to you, the healing is in accordance with your re-action to it. If you accept the call as being serious, something requiring attention, or something that must be overcome or destroyed, that reaction to it makes it impossible to have an instantaneous healing. On the other hand, if you are alert when the call comes, and do not react to it in that manner, but instantly realize, "I and my Father are one"—and actually have that consciousness—then the healing takes place.

That is why (and please remember this) you never can help anybody five minutes after the call for help comes. All healing work must be done when the call touches your consciousness, because it is your reaction to it that determines the healing. You cannot say, "I am too busy to give a treatment," because then you have acknowledged the power of error, and your treatment is not going to be effective. Every healing is at the point of contact. Of course, it is absolutely true that if you are, or when you are, at the very height of spiritual consciousness, and these calls come, you will instantaneously meet the claim. If you are not on these spiritual heights, the call will come a second time, a third, a tenth, a twentieth time, or a thousandth time, if your consciousness is not ready—if it is not at that high place where it does not react to erroneous claims.

Each time a claim presents itself to your thought, whether in the form of a patient's telephoning, telegraphing, writing, or visiting you, it must be met at that time. If I were sitting here this minute and some problem of a patient came to my thought, it must be met at once. Even though I might be talking to you, I must meet that claim when it presents itself to my thought. There is no use saying,

"When I am alone tonight, I will give a treatment."
A treatment is always at the standpoint of contact.
When the claim touches the practitioner's consciousness, that is when the treatment takes place. That
explains why it is just as possible to take care of
a hundred cases a day as it is to take care of three.
If a hundred cases can be brought to your consciousness, then a hundred cases can be met at that
second when they are being brought to your consciousness. As a matter of fact, they must be met at
that moment. There is no time element in healing.
All healing is instantaneous healing. The practitioner
may have had to give a thousand treatments, but
the healing takes place in *one* of those treatments.
There is no such thing as gradual healing; all healing
is instantaneous. Either a case is met, or it is not
met. When it is met, it is completely met, although
it may take a week or a month for all the evidence to
drop away and for the patient to discover that he is
completely healed. But the healing takes place at the
moment of contact.

For example, a person may have a sore, may ask
for help, and may be instantaneously healed; but
it may take three days or more for the new skin to
form, so that he can say, "Well, that is complete
now." It is not complete when the evidence testifies
to its completeness; it is complete at the moment
when the "click" takes place. The healing takes
place at the moment of contact. But when it does
take place, at that instant of contact, from then on,
it makes no difference whether the entire evidence
disappears in a minute, or whether it gradually
disappears over the course of two or three weeks. It

was the awareness of truth at the moment of contact that determined the healing.

Give every call made upon you an instantaneous response. Never, never, think in terms of, "I must give that person a treatment tonight." Meet every claim at the instant it is presented to you. Never think about giving it a treatment later. If the work were done at the moment of contact, it would be a waste of time to think of it an hour from that time. You may never have to think of it again. You must understand that healing work is done by a state of consciousness at the time of contact, not at a future time. Otherwise, healing would be dependent on time, on human effort, or on human thinking; and healing is not dependent on any of these things; it is dependent only on touching the Christ. When the claim touches the Christ, the healing takes place. If you are walking along the street and you become aware of any form of discord, meet it in your consciousness immediately, and then walk on and forget about it. If it comes back to your thought, meet it again. Each time it presents itself to you meet it. How? *By not reacting to it!* That is the secret of healing—*no reaction.*

No Reaction to Error

Are you convinced that nobody ever dies? Do not deceive yourself. Do not say, "Oh, I know that life is immortal; but of course, you know that there is such a thing as passing on." No, passing on is only a gentler term for dying. That does not mean that there are not many people who are experiencing what we term "death," but it is not a necessity. Life is eternal, here and now. Life is immortal, here and now. All the world may believe that death is a necessity, but what the world is thinking about death or what it is doing about it is not your concern. Your concern is to be the light of the world, in so far as you know the truth that God is life, and therefore, life is immortal and eternal. Let every claim of death that comes to you hit up against that wall. Do not react to it; do not worry or fear for your patient.

That does not mean that we are not to have compassion. We would not be in this work unless we had a large measure of compassion. We would not be devoting our life to the healing ministry if we did not want to be of help. But how can we be of help? By sympathizing humanly, by feeling sorry for our patients? No, by *not reacting*. Do not react. I am sure that that is the meaning of the Master's teaching: "resist not evil;[1] agree with thine adversary;[2] put up thy sword."[3] Do not react. Do not admit that there is a power that you have to fight or combat. Then, when somebody tells you about a problem, you do not react to it; you are not afraid that it will not be healed or met; you do not recognize that there is anything that has to be healed or that has to be met.

In reality, death has no power. So if a person says, "I am dying," you will not be overly disturbed. That indifference to the appearance or lack of reaction to it is the healing consciousness. Jesus' reaction to

[1] Matthew 5:39.   [2] Matthew 5:29.
[3] John 18:11.

Pilate was, "Thou couldest have no power at all against me, except it were given thee from above."[1] That is a correct reaction. Your response must always be of such a nature that it shows a complete lack of hate, love, or fear of error. If you do not hate, fear, or love error, you will not react to it.

Often there comes the temptation to say, "Ah, here is something I must do something about. As soon as I finish this dinner, I will go inside and give it a treatment"; but sooner or later we must all reach the place where nothing tempts us or finds a response within us. Successful healing work is dependent on just such a lack of response. The healing must be done at the point of contact, at the moment of contact; and when it is, you will not have to give a treatment afterwards.

Error in any form is no thing, no person, no circumstance, no condition. But it presents itself to you *as* person, place, thing, circumstance, or condition, and that is where you have to be spiritually alert. When it presents itself, you must instantly take care of it. Instantly dissolve it, by not reacting to it with any fear, hate, or love. It is very simple—just three words: fear, hate, love. Do not react with fear, hate, or love; and the problem is met. When we do not meet our problems—and I do not claim that we are meeting them 100 percent—it is because we have reacted to the problem with fear, hate, or love.

So never deceive yourself. When you fail, know why you fail. And do not be afraid of it, because it is an opportunity to pick yourself up and start over again with a higher understanding. When you do

[1] John 19:11.

151

not instantly meet a case, it is because, consciously or subconsciously, you have responded with hate, fear, or love of the error. Please believe me: It is reaction that counts. It is your reaction to a call for help that determines whether there will be a healing and whether it will be a quick healing or a slow healing. Actually, there is no slow healing. All healings are instantaneous; but whether you meet it at the time of the first treatment or the last, depends upon how you maintain a state of consciousness which does not react.

These two points contain the principle of Christ healing. If, first, we could always maintain that conscious oneness with God—that idea of our complete oneness, Self-maintenance, Self-sustenance—living continuously in that consciousness; and secondly, not react to the claims that come from without, there would be nothing left for us to do.

The question is often raised: "Do you have to be asked before you do work for another?" In other words, "Is it necessary for a person to ask for help before you give him help?" Generally speaking, yes. Either an individual, himself, must ask for help, or someone must ask for him. In other words, the one needing or desiring help must be brought to the consciousness of the practitioner. Some relative or friend may be the one to ask for the help, but in so doing, he is bringing the patient to the consciousness of the practitioner, or bringing the problem to the consciousness of the practitioner. In one way or another, there should be a request for help.

Very often, when he was asked for help, the Master said something like, "Do you believe that I can do this; do you have faith?" Even the asking was not quite enough. There had to be a little something more even than the asking; there had to be some degree of faith. But, strangely enough, healings take place without it. We have all had business associates or relatives or friends who were ill but who would not turn to Truth, and we, ourselves, took up work for them because their lives touched ours at some point. And they had healings through that work. That happens frequently.

The ideal situation is where some person really wants spiritual healing and asks for it. The fact that I had not been asked, however, would not hinder me from knowing the truth. Whenever I become aware of any form of error, whether it touches me by coming to me over the radio, by reading about it in the newspapers, or by hearing friends, relatives, or patients discuss it—no matter who, what, why—the moment the suggestion of error touches my consciousness, I am on the alert to meet it right at that moment. I do not wait; I do not wait to be asked; I meet it. The person involved may not benefit by my work: the measure of his receptivity or responsiveness to truth is his own demonstration. When he specifically asks for help, however, he is more likely to receive it. But never wait to be asked for help. Never, never. The moment you become aware of error—the moment that any suggestion of error comes to your consciousness—do something about it, and do it at that very instant. And, remember, the doing is your lack of response or reaction in the form of either hate, fear, or love, of the error. Do not react with either hate, fear, or love.

Handling the Suggestion of a Cause for Error

Do not be afraid of fear. Do not be afraid of ignorance. Do not be afraid of sin. They are not power. Sin is not a power for evil, but neither is sin a power for good. You cannot get pleasure out of sin any more than you can get punishment out of it, once you have realized that it is not power. Do not be one-sided and say, "Sin cannot do anything to me; it cannot cause any evil condition"; without, at the same time, realizing that sin cannot give any pleasure, either. Sin cannot enrich you and it cannot impoverish you. Sin cannot punish you, but it cannot cause pleasure, either. Sin is a false belief, an illusion, a false sense of reality; it has no power to give you pleasure or pain.

At times in helping people, the thought may come to you that there is something operating from the "other side." I am sure that most practitioners, at some time or other, have had cases in which they directly received the impression that there were forces of evil working from the other side—that is, from what we call "those who have passed on." One thing you can do is to handle this suggestion from the standpoint of neither hating, fearing, nor loving error, not giving it power, not reacting to it, but agreeing that it is not a power and does not have power. There is no such thing as either evil or good power being transmitted from one person to another, whether they are on this plane of consciousness or on any plane of consciousness. Since each one is consciously one with the Father, each one is Self-maintained and Self-sustained. Therefore, there is no parasitic thought; there is no drawing thought; there is no leaning thought which can operate as law. Through knowing this, you set aside that particular phase of karma.

If something is revealed to you in your work as a possible cause of inharmony, do not hesitate to handle it as *no* cause. Perhaps it is being revealed to you what the seeming cause is; and if it is, handle it; but handle it in the same way as the belief in karma. Meet it instantly with the recognition, "Well, that is not cause either. Neither can that have any power." Do not handle it as if now you have discovered some new form of error—there are not any new forms, even though the claim is legion. Every claim must be handled in the same way. The practitioner realizes that "I and my Father are one."[1] That is the relationship that exists, and the only relationship that nullifies karma or the belief in any cause separate from God.

A Divine Idea Contains within Itself the Power of Fulfillment

The question may arise as to the correct treatment for success in some particular enterprise such as, for example, a theatrical production. Of course, you must realize that there is no treatment that anyone can give that will make a show prosperous that has no reason for existing or being successful. The treatment for any play or for any book should be along this line: Does it contain a divine idea? Is it an expression, or is it the symbol of an expression of

[1] John 10:30.

love, truth, or beauty? Does it contain within itself some semblance of a divine idea? If so, the divine Intelligence that brought it forth has saved but a remnant, and that remnant is always a big enough remnant to make it productive, successful, and fruitful. You can apply this truth to a moving picture; you can apply it to a play; you can apply it to a book; you can apply it to a teaching. If a teaching has within itself the seed of truth, of love, of service, of any good; then that teaching must be fruitful, because the Mind that formed it, the Mind that gave expression to it, has also saved out a remnant of those who are essential to its recognition, support, and fruitage.

This same kind of treatment would apply, also, to the work of a practitioner or of a teacher. If a practitioner or a teacher is imbued with the Christ; if within his activity or ministry there is a spiritual idea, a spiritual power; if within that practitioner's or teacher's consciousness, there is the showing forth of the divine idea, then the same Mind that presents the divine idea as practitioner or teacher, also fulfills Itself as fruitage—the remnant of those who are there to recognize that activity, to support it, and to respond to it. You remember the story of the remnant that was saved out for Elijah. The remnant was really not saved out for Elijah; the remnant was saved out for God, and God's message. It did not make any difference whether it was Elijah or Elisha proclaiming it, or whether today a practitioner or teacher is revealing it. If it is a message of truth, then the same Mind or Intelligence that produced the idea also provides those who have not bowed their knees to Baal. It also provides those who are receptive and responsive to the message. This is important. Whether you are going to produce a moving picture or a play, or whether you are going to write a book, or whether you are going to give the world some new truth or a new presentation of truth, ask yourself: Is there a divine idea in it? Does it represent some spiritual idea of life, truth, beauty, harmony, service? These questions would apply whether you were operating a hotel, a summer resort, or a rooming house; or whether you were establishing a school. The particular form of the activity is not important. The important question is: Is the activity the embodiment and presentation of a divine idea? If it is, it has within itself the seed of success, since the Mind that formed the idea, that brought it into consciousness, brings it to fruition.

Always, Mind has saved out a remnant of those receptive and responsive to every divine idea. You can apply this to any and every kind of activity. If it represents an idea of service, if it is symbolic of some spiritual idea, it will come to fruition. On the other hand, you cannot take some old, worn-out idea and expect it to prosper. Neither can you produce a play or a picture and expect a spiritual treatment to help it, if it does not have within itself the power of fulfillment.

Making the Treatment Individual

The moment a claim is brought to the practitioner's consciousness, the practitioner meets it, and that makes it individual to the person who

157

brought it to the practitioner. If you come to me and say, "I have a headache," I meet that in my thought instantly by not reacting to it as though it were something of an evil nature, and you receive the response, thereby making it individual. It is individual, whether or not you receive the response by reason of the fact that you have come to a practitioner and brought the claim to him. Whatever truth is active in the practitioner's consciousness makes the treatment individual to the person who has brought the claim to him. In the same way, if you say, "My child is ill," the treatment becomes personal or individual to the child because you have brought the child and the child's claim to the practitioner's consciousness. The practitioner does not have to know the name of the patient or the name of the claim or the name of the disease.

No matter what name the patient or you might give to the disease, you have no assurance that it is the correct name. Even a doctor often does not know what the disease is, because sometimes a thorough diagnosis is wrong. The records of hospitals show that only forty-five percent of the deaths that are checked by an autopsy are the result of the disease for which the patient was being treated. Those are official records—medical records. Therefore, when a patient tells you what his claim is, if he has had a thorough medical examination, he may be correct and then again he may not be. What is going to happen, then, in the case of the other fifty-five percent of incorrect names of disease given you by patients? If there has not been a thorough physical checkup, they may be only ten or twenty percent correct. In that case, you would be eighty percent wrong in your treatments, if your treatment depended upon knowing the name of the disease, because you would be treating the wrong thing.

Let us be clear on this. Very few of the claims that are brought to a practitioner are ever diagnosed. Therefore, there is little chance of a patient's giving him the correct name of the disease. At best, the patient says, "My stomach hurts." If you knew all the different kinds of ailments that can happen to a stomach, you would know how ridiculous it is to direct a treatment to the stomach, or anything around the stomach. And how frequently patients have been treated for heart disease who have been suffering from gas pains or indigestion.

Not only is it unnecessary to know the name of the disease, but you do not need the name of the patient. The name that a patient gives you may not be his given name. It may be a stage name, a pseudonym, a nickname, or an otherwise assumed name. A married woman nearly always uses her husband's name. Demanding the name is ridiculous. Stop that nonsense. In the first place, there is no disease. Secondly, there is no person who has a disease. So of what significance is the name? There is a claim of a selfhood apart from God. There is a claim of an identity apart from God. There is a claim of a condition apart from God. But its name is legion. It has infinite form and an infinite variety of names. So stop dealing in names, and meet disease as suggestion. That is what you are dealing with—suggestion. Meet that instantly when it comes to thought. If you meet it at that moment, it will translate itself into harmony in the patient's consciousness.

Never try to make a treatment personal. Never direct it toward any one. Meet the claim in your own consciousness when it is presented to you, but do not identify it with a person. The person will get the benefit of the treatment, even if you do not understand how it is accomplished. The mere fact that you have taken him into your consciousness makes it binding upon him. But, whether you understand that at the moment or not, please believe this: *Every claim, every suggestion, must be met in your consciousness at the time of contact.* Do not put off the healing even for five minutes.

CHAPTER TEN

SPIRITUAL EXISTENCE

MEDITATION is valuable, even if the meditation lasts for only one or two minutes—even if it is only a few minutes snatched for this purpose during the noon hour. It is important, furthermore, never to retire, never to go to bed, just as a human being; because then you would have nothing more nor less than a night of human sleep, which might or might not be restful. Acquire the habit of never doing anything without first opening consciousness to the inflow of Spirit, of never engaging in any human activity without first opening consciousness to the inflow. Never begin any human activity—whether at the beginning of the day on awakening, whether it is preparing a meal, whether it is going out into the business world, whether it is undertaking household duties, or whether it is retiring for a nap or for a night's sleep—without specifically opening consciousness to the inflow of the Spirit.

For a while you may not get any results; that is, you may not be consciously aware of any results. But you will never open your consciousness to God without getting a result, even though at the time you may not be aware of the result. In other words, you may meditate, you may open your consciousness, and you may feel no response. Do not let that disturb you. That has nothing to do with it. I went on in that same way for eight months, meditating five and six times a day, and never in all that time, having any answering response. Of course, I did it alone. I did not receive my inner teaching until after the meditation had been successfully accomplished. I only found my inner Teacher when I found the ability to "be still, and know that I am God."[1] For you it will be much more simple.

As you continue meditating—especially as you have the opportunity to do it with others who have achieved the ability to meditate—it will become more and more simple, and you will feel the response much more quickly. But do not be discouraged if there seems to be no answer, if you seem to be no more spiritual after the meditation than before, or if you do not get any response. Remember that behind you there are hundreds of generations of people who have lived in the outer world, living completely in the realm of effect. That is the heritage of a human being, and that is the thing that you must break through. In time, if you persevere, you will find yourself automatically settling down into the center of your own being; and from that point on, you will feel yourself to be an avenue through which all of the Spirit continuously pours Itself. You can almost feel how it flows out from the center of your being.

Remember not to be too concerned about human beings. You are not on the human plane of existence. That does not mean that you should become cold and heartless. It does not mean that if somebody needs food, you are to give him a treatment and

[1] Psalms 46:10.

162

withhold the food. If somebody needs clothing, do not withhold it because you are so metaphysical. I do not mean that. I mean that even while suffering it to be so now, do not accept the appearance as the reality, but always stand fast on the inner plane, realizing the presence of God.

Continuity of Individual Identity

Now we come to another question: "Do you believe that you would be living as an individual, if you had never experienced human birth?" Regardless of what you may now think, ponder that idea in the weeks to come. What would have happened to you had you had not been born humanly? Where would you be? What would you be doing? It may give you an insight into what you may experience after the world says that you are dead. In reality, you will never be dead, but there may come a time when the world will believe that you are dead; and it would be wise for you to have some idea of what you will be doing, and where, and when, and how.

"Before Abraham was, I am."[1] That means that Jesus existed as an actual, individual entity and identity before Abraham's human existence. It means that, before Abraham, you existed as an individual, as a spiritual entity, as a spiritual identity. God, in manifesting Itself individually, could not begin to express Itself at a certain time in a certain place. God's manifestation of Its own being has always existed. God's manifestation of Its own being has existed since time began, since God, Itself,

[1] John 8:58.

163

began—not that God ever did begin, because God is timeless and spaceless, God is infinite; God is eternal. But God is eternally expressed; God is eternally manifested, and has been, ever since God has been God. That manifestation, that expression, is you, and it is I. Nothing can be added to God and nothing can be taken from God. God has been and is fully manifested from the beginning. Therefore, if you are the God-entity, in any form, the God-identity, or the God-individual, before Abraham was, you have had conscious identity. I have had conscious individual identity ever since God has. And that is forever. By that same token, "I am with you alway, even unto the end of the world."[1] In other words, as long as God is God, God will individualize Itself, or individually express Itself, as individual being—spiritual being. Do you see how pointless it is to look at a human being and begin thinking about his age or his condition? That picture before the eyes is the illusion of human sense.

The fact that we have been drawn together from every part of the world, representing almost every religion, with varying degrees of education and from diverse backgrounds, is sufficient indication that somewhere on the path we have touched each other in consciousness. We have existed before this experience. How could we be of one mind, of one Spirit and consciousness, if somewhere, somehow, we had not touched each other in consciousness? Once you catch the realization of this truth of your immortal individuality, of the fact that you have existed, pre-existed, co-existed, since God began,

[1] Matthew 28:19.

and that you will individualize the life that God is unto eternity, you will begin to understand the spiritual universe and spiritual existence.

Then will come the realization of why we are on this spiritual path, why we have been drawn together. It cannot be for the purpose of developing a heart that beats a little more normally according to the world's standards, or that ten or a hundred dollars a week should be added to our income, or that we should find a more comfortable house in which to live. It surely was not to that end that we have come to this study, although the effect of this study will be better health, more happiness, a greater sense of peace within, probably a better home in which to live, and perhaps a greater sense of supply. These will be some of the effects of our study. But the real purpose is to awaken us to our true identity; to awaken us, so that when we are awakened, we shall see Him as He is, and be satisfied with His likeness. The "He" to whom we are to be awakened and which we are to recognize is our own spiritual identity as Christ—our identity as the Son of God, as the spiritual image and likeness of God.

It is our individual being—our spiritual identity— to which we are to be awakened. That identity has existed and co-existed with God from the beginning. That individual identity will continue to be individual you and me until the end of the world, that is, until all mortal concepts disappear, and we realize the spiritual universe. That was the vision of John. That was the vision of Paul who wrote about the "house not made with hands, eternal in the heavens."[1]

[1] II Corinthians 5:1.

That spiritual identity is the *I* which has existed throughout all time and which will continue to exist for all time to come.

According to human values, we all appreciate motherhood, fatherhood, and parental and filial relationships, but we know from experience that they are not always as beautiful as they are sometimes pictured. For many years I, myself, was unable to discover any reason for my having been born. Others may not have had this experience, but at one period of my existence, I had to find some reason for living. Furthermore, as I looked about, I wondered why other men and women were living— working eight hours a day, nine, ten hours a day, with their only recompense a place to sleep, and ultimately, a hole to crawl into. It did not seem very purposeful or meaningful. Now I see what life can be when it is lifted above that mortal, human, finite, physical sense—when consciousness expands, and we catch the vision of each other as spiritual beings. We find a joy in human companionship hitherto unknown. That comes when we are seeing through spiritual light, not through the dark glass of manhood. Because of this vision, I am more than ever convinced that spiritual friendship, spiritual companionship, would be a part of our existence even without the process of human birth. In fact, I know from the inner companionship I have experienced, that all who have existed as individuals—as God manifesting Itself as individual being—all of those still exist. They not only exist, but they commune with us; they tabernacle with us. We are not aware of this until we open the spiritual center of our being, and find them there; we are unaware of their existence, because they do not exist as mortals; they do not exist as human beings; they do not even exist as dead spirits, or the spirits of the dead. They exist, as I exist, as individual being, but as individual beings who have always been alive and have never died. On that higher plane of consciousness, you will never meet those who have lived and died; they have always been immortal. You find them in their immortality and not in the human sense of manhood or womanhood.

Healing work, which is the proof of our work and of the rightness of the message, becomes easier, less labored, and much more fruitful, as we perceive the spiritual nature of the *You* that you are and the *I* that I am, as we learn to drop this physical sense of existence. Now all this may sound abstract, or absolute, but please believe me, it is not. It is possible right here on the level where you are now, and where I am now; and it is brought into manifestation and expression in the degree that you and I realize that our function in this work is not merely to make a physical body more comfortable physically, or to make a material purse richer. As you rise above that stage of the work, you will no longer center your thought on the material plane of satisfaction—on the physical, mental, or even on the financial plane. Then you will begin to think of the spiritual significance of individual being and spiritual supply, and you will find an entirely new world. That new world will appear here as improved humanhood. It will appear as an improved body, or as an improved pocketbook; but it will not be an improved anything and you will know it. You will consider these outward effects of no importance, because you will know that they are just the translation of the divine law into human terms.

As you open your consciousness for the inflow, you will find that the Spirit will really go before you and do that for you which you had expected to do humanly. Ultimately, you will find that you rarely have much to do humanly—that always the Spirit goes before you to make the crooked places straight, to open and do those things that, heretofore, you have thought you had to do. Spirit is a reality. Spirit is a power. Heretofore, we have merely said so; but now we really have to draw It forth and watch It at work. Spirit is God; Spirit is truth; Spirit is omnipresent, omniscient, omnipotent. Once we have the conscious feeling of the Presence, It lives our lives for us. But there must be the conscious communion. There must be the conscious oneness or conscious at-one-ment. There must be a conscious awareness of the Presence, and that all takes place through the opening of consciousness to Truth through meditation in one form or another.

No Predestination in God

Sometimes the question is asked: "Do you believe that each one of us must go through certain experiences during our lives, that certain pictures present themselves to us, or are destined for us, according to a foreordained pattern, even to the experience of our coming into some form of truth work at a particular time?"

No, I do not believe that there are any such patterns or pictures. God is Spirit, and God has no awareness of human pictures. It is an impossibility that God could believe that we have to be run over by an automobile, or that we must become ill with a certain disease. It is impossible to believe that God ordains that we should marry, be unhappy; or that we should work hard, faithfully, honestly, sincerely, accumulate some degree of financial competence, and then have a panic or a depression or something beyond our own control wipe it out for us. No, these things I do not believe, nor do I believe that God ordains that some children should come into the world healthy and wealthy, and that others should come into the world poverty stricken or deformed.

God is individual, spiritual consciousness. If we were consciously aware of that, then our experience would be God experiencing Itself as us, and our life would contain nothing but the harmony of God. The experience of the prodigal son is one to which I often refer. The son probably became tired of receiving all his good from the father, and wanted to go out and make a name for himself. That state of consciousness is our humanhood. Humanhood is the "prodigal son," wandering around in life, claiming to be Mary, Joe, or Joel. It sets up a separate entity and it creates for itself all of the experiences through which it goes. Yet, all the time it is really God made manifest. The proof of this is that everyone in the history of the world who has touched God consciousness has been freed of these mortal patterns—has been freed of sin, disease, lack, limitation. Life to such a person takes on an entirely different pattern—a pattern of freedom, wholeness, abundance, and happiness.

Some people, however, who have already touched God consciousness, have had other forms of suffering come upon them, perhaps because they later accepted a limited concept of life, and set out to reform the world. In so doing, they brought upon themselves persecution and crucifixion. If each one of us were to realize this God consciousness and, at the same time, set the other person free to realize this for himself as well, then the religious leaders of our world would not have had to go through such struggles. If I were to attempt to attract crowds to this message by preaching on the street corners, I might receive a very unpleasant reception, because I would be trying to bring Spirit to the human mind which is antagonistic to It.

On the other hand, if I abide in the center of my being, if I sit in my office or home and rest content in my conscious oneness with God; one here, another there, and two or three in another place are attracted to me; and just as a remnant of those who had not bowed their knees to Baal was saved out for Elijah, so do I find the remnant that my state of consciousness has drawn to me. Then there are no antagonisms and no arguments—only a state of receptivity.

I do not believe that human problems have anything to do with God, and for that reason they are not foreordained. They are only foreordained from the standpoint of humanhood. If we adopt stealing as our means of a livelihood, it is foreordained that we will end up in jail, if we live long enough. But that is a pattern that we have drawn, not one that God has drawn. There is a striking example of that in the man, Starr Daily. The foreordained climax to the pattern he had established was a twenty-year prison sentence; yet one touch of the Christ nullified the whole human pattern. Three years after the moment of his Christ realization, he was released on parole, even though a parole board stated that he could never be paroled. A human pattern is never spiritually ordained, nor is it ordained to be permanent, even humanly; it is merely a question of when and how soon the Christ comes.

The theme of this message is: *spiritual identity, spiritual activity, spiritual power*; their development within our own being; and the need for touching within ourselves that spiritual Center from which flow spiritual activity and spiritual power. Once that spiritual Center has been touched, and the power of Spirit has been released, It really lives Itself as our experience. What Paul says becomes literally true: "I live; yet not I, but Christ liveth in me";[1] or the Master, "I can of mine own self do nothing.[2] . . . My doctrine is not mine but his that sent me."[3] The essence of this message is that the Father is really living our life, doing all things, and being all.

Sincerity and Integrity Prerequisites for the Search for God

Spirituality, however, does not come forth in a day, in a week, or in a month. Yes, it is true that Saul of Tarsus became Paul in a blinding flash. But remember the number of years that Saul of Tarsus had been studying truth under the guidance of a

[1] Galatians 2:20.   [2] John 5:30.   [3] John 7:16.

spiritual teacher. That his spiritual guidance may or may not have been correct is not the significant factor. What is significant is that Saul was God-hungry, that Saul was so intent on God that he was willing to be a party to the persecution and murder of others for what he considered to be Truth. There was an inner devotion to Truth or God. So with us: what is important is the motive and the intent. If we persist in following a religious or metaphysical study for some material good that we are seeking, we shall never be a Paul; we shall never have the experience of the illumination. If, however, we are God-hungry, if we are intent on learning the true nature of Cause, rather than demonstrating effect, then it really makes no difference whether we pursue that path as a Roman Catholic, as a Hebrew, as a Protestant, or as a follower of some one of the numerous metaphysical movements: we will reach the goal —realization. Our search will carry us from one stage of consciousness to another; it may even take us from one church to another, or one teaching to another, but in the end it will carry us out of the human sense of church. Just think how wonderful it is that a man who was so intent on Judaism as Saul should have been the very one to destroy the belief that it was necessary to be a Jew before one could become a Christian. The light in his consciousness was so complete that Judaism faded out in his vision of Christianity.

If we could learn all the truth that is contained in all the scriptures of the world, it still might not lead us to the spiritual experience. But as long as we are on the path of seeking the Spirit, and the spiritual way of life, then the more we associate with those on the path, the better it will be. The more we can be together in the fellowship of the Spirit—whether it is in the form of attending lectures, classes, or group meetings—the more helpful it will be. Such fellowship leads to the unfolding of consciousness, unless somebody should attempt to crystallize these associations into an organization, so that the Spirit is lost in the outer form. It is unfortunate that it is necessary to have even as little organization as there is in The Infinite Way to keep the message printed, published, and recorded. That does require some organization, but I am sure it will never become a church organization with church memberships, and for this reason: I long with all the intensity of my being to see every individual free in Christ; I long to see every individual so at-one with God that we are only companions to each other on the way—helpers when one of us slips a little or needs encouragement.

Therefore, let us never indulge such human pastimes as judgment, criticism, or condemnation of each other, because each one of us is going to have to work out his own spiritual unfoldment in an individual way. The way that I work mine out may not appeal to all of you, but that is my individual demonstration, so let me have the freedom to see and do things in my own way. Each one of you in turn will do things with which some of the other students may not agree. Let each one have the privilege of working it out and even failing, if that is necessary. Failure may serve a very good purpose in revealing the incorrect things we may be doing. Instead of criticizing or judging or condemning, let us support each other in this activity. No one could be in this work with any motive but that of spiritual development. To do otherwise would be a violation of spiritual integrity. We cannot put on the Robe, and then violate its ethics or teachings or morality. Any such violation will prove to be a boomerang. Out in the world men can lie, cheat, steal, or defraud, and their evil deeds may not return to them for a long period of time; but it is not so with one who is on the spiritual path.

A person who has opened his consciousness to spiritual truth, pays a heavy penalty for any conscious error in which he indulges—even for the mistakes he makes. An honest mistake will bring a degree of suffering to him, since that mistake must be pointed out to him in order for him to change. But conscious error—ambition for place or position, greed for money, lusting after the flesh—indulged in while wearing this Robe carries with it a heavy price. Let us as individuals live up to our highest developed sense of spiritual right. Do not think for a minute that I claim that I am or that anybody I have ever known is fulfilling the fullness of the Christ. Our responsibility is to make the effort to live up to our highest developed sense of spiritual good. As long as we are doing that, we are on the right path. It is only when we come down from that level, and through some human means or some human desire, find our selves in conflict with the action of the Spirit that trouble descends upon us.

The Spirit is a freeing action, and It frees us from material concepts and material forms of existence;

but this activity can be a terrifying thing when it strikes up against the opposite quality of spiritual dishonesty. I think that is why I use the term *spiritual integrity* so much. We can do many things humanly that may not seem right to the world; but when we are on the spiritual path, it is then necessary to live up to our highest unfoldment, our highest developed sense of spiritual good. Then we do not have to fear what mortal man can do to us; we do not have to fear the past, the present, or the future. Here, too, our history as human beings may not always conform to our spiritual heritage. Therefore, let us learn not to judge according to appearances. Let us not be too concerned about each other's human history. We come out of varying backgrounds of sin or purity, disease or health, and ignorance or wisdom. But though the sin be as scarlet, it will be white as snow once we touch the spiritual level of consciousness.

One of the great sins of organization is that often after it accepts an individual in Christ, it then proceeds to ferret out his past and sit in judgment upon him. Instead of working through a sense of forgiveness and understanding, it still applies the same code of human conduct or human punishment or human action as before. Even on this spiritual path, we make human mistakes. It has been done over and over again in the Protestant ministry, in the Catholic ministry, in the Hebrew ministry. And we all know that in the metaphysical ministry people well along the path have been subject to temptation and have fallen.

So let us not adopt the attitude of the world—

criticism, judgment, or condemnation. Rather let us see if we cannot work together, and with our enlightenment lift each other up so as to make it impossible for any one to fall by the wayside again. In other words, even though there is a sense of humanness among us, let us not judge humanly. Let us not act as the human world acts. Let us not work from the standpoint of expulsion or ostracism. Let us rather take the attitude that we are all one; and, therefore, our purpose is upliftment, not punishment, or excommunication. This is a very important point. Remember this, because it is only that state of consciousness which will know how to forgive an enemy, how to forgive those who despitefully use us, how, in other words, to fulfill the Christian doctrine of "love one another."[1] Love not only your friends and your neighbors, but love those who persecute you and hate you. Love! Love! Love! Forgive! Forgive! Forgive! And then, finally, reach that state of consciousness in which you no longer take the mental sword of criticism, judgment, or condemnation. When that time comes, your consciousness will have become the light of the world, because in it there is neither love, hate, nor fear of error.

[1] John 4:7.

CHAPTER ELEVEN

THE ALLNESS OF GOD

THE primary purpose of our work is to bring forth our true identity as Spirit, as God made manifest, as life, individually expressed in all of life's harmony and perfection. We, in our work, do not attempt just to turn sick people into well people, or poor people into rich people. Improving humanhood is not our main object. The fruitage of our work is improved health and supply, but the improvement of material conditions is not its prime object. These are only the "signs following." The primary object is to reveal God as individual being, to reveal that there are not God *and* man, but that there is only God, God appearing as individual you and individual me to reveal that "I and my Father are one."[1] There are not both a God *and* you, but since God is infinite, and God is all, then God must express Itself, manifest Itself, *as* you and *as* me.

In this oneness, there is no room for sin, disease, lack, or limitation. There is no room for war or for unfair competition. There is no room for the evils of capitalism or the evils of communism. There is only room for the understanding of true being—the understanding of what it means to be God manifested individually, in all of God's glory. You will

[1] John 10:30.

177

remember the prayer of the Master: "Father, glorify me with thine own self, with the glory which I had with thee."[1] Think what it would mean if we could stand forth here and now in all of God's glory. Think how impossible it would be to lack anything if we were showing forth the allness of God, if we were showing forth the truth of that statement, "Son . . . all that I have is thine."[2] According to Scripture, it is true that all that the Father hath is thine and mine. Once you and I begin to show forth that allness of God, how impossible it would be for any form of envy, jealousy, malice, or strife to enter into our daily experience. And that is the object of this work. The Infinite Way is not merely for the purpose of setting up better human beings, but to reveal the allness of God as individual you and me.

In all religions there are promises of Omnipresence. We have to go one step further; we have to *demonstrate* Omnipresence. To us the presence of God must become a living reality; God must become as real to you and to me as we are real to each other. It must ultimately be as possible for you to tune in to God as for you to tune in to your practitioner on the telephone. God, through this study, through meditation, and through inspiration, must become, not a word that we talk about, not a being to whom we pray, but an actual companion on our pathway, through life.

The object of this work is to make God real—to make God as real to you and to me as he was to Abraham, Jacob, Moses, Elisha, Elijah, Jesus, John, Paul, or Peter. God becomes an absolute living

[1] John 17:5.   [2] Luke 15:31.

reality—a presence, a power, a companion, a healer, a supplier. We shall not find God in books and we shall not find God in churches. Books and churches are merely the avenues which enable us to open our consciousness to the inflow. God ultimately will be revealed where Jesus said It would be revealed—within: "The kingdom of God is within you[1] . . . I can of mine own self do nothing[2] . . . the Father that dwelleth in me, he doeth the works."[3] Where is the Father? Within me. Of course, that does not mean inside this body. God is not in our physical body, but God is within us in the sense that God is our very own being. God is not separate or apart from you or me. In this case, the word "within" does not actually mean within some part of the body such as the brain or heart: it means that God is not something outside or separate or apart from our own being. God is not separate or apart from our consciousness. And before long we shall see very clearly that God *is* our consciousness.

Man Is Not a Reflection

Most metaphysical teachings would call us "man." Their synonyms for the word "man" include idea, image, likeness, reflection, expression. Nearly all of them teach that you are an idea of God, but The Infinite Way teaching does not agree with that concept. This teaching stands on the fullness of the Master's unfoldment, on the fullness of his realization that in his humanhood, he, of himself, could do nothing:

[1] Luke 17:21.   [2] John 5:30.   [3] John 14:10.

I am the way, the truth, and the life.[1]

I can of mine own self do nothing.[2]

The Father that dwelleth in me, he doeth the works.[3]

Have I been so long time with you, and yet hast thou not known me, Philip?[4]

I and my Father are one.[5]

Did you ever see one? Hold up one of your fingers—just one finger and not two. Think of that one finger as the symbol of the oneness expressed by the "I and my Father."

Always remember: I and the Father are one. Unless you can agree with that teaching of oneness, understand it, and feel the rightness of it, you will never be able to take the next step and realize: All that God is, I am; all that the Father hath is mine. Now hold up two of your fingers and notice that no matter how close together you can bring them, you do not have one, or oneness. You still have two-ness. As long as you have two, you will be striving to bring them together, or expecting one of them to pray to the other, or to have one of them worthy of the other. But if you can agree that I and the Father are one, as much as one finger is one, then you will find that all that the Father is, I am, and all that the Father hath is mine; you will understand that when you pray, believing that you already have, you do already have. Two fingers represent God *and* you. One finger is our symbol—God manifest *as you*. It is the Word made flesh—not the Word *and* flesh, but the Word *made* flesh.

[1] John 14:6.   [2] John 5:30.   [3] John 14:10.
[4] John 14:9.   [5] John 10:30.

The basis of our work is oneness—omnipresence. It is not one thing present together with another thing. It is omnipresence—"I and my Father are one." In this oneness is your completeness. In this oneness, God is made manifest as individual you and me in all of Its glory. "Glorify thou me with thy glory." The first important concept that must be changed in coming from any metaphysical teaching to The Infinite Way is that you are *not* an idea; you are *not* a reflection. Look at a reflection of yourself on the wall and ask yourself how you would like to be that reflection.

We are not reflections; we are not ideas; you and I are life eternal. If we were other than life eternal, there would be a law, a God, a something, acting upon us, whereas: I am the way, I am the law. I was given dominion over the things of the sea, over the things of the earth, over the things of the air, and over the things of the sky. In that oneness is dominion—the dominion of God made manifest as individual you and me. You should study this very carefully, turning to the Father within, and praying for light and guidance on this point, because on this revelation rests the entire demonstration of harmony.

The moment you believe that there is some other power—some power outside of yourself, separate from yourself—that can act upon you, even if you believe it is a good power, you are exposing yourself to the possibility of its opposite, an evil power. There is no power acting upon you. Life, God, or Soul is the *only power;* God, Soul, Spirit, and Truth are the reality of your being. If there is only one Life, and that Life is your life, then God is your life. If there is only one Mind, then God is your mind. God is your Soul. God is your Spirit. We are told that even "your body is the temple of the Holy Ghost."[1] What else is there to you but life, mind, Soul, Spirit, and body? And all this is God—God infinitely manifested in all Its glory as you and as me.

The history of the world, and surely the history of the religious world, contradicts any such teaching. But history has very little proof of harmony to offer us. We have only to look at the history of the world to find a continuous record of the belief that we are something separate and apart from God. On every side there are wars and other chaotic conditions. If there is to be any hope for us as individuals, it will have to be found in the message and the mission of the Master; and that message and that mission without misinterpretation. The Word itself must suffice. We must accept as our principle the words of the Master, not as a teaching applying to an individual of two thousand years ago, but as a principle of life which we can follow. On that point of oneness, of conscious oneness with God, rests the foundation of all else that is to come.

The Human Mind Is an Avenue of Awareness

A second important point in the message of The Infinite Way is also in disagreement with most of the teaching of the metaphysical world: The human mind is not a power; human thought is not a power; even good human thought is not a power. Those who have attempted to heal with good human thought

[1] I Corinthians 6:19.

will testify to the fact that it is not a very great healing agency. If we are dependent on the human thought of a practitioner, we are in a very precarious situation. You know that many practitioners, at some time or other, prove to be very human. If that should happen to be the case when you need help, how would you get your help? If the practitioner happened to be asleep when the call came, what hope would there be for the patient? No, human thought is not a power. Human thought cannot make two times two become four. The principle of mathematics establishes that fact. Human thought cannot violate the principle of mathematics by making two times two become five. God's thoughts are not your thoughts, and your thoughts are not God's thoughts. "Which of you by taking thought can add one cubit unto his stature?"[1]

If in treatment we use the human mind to bring about a healthy heart, liver, or lung, we may possibly achieve our objective. But tomorrow is another day, and why should not one or another of these organs become sick tomorrow, even though it has been restored to health today? Next month is another month, next year another year, and before we realize it, the years have added up to three score and ten. After that, of course, there is no use praying for a good heart or liver or lung; it is too late. Even scripture tells us that. It has been said that the study of metaphysics prevents untimely death, but what is a timely death? If you believe in the timeliness of death, can you pray for a good heart after seventy, eighty, or whatever your conception of a proper life

[1] Matthew 6:27.

183

and contagion from certain germs. There is a universal belief in vitamins and calories. There is a universal belief in anything and everything under the sun, except the power and presence of God. That is not so universal. There are only a few of us trying to maintain our firm faith in and reliance upon that truth.

If we understand that the human mind is an avenue of awareness, we will not make the mistake of trying to do away with the human mind; but we shall be very grateful that we have it to use as an avenue of awareness. Through this mind and its thoughts, we can become aware of the truth of being; we can become aware of the beauties and bounties of the world. It is through thought that we become aware of each other. Through thought, God, Truth, imparts Itself to me and to you. Through thought, we become receptive to the divine ideas, the spiritual ideas of life. Therefore, we are not trying to negate or eliminate either thought or the human mind, but rather are we going to utilize it as one of those avenues given to us for the harmonious expression of daily experience. However, we are not going to use that mind as a power; we are not going to use that mind to demonstrate health or wealth or opportunity: We are merely going to use that mind to become aware of the health and the wealth that already exist as the natural state of our being. This teaching cannot be built on the old metaphysics, because no amount of human thought-taking is going to bring about health or wealth. Only God can do that, and God *is* the very life of our being.

Difference between Prayer and Treatment

We shall go on now to another point in which there is a lack of agreement—perhaps not disagreement, but in which there is a difference in language and a difference in application. In The Infinite Way, prayer and treatment are not the same thing. Treatment is not a synonym for prayer; prayer is not a synonym for treatment. In this teaching, treatment is the truth that you and I know, the truth that we think, declare, or affirm in contradistinction to the error that is appearing. In other words, when I say that God is the law and the reality of my being, that God is my life, my Soul; when I say that God, the life which is God, is the eternality and immortality of my being; when I say that Christ is the law unto my being, and there is not a material law to act upon me; when I declare or affirm my oneness with God; when I declare or affirm the nothingness, the non-reality, of any form of error, that is treatment. In some metaphysical teachings, this would be considered prayer, but not in our work.

In The Infinite Way, affirmations and denials have not been entirely eliminated. We do not do away completely with affirmations and denials, but we do not think of them as prayer; they are treatment, a statement or restatement of truth within our own thought. The purpose of the treatment is to remind ourselves of the truth of being, thereby lifting ourselves to that place where prayer is possible.

Prayer is the word of God which comes to us. Prayer is not something we do. Prayer is not a

186

voicing of anything for God to hear. Prayer is not a petition nor is it an affirmation. Prayer is really the word of God coming to us. It is the "Peace, be still,"[1] that is voiced within our consciousness. It is an assurance that comes to us within, which says: "Be still, and know that I am God. I am on the field. Stand still and see the salvation of the Lord." When a practitioner or a teacher says to you, "Stand still, and see the salvation of the Lord," that is treatment, not prayer. You are being reminded of some truth, the purpose of which is to bring about a certain stillness in your thought, a certain quietness, and an ability to be receptive, so that you may hear within you a voice saying, "This is the way, walk ye in it."[2]

But when you hear this voice within your own being—and when I say hear I do not necessarily mean audibly hear; I mean hear in the sense of becoming aware of, sensing, feeling, or becoming conscious of—that is the Word. If you become aware of something stirring within you, if you become aware of a sense of peace descending upon you, that is prayer; that is the Word coming to your consciousness. That is communion. Prayer, or communion, is the relationship existing between God, the Father, and God, the Son. It is the relationship between the universal infinite Being and you. It is infinite, yet individualized in expression. This is the relationship which makes it possible for you to hear and receive divine guidance, divine healing, divine direction, divine protection, or whatever it is that is necessary in your experience.

[1] Mark 4:39.   [2] Isaiah 30:21.

I know from my own experience that healing takes place for my patient when something within me says, "All is well"; or "I am on the field"; or "Do not worry; I am there, too." To the Master it came as: "I can of mine own self do nothing."[1] In other words, even though the Father and I are one, this part of me that appears to the world as a human being is not really the presence or power of God. The presence and power of God is that which is invisible to your eyes, but is very, very visible and audible to your spiritual senses. When I am still, when I am quiet, when I am receptive, this assurance comes to me. Sometimes it comes in words, sometimes in quotations, sometimes in original thoughts, sometimes just in a feeling of well-being; and then I know that all is well with those who have called on me for help. Emerson called it the "Oversoul." It is really Omnipresence—the very infinite presence and power of God, consciously realized.

God is omnipresent; God is always present. But it is our conscious realization of this that does the work. It is not simply the fact that God is omnipresent. God is omnipresent on every battlefield in the world, right where men are being killed. That God is omnipresent, that God was in reality on the battlefield, did not help those needing help. No, it takes conscious realization of the presence of God in order to make God available in whatever need there may be. Never think for a minute that there is any place in the world that is not filled with the presence of God; but never think for a moment that that is going to be of much help to you, except in proportion to your

[1] John 5:30.

conscious realization of that truth. It is conscious realization that is prayer. Praying and repeating the 23rd Psalm or the 91st Psalm, or voicing all the metaphysical truths you know, such as, "I am rich, and I know it," or "I am well, and I know it," will not do the work. Some of you know what could be happening to you at the very moment you are making these statements. Repeating words does not do the work. It may lift your thought to that place where the work can be done—to that place where you have a conscious realization of the presence of God.

Right here is a point of demarcation between this and much of the metaphysical work in the world. The Infinite Way is an unfoldment which says that you and I, as well as Jesus, Moses, and Elijah, must have a conscious realization of the presence of God. It is not going to do us any good to walk around saying, "God is love, and God is present; God is love, and God is present." Unless, and until, we actually feel the presence of God, unless we can lift ourselves to a state of consciousness in which God becomes tangible and visible and evident in our own experience, it is all in the realm of treatment and not prayer.

Treatment is correct in its place, and all of you who are familiar with my writings know that a considerable amount of space is given to the subject of treatment. I am very thorough in the teaching of treatment; because I believe that at certain stages of our experience, it is not only necessary to treat, but that treatment forms the very foundation of our understanding of truth. At least, it is the letter of truth, upon which we may build the structure of spiritual understanding.

To know the correct letter of truth is a good foundation for the revelation, unfoldment, and spiritual discernment of truth, the spiritual consciousness of truth. Naturally, after a while you will have no more need for treatment than you have use for stating or repeating the multiplication table. When you have occasion to know the product of 12 times 12, 144 comes to thought immediately without conscious effort.

No matter how much you learn of treatment in any metaphysical work, no matter how perfect you become in stating the truth as it is found in The Infinite Way writings, please do not have too much faith in it, or you may stumble and fall. It is not the statement of truth that does the work; it is the inner realization of truth. It is not how much you can declare God, affirm God, or petition God. It is not how many statements of truth you know. On the contrary, it is much better for a student to use two or three statements as reminders of truth; meditate upon them; ponder them; and then rest, and let God do the work. Let spiritual consciousness unfold.

All this repeating of statements of truth is self-hypnosis—auto-suggestion. No one ever has to use force or power in this work. Nothing is more true than that it is "not by might, nor by power, but by my spirit, saith the Lord of hosts"[1]—not by physical might, and not by mental power, but by *My* Spirit.

Regardless of how much you may declare that I and the Father are one, it does not have any real

[1] Zechariah 4:6.

power unless you know what the Father is, and unless you know who *I am*. Two things must be known: Who am I? and, What is God? Ultimately, in the end, we will know that they are one. But until we have reached that point, let us not accept blindly some statement about God or about ourselves.

That word *I* contains the entire secret of Hebrew Scripture. That word *I* contains the entire secret of the ancient Hindu Scripture. That word *I* contains the secret of the Master's revelation. Only through this understanding of the word *I*, can you understand that "I and my Father are one," or "I am the the way, the truth, and the life." And without that understanding, what good would any treatment be? What good would any treatment be that did not embrace within itself the wisdom of truth! It is assumed that a treatment is the embodiment of truth, or expression of truth. Unless we know the truth about the *I*, unless we know the truth about the Father, unless we know the truth about body, a treatment is not really worth the time it takes to give it. Even a mental treatment, even a statement of truth, must be literally true to be even a little bit effective; and, in order to lead to the consciousness of truth, a treatment must be a declaration of truth.

The Deep Things of God Revealed through Meditation

We now come to the subject of meditation. If you follow along the path of The Infinite Way, you will learn a great deal about meditation and its practice. Without it you are merely living as a human being, and as such you are subject to all of the conditions of humanhood, just as is every other human being in the world. When, however, you develop the ability to meditate, to open your consciousness to the inflow of the Spirit, then you have the conscious awareness of the presence of Spirit, of God, of Life, Truth, and Love, with you from morning until night, and from night until morning. It is this *conscious awareness* that is your safety and your security.

God is infinite good. But this good is experienced only through the conscious recognition, or conscious awareness, of the presence and power of God. Therefore, as we follow the instruction in the chapter on "Meditation" in *The Infinite Way*, we shall find that from waking in the morning until retiring at night, never for a moment do we leave God out of our consciousness. We make God the very center of our consciousness, the very activity of our consciousness. When we do that, something happens to most of us. Very few of us who have been in this work any length of time are permitted to sleep a whole night through. Somehow we are awakened with another reminder of God's presence and power; and it is that reminder in the middle of the night that often proves a benediction to our friends and family and patients, since in that stillness and quietness of the night it is easier to receive this conscious awareness of divine Presence and divine Power. Naturally, that blesses all those who are a part of our consciousness.

As we fill our thought, our consciousness, with this realization of God, an extraordinary thing happens to us. A greater sense of quietness descends upon us, a greater sense of peace. With the realization of God's presence we have a confidence that all is well, and we know why. We cannot escape from God once we have made God the reality of our being. That makes it possible for the deeper meditation. It is in this deeper meditation that we really learn the deep things of God. There are deep things of God to be known, and these deep things of God are shown forth in our experience. For example, we were not born to be only business men and housewives. We were all born for a spiritual purpose—to perform a spiritual function, to be some part of God's plan. In the degree, however, that we are attached to the human world, we are not about our Father's business. And that is one of the reasons we are in this work— to get back to the Father's house. Instead of living this prodigal experience, instead of earning our living by the sweat of our brow, one of these days we shall return to the Father's house and the Father consciousness, and there find a jeweled ring and a purple robe—find that we have nothing to do but bask in the Father's love.

CHAPTER TWELVE

GOD CONSCIOUSNESS

To know our true identity is to solve every problem of so-called human existence. Actually, we are not living a human existence. Our existence is spiritual and divine, but because we do not know our true identity, it has become filled with discord and inharmony. If I know that I am *I*, and that that *I* is infinite Being, there can never intrude a thought of lack, limitation, discord, inharmony, jealousy, malice, or lust. When I know that I am *I*, and that this *I* is the infinity, the allness of God's being made manifest, the Word made flesh, then only can I realize that *I* am Self-sustained and Self-maintained.

Some day all of us will admit that *I* is Self-created:

I, the very consciousness of my being, formed me before ever I was in the womb. I would not have been there at all if *I*, the divine consciousness of my being, had not been expressing Itself in just that way. *I*, the divine consciousness of my being, formed my body after its own image and likeness, as my vehicle of expression. I can no more be separated from my body than I can be separated from my life. My body is the form in which my

194

life is appearing. My body is an expression of my identity. My parents did not create it. *I* created it. My consciousness created it and my consciousness is maintaining it now in its present form. If my consciousness were to change, my body would change. If my consciousness of supply were to change, my supply would change. Always, consciousness is forming its own body, its own image and likeness. My consciousness of home has made my home whatever it is. My consciousness of business, of a practice, of health, expresses as my home or business or practice, my health or my wealth.

Those who understand this principle and who have seen some of the slums or ghettos of New York City will understand that only the state of consciousness of the people living in them created those ghettos. In the city of Chicago, where not too many years ago there were open plains, and people could have built any kind of a home they wanted on those plains, slums and ghettos have grown up. In California, with all its wide open spaces, pure clear air, and bright sunshine, there are also slum areas. Every city, every village, every town has its slums. Where do they come from? People bring them with them. First, they carry the slum-idea of home in their consciousness, and then they build outwardly that which has already been built in their consciousness. People, with limited concepts of homes and houses, plant those limited concepts wherever they go to live, and when they move from place to place, they carry their slums with them. Why? Because their consciousness out-pictures as their way of living. It is true that many people have emerged from the slums, but they are the people who have eliminated slums from their consciousness. Until there is a change in a person's consciousness of home, there is no change in the outer conditions.

There are times when we wonder why it is that we are the same this year as we were last year or the year before. Sometimes we wonder why, after years on the metaphysical path, no change has come. There is only one reason for it: our consciousness has not expanded. We have remained at the same level of consciousness, and because our consciousness has not expanded, conditions for us have not changed or improved. You can prove this for yourself. Nothing in your outer world will change, unless, and until, a change first takes place in your consciousness.

Your Consciousness Is Your Supply

Actually, consciousness is God. God is individual consciousness. God is your consciousness and mine. Were we to recognize and acknowledge that truth this minute, and each day remind ourselves: "My daily experience is not coming forth from my limited human background, my limited education, or my limited home environment; but my daily experience is the expression or the emanation of the divine Consciousness which is God," we would find many changes taking place in our experience. We would then be bringing forth the harmony of God, rather than the inharmony and discord of limited finite human sense.

It is neither your fault nor mine that we have been carrying ghettos of one kind or another with us. It is because we were not taught in the beginning that God is our consciousness, and that we can experience the infinity of God merely by recognizing that truth. Had we been taught that the principle as shown forth by the Master in feeding the multitudes is an ever present, omnipotent principle, here and now, our lives would be different. We should not be worrying, fearing, doubting, and thinking about how we were going to get along. We should not be concerned as to whether the stock market was rising or falling, or whether the cattle market was up or down, since we would know that all that exists as effect—the effect of our own consciousness, when we realize God as our consciousness.

Jesus had only a few loaves and a few fishes, and yet with those few loaves and fishes he fed the multitudes. If he proved nothing else, he proved this: that the substance was not in the amount of fish and bread he had, but in the Spirit that animated all existence. Some years ago, I was under the dire necessity of learning the nature of supply. At the point of rock bottom, I was forced to make my demonstration of supply. That is one reason why I can tell you not to be afraid of your problems. Work at them. Many times they will prove to be your greatest blessings. You will not recognize the truth of this while your problems are with you, but later on you will say, "Oh, what would I have been, or where would I have been, had it not been for the depth of that problem!" It is the depth of our problems that forces us to dig deeper into this ocean

home, and all your relationships—social, financial, commercial.

When you know the nature of God, the nature of Omnipresence, when you know God to be divine Consciousness, individual consciousness, your consciousness and mine, you have really grasped all that the Master asked of us, when he said, "Seek ye first the kingdom of God and his righteousness; and all these things shall be added unto you."[1] Find out what God is and where God is. Find out the nature of God. That is your whole duty in life. You have nothing else to do. You have nothing in the world to demonstrate. If you are reading this book with inner vision, you can, at this moment, stop working on any problem. Accept only one problem: *What is God?* What is the nature of God? What is the principle of life?

When you have found the answer to the question, What is God? when you really have come to that place where you can say, "I know now that God is individual life, mind, Soul, consciousness"; then you will discover that you have no further problems. Having found God as omnipresence, as the actual reality of your being, you will also find God in Its infinite form and variety, which will include transportation or dollar bills or carrots or potatoes. It appears in all forms, since God is not a person. God is the eternal, immortal, omnipresent substance of the universe. God made all that was made. Out of what? God being all, God, Itself, must have made all that was made out of Itself.

If you can find God as Consciousness—and more

[1] Matthew 6:33.

especially, if you can find God as *your consciousness*—then you will find God appearing in all the forms which God assumes: husband, wife, friend, employee, and even enemy. Mark my words; even your enemy. That is why you have to love your enemies as deeply and sincerely as you love your friends, because God is the very substance, law, and principle of those whom you may have been believing to be your enemies. Actually, they are not your enemies at all. An enemy is a false concept that you have entertained of someone. In fact, most of us entertain false concepts of each other and of the world. This is very easy to understand, if we stop to think about what we are actually seeing in the universe. To begin with, God made all that was made, and anything that God did not make was not made. All that God did make, however, is good. Therefore, if what we are seeing does not measure up to that pattern, it is not because there is anything of an erroneous nature in the world, but because we, individually or collectively, are entertaining a false concept of creation, and of each other.

Begin with this simple practice: first, find out *what* God is; then, find *where* God is. When you find God to be the consciousness of your own being, when you find that God is your very consciousness, your very awareness; you will have found all the forms as which God appears. You will then find God unfolding Itself—Consciousness unfolding Itself, revealing Itself—as your daily experience. Never forget this: that which appears as our daily finite experience, is our sense of limitation, appearing as a lack of education, or lack of opportunity, or a lack of a satisfactory environment. All of that is appearing as our limited daily experience. When, however, we begin to realize this great truth of being, that we are not limited to the finite sense of consciousness, that we are not limited to our personal sense of existence, but rather that God, the infinite consciousness of our being is the source and the form of our life; then, watch the miracles that begin to occur in our experience.

Treatment by a Practitioner
Is Always a Self-Treatment

The world belief of a selfhood apart from God, of a life apart from God, is so strong that many practitioners whom I have met have come under a sense of heaviness which comes from the fact that they do not always live at such a high level of spiritual consciousness that they are able to laugh off this world hypnotism. The sincere practitioner must sit down occasionally, sometimes frequently, and do some serious treating. Let me be very clear on this point: this treating is never a treatment of the other person. I have never in my life given a treatment to anyone. I have never addressed a treatment to any person on earth. I have never taken the name of the patient into my thought, or the name of the disease. So far as I am concerned, I do not believe it would do me any good to know the name of the disease; and I do not believe that the patients, themselves, know the names; and I am convinced that even the doctors do not always know the name of the disease. As a matter of fact, it would be much better if I did not know the name, since our work does not lie in the realm of healing physical bodies or physical diseases. We have agreed in this work that I and the Father are one: that One is Spirit or God. The only truth, therefore, that must be known is the truth about God. God, being infinite, includes all that appears as individual you or me, and that treatment excludes all diseases.

In the human picture there is height, width, depth, but all of that is only a false sense of what is really going on, since Spirit knows no height, width, or depth. There is no such thing as a three dimensional Spirit. Spirit is infinite and eternal life, and even though It expresses Itself individually, It does not express Itself as finite form: therefore, there is no space element or time element in treatment. In treatment, we are absolute in the sense that God is absolutely *all*, and in all, and through all, and as all. We are absolute in the sense that our treatment begins with God and ends with God. It never comes down to the human level. It never takes cognizance of any phase of human experience. It never tries to still the waves of the ocean. It just says, "Peace, be still"—not to the waves, but to our belief that there is a finite condition anywhere.

My treatment is always self-treatment. All of my work begins with the word "God." I may *translate* that word. I may re-interpret it. For example, when people come with claims of a mental nature, instead of using the word "life," I may use the word "mind," and realize that God as mind is forever expressing Its intelligence, Its infinite wisdom, omnipresence, and guidance. But always, I keep my treatment right up there on the level of God, and there I stay. I begin with God, and I end with God. No human being and no human condition ever come into my treatment. Why? Because if they did, my treatment would not conform to the Master's treatment. The Master's injunction about treatment was: "Take no thought for your life, what ye shall eat, or what ye shall drink."[1] Certainly, human thought is seeking extra supply; it is seeking a few more years to add to that date on the tombstone. Certainly, the human world, the nations of the world, are seeking ease in matter.

So we, in this work, are not attempting merely to postpone a date on a tombstone; we are not trying merely to give you a healthy body for a few extra days or weeks or months; we are not here to help you increase your supply ten dollars a week or a hundred, or a thousand. Our work is to reveal to you that God is your immortal life, and therefore, your life is not subject to death or accident or sin or disease. Our work is to show forth that God actually is omnipresent. In other words, you are the very presence of God, and you are no more subject to material conditions than is God, Itself. Only the belief that you are something separate and apart from God can cause you to go on from year to year with the same old aches and pains and lacks and limitations. The moment you catch the slightest glimpse of the truth that "I and my Father are one,"[2] that God actually is the life of your individual being, it is a marvelous thing.

Catch one little glimpse, one little grain of the

[1] Matthew 6:25. [2] John 10:30.

203

truth that God is your life, God is your consciousness, and you will find that you have no personal life, either to gain or to lose. The only life you have is God, Self-maintaining and self-sustaining Life. You will find the miracle that this vision brings into your experience. Let God express Itself as you. Let God, the divine Consciousness of your being, come forth as your daily experience while you watch. Become a beholder of God living your daily experience, and see how great and how infinite it is.

The Threshold of a New Spiritual Age

The Infinite Way is not an organized movement: it has no membership; it has no dues; there are no financial obligations. But it is a movement; and it is a movement that is spreading throughout the world. I do not necessarily mean my work only; my work is but a part of something that is happening through-out the world in many forms, in many ways, in many countries. I do not know the reason for this. I only know that somewhere about 1924 the world passed from a very mental and mechanical state of con-sciousness into the beginning of a spiritual move-ment, a movement which, ultimately is going to encompass the entire world. In other words, we are coming into a spiritual age. That does not necessarily mean that there will not be another war or that there will not be atomic bombs. There may be. Such things may wipe out much of the materialistic thought of the world. It may be that the new spiritual age will be founded on the remnant, on those who remain after the holocaust. Never doubt but that we are at the beginning of a spiritual age. We are at the beginning of an age in which the acquisition of things or persons will be of very little importance. The realization will be that I and my Father are one, and that the place whereon I stand is holy ground; and therefore, right where I am, all that the Father hath is mine. I will live here in my sense of completeness, and you will live there, and neither one will envy or quarrel with the other. There are signs that that age is definitely here.

As a part of that spiritual surge, let us say that I, in my individual way, have caught a little glimpse of that, and through that have attracted to me those ready for that upsurge of Spirit at this particular time. In many parts of the world, however, others have also felt this same surge of Spirit. Others have caught this vision of the Spirit, and are attracting to themselves little groups, and in some cases very large groups. What has happened is that not only materiality has failed, but mentality has failed.

Let us be willing to admit that there *is* God. God *is*; and God is omnipresent. If our daily affairs are not showing forth the fullness of harmony, health, wholeness, happiness, peace, and joy, it is only because we have not yet tapped that spiritual Power. Talking or reading about it is not going to do it. Talking about it, reading about it, and coming together in groups are only steps on the way. Each one of you must do what I had to do: prove it; demonstrate it; show forth that God *is*, and that God is available here and now. There is but one way in which this can be done: first, the recognition of

God as omnipresent—the recognition of God as the Soul or Consciousness of your being and of mine—and second, the reliance on It. For instance, if you have some simple shopping to do tomorrow, instead of leaving home and saying, "Well, I shall have to shop in this store, and that store, and the other store, and I hope that I shall not have to go on to the fourth or fifth," take a few seconds for the realization of the presence of this spiritual Power. Sit down for a moment of meditation, not to think about material things, but to think about the presence of God, and then wait until you feel that "click", that little assurance of God's presence. If you do this, you will find the articles you wish to purchase so quickly and effortlessly, that you will have the greater part of the day left for study, meditation, and communion.

By this simple method, every experience of your family life, from the simplest things to the most complex, becomes easy, peaceful, and successful. You know that God is. You declare that God is. Now prove It. Sit down and get the feeling of that presence of God, and watch how It goes before you to make the crooked places straight. Watch how It opens up the lanes of traffic for you when you are driving. Watch how It does all things for you in your experience—how It even changes the attitude of other people toward you, and changes their relationship to you, and yours to them. The things that you and I cannot do humanly, It can do for you, if you feel this It. That is the secret, you see. There is an It called God. God *is*. But God is only available to you and to me in proportion to our contact with It.

There has to be a contact. You have to be *in* and *of* that God consciousness in order to attain it.

No Transference of Thought in Treatment

Although we use treatments, treatment is the smallest part of our work. Treatment is only used for the purpose of preparing ourselves so that we can feel God—sense God's presence, get the conscious awareness of God's presence. You never have to think of your patient. You never have to think of his beliefs, because the all-knowing Mind already knows what Its business is, and the moment you have contacted It, It goes about and fulfills Its mission. You may ask, "But how does that treatment reach my patient?" The fact that your patient has asked for help has made him a part of your consciousness. There is only one Consciousness, and if you consciously bring yourself to a practitioner's thought, you are in his consciousness. That is how patients get their help.

Our work does not consist in the transference of thoughts. Our work is contacting God, the one Life, and then letting that Life express Itself in me and in you. It is true that you may ask a practitioner for help, or reach out to him for help by telephone or telegram. As a matter of fact, at a certain stage of consciousness, you will find it possible merely to think of your practitioner and immediately receive your help. It will not be necessary even to write, telegraph, or telephone, but only to think of him, and the help will be there. The reason is, that in thinking of him, you have tuned yourself in to his

God consciousness—not his human consciousness. Whatever of truth, therefore, is manifesting itself as the practitioner's experience, automatically becomes yours.

When you turn to a practitioner, you are not turning to a person. The practitioner as a person can do nothing more for you than you can do for yourself, unless he has attained a greater measure of the Christ consciousness than you have. If he has not attained a measure of the Christ, he cannot help you. That is the reason one practitioner does better healing work than another; that is why one practitioner gets better results than another. It is not that God is different in different cases. It is only that one practitioner has attained a greater unfoldment of God consciousness, and, therefore, greater results come forth. That is why the Master's work resulted in more healings than did that of his disciples. As a matter of fact, the disciples never hesitated, when they failed in a case, to bring it to the Master. Why? It was the same God; it was the same Truth; it was the same Consciousness; but the Master attained a higher awareness of It. Every individual in the world has access to the same Christ consciousness to which Jesus had access. The difference lies in the degree of Christhood reached and maintained by Jesus as compared with that reached and maintained by you and me.

Some practitioners devote their entire lives to the Christ ministry—morning, noon, and night, and all night long. They have no other interest. They have given up their social life; they have given up their concern about the goods of this world; they have given up their concern about their family life. Their whole heart and soul and mind and body are in this ministry. It is natural that such practitioners will bring forth greater fruitage than the practitioner who divides his day into three parts, giving one part to the ministry, one part to social and family life, and the third part to sleep.

Omnipresence

A successful practice requires a life dedicated to the recognition and realization of omnipresence:

Omnipresence is the presence of all. Omnipresence is all-presence. Allness is where I am. Therefore, there is never a need to look out to a person, circumstance, or condition for anything necessary to my unfoldment. All that God is, I am. In this Presence, in the very presence of *I Am*, is the fulfillment of all that God is. God fulfills Itself in all Its fullness, in all Its entirety and Its completeness, as the very Presence that *I am*. In this awareness of Omnipresence, there is no need to fear either man or circumstance, since the full protection of the Father accompanies this Omnipresence. There is no need to seek outside for supply, because in this Omnipresence is the presence of *all* of God's supply. This Omnipresence is the presence of all God's children; and this assures me of companionship, of friendship, of right associations and relationships. I need not seek outside my own being for any person, companionship, association, or relationship, since

Omnipresence is the fullness of the Godhead bodily.

Omnipresence is the full power of God, and that power is good; that power is love. We do not humanly address or guide It—we realize Its presence, and let It do Its work. It was this Omnipresence that enabled the Hebrew prophet to pray, "Open his eyes, that he may see."[1] He prayed not for more warriors, for more troops, nor for a greater supply of anything, but only that his servant's eyes might be opened.

Regardless of what the need may appear to be, It, God, is omnipresent as fulfillment. It will do you no good to pray for it. Only pray, "Open thy servant's eyes," so that when those eyes are opened you may behold that right here and now is all that you will ever need for the fulfillment of your experience. Remember: "Before Abraham was, I am.[2] . . . I am with you alway, even unto the end of the world."[3] We do not seek It; we do not implore It, we do not petition It. We just realize Its presence, and wait until the feeling of reassurance comes. Then you will know that this consciousness of yours is the substance of all form. This consciousness of yours appears outwardly as the protection you need, or the dollars you need, or the home you need, or the friends or companions you need, or the health, or the new heart or liver or lung. Always it is this consciousness that is appearing outwardly. Our prayer is, "Open my eyes that I may behold fulfillment and Omnipresence."

[1] II Kings 6:17.   [2] John 8:58.
[3] Matthew 28:20.

CHAPTER THIRTEEN

INDIVIDUAL CONSCIOUSNESS

THE principle of life, which we all must learn, is that we cannot have anything until we first have the consciousness of that thing. If we were given a million dollars, we probably could not hold on to it, unless, in some way, we had developed the consciousness of a million dollars. That is one of the reasons why fortunes are lost. Those who inherit fortunes, even some of the people who earn them, cannot keep them, because if there is not a consciousness of wealth behind the inheritance or the amassing of a fortune, it will be dissipated, sooner or later, in one way or another. The same principle applies to every situation.

In order to have a beautiful home, it is necessary to have the consciousness of a beautiful home. Without that, a home would be only a house, and either its owner might or might not decorate and furnish it in good taste, or it might be furnished by someone else in conformity with the prevailing fashion of the day. The principle of life—*the* principle of life—is consciousness. We must have the consciousness of a thing in order to have the thing itself.

The first step in this work is attaining the conscious awareness of the presence of God. There are many ways of doing this. One method is outlined in

The Infinite Way in the chapter on "Meditation," in which, upon awakening in the morning, you fill yourself with the consciousness of truth, with the realization of God's presence. Then, throughout the day, you should continue to recognize and realize the presence and the allness of God. Whether you are receiving or disbursing money, whether you are eating or drinking, always recognize God as the source. Acknowledge God, acknowledge Christ as the reality of your being. If you persist in that throughout the day and evening, even if for only brief periods, you will find that within a short time, your thought will become so spiritualized that your outer experience will be transformed.

The statement, "I live; yet not I, but Christ liveth in me,"[1] is enough to make anyone's life a success. If only we could catch the vision in that statement; if we could catch the inspirational meaning, the inner or esoteric meaning, of those words; that one statement would be a sufficient foundation for a successful life.

Conscious awareness of the presence of God, therefore, is the first step in developing spiritual consciousness and a life that flows out from the spiritualization of consciousness. Begin the development of this consciousness by taking a statement from the Bible, gaining an actual awareness of its inner meaning through meditation, and then carrying it with you throughout the day. Through following this practice, you will soon have a clear understanding of what the Master meant, when he said to the disciples who wanted to give him food, "I have

[1] Galatians 2:20.

meat to eat that ye know not of,"[1] and what he meant when he said to the woman at the well, "But the water that I shall give him shall be in him a well of water springing up into everlasting life."[2]

In other words, this consciousness of Truth, this realization of Christ, is spiritual meat and spiritual drink—the spiritual wine and the spiritual water—and having it, you can never hunger, and you can never thirst. *But each one of us must carry it on as an activity in his own consciousness*, because unless there is this activity taking place in consciousness, just sitting in a chair and waiting for God, or for Christ, to do something might result in a very long, monotonous wait.

It is a simple enough thing to say, "I and my Father are one,"[3] and to repeat it a hundred times; but saying it or repeating it will not make it so. As a matter of fact, it is already true; but even its being true is not sufficient. *There must be a conscious awareness of it.* Humanly, of course, such a statement as "I and my Father are one" is ridiculous. It does not make sense. But if we can gain the sense of oneness, and actually achieve the realization that the *I* of God and the "I" of me are the selfsame *I*; that the "I" of me and the "I" of you are the selfsame *I*— if we can gain that, we shall have gained the entire demonstration of the Master. It was almost the end of his ministry before he revealed that "he that hath seen me hath seen the Father."[4] Now we, ultimately, must gain that same consciousness. Otherwise, we shall have a life separate and apart from God, a life

1 John 4:32.   2 John 4:14.
3 John 10:30.   4 John 14:9.

213

that can be born and a life that can die, a life that can be diseased and a life that can change. If, however, we have that life which is God, we shall not experience a change of life, an end of life, or the decomposition of life. If we have the life which is God, our demonstration of eternality and immortality is complete.

Reality and Unreality

The next thing we must bring to conscious remembrance is the nature of that which appears to us as error. In the metaphysical world, error is understood to be a negation of truth, a denial of truth, or the opposite of truth. Above all things, we understand it to be illusion, or non-reality. Many students misinterpret the words non-reality, unreality, and unreal. When they declare that sin or disease is unreal, they believe that that means that the sin or disease is non-existent, and therefore, they ignore it. To say that sin and disease are unreal does not mean that they are non-existent. It does not mean that there is not something *appearing as* sin or disease, but it means that that appearance has none of the qualities of reality.

The meaning of the word "unreality," in this sense, is not the commonly accepted definition of the word. It is used here as the term is used in philosophy. The word "reality" in that sense means that which is permanent, that which is eternal, that which is infinite, that which always has been and always will be. In that sense of the word, you would understand instantly the unreal nature of disease. There was a time when the disease did not exist and there will be a time when it will not exist. It is not real, because it has no substance to maintain or sustain it. It exists only as a finite sense, as a false sense, in the same way in which two times two are five exists— not as reality, not as an entity or identity; but as an appearance, belief, or illusion, or a false sense of mathematics.

This is of vital importance to us because the whole world is trying to get rid of sin and disease as if they were realities, as if they had an actual existence. The ministry is trying to heal sinners and remove sin. The medical world is trying to remove disease, and many times they succeed. But that is not our work nor our world. "My kingdom is not of this world."[1] If we, as metaphysicians, approach the subject of sin and disease as if they exist as reality, and as if we are expected to do something about them, or to use some power or force to remove them, we are on the same level of consciousness as the material or mental world. Now, remember, spiritual work is not on that level. You will find in *Spiritual Interpretation of Scripture*[2] and in other Infinite Way writings a complete exposition of the nature of error, and especially the nature of material and mental belief as distinct from spiritual reality.

Let a practitioner begin with the premise that his patient actually has a disease or a sin, and, mark my words, he will not be able to bring about a healing at all, because there is not a spark of spiritual truth

[1] John 18:36.
[2] By the author (Willing Publishing Company, San Gabriel, California, 1947).

in any statement or thought that claims that any person has a condition that is not a part of God's being, because God's being is *all*.

If you are going to take your stand on the truth that "I and my Father are one,"[1] please understand and immediately recognize that what you are beholding with your senses is a false sense of reality; you are not only watching the tracks come together, but actually believing that they do. In the healing ministry of The Infinite Way, our standpoint is God—God omnipresent, omniscient, omnipotent; God, the Life of all being; God, the Spirit and the Soul of individual being. Therefore, all is perfection. We let every belief or appearance strike against that spiritual wall, that spiritual consciousness which we have built, and then we say to any and every form of error, as the Master said, "Thou couldest have no power at all against me, except it were given thee from above."[2] We hold that wall against every belief or appearance that may hit up against it. We do not say, "What caused this?" or "What can I do about it?" No, our response is, "What is there to hinder you? Pick up your bed and walk."

Never forget this. If you forget everything else, do not forget this one point, because you can heal, and anyone in the world can heal, if you can catch one single glimpse of the truth that there cannot be God *and* reality in sin or disease. In the beginning, you may only heal or bring about improvement in the smaller things, or so-called minor things, of life. But as you build this consciousness, as you become more and more aware of error as unreality—a

[1] John 10:30.   [2] John 19:11.

non-power, a non-force, a non-existent entity or
identity, a substance-less form—then healing becomes a very, very simple thing.

All that is necessary after that, is to wàtch that
you do not accept any of the world's prejudice or
bias. Never believe that this truth is not equally true
of Catholic, Jew, Protestant, Hindu, or Moslem;
because if you do not see its universality, you lose
your vision. Unless you can see God as the reality of
all being; unless you can see that no sin, sickness,
or limitation differs from another, that all exist as
illusion—unless you can see that, you are lost. If
you can see that God, in Its infinite eternal omnipotence, omniscience, omnipresence, is the life of
individual being; and if you can be big enough to
include the entire universe in that life, then you have
begun your healing ministry. But if you accept into
your thought any difference or distinction between
one race or another, one nationality, one religion, one
creed, one metaphysical movement or another, then
you are lost. There is no distinction or difference:
we are all one in Christ Jesus.

Consciousness Is the Substance of All Form

God is consciousness. God is your consciousness
and my consciousness. God is individual consciousness, and that consciousness is the creative principle
of the universe. This truth must be firmly established
within us, for this reason: As human beings, we have
been brought up in the belief that substance and
reality are in the world of form. In other words,
we have been taught to respect, let us say, for

example, money—to love it, to hate it, or to fear it. At least we have been taught that there is some great value in it, because the world is struggling for it, and struggling hard. It not only wants to have money for current expenses, but it wants to have it to save and put away—very often "where moth and rust doth corrupt."[1] There is a sense of security, of well-being, of expansion, when one has enough money. I am speaking now of the world, and also of you and me, before we gained some awareness of this truth; and despite our progress on the path, there may even yet be a lurking bit of the money thought in us.

Christ consciousness is a state of consciousness in which any form, as such, becomes unimportant; in which no attempt is made to get, acquire, or achieve any form, but in which is recognized the truth that whatever and wherever the need is, the answer appears. Since the place whereon I stand is holy ground, and all of God is here, then God makes Itself manifest as whatever form is necessary at any particular time. When you can see this, it would make no difference to you what is going on out here in the world. There would be no attempt to acquire money, houses, automobiles, transportation, or airplanes. I do not mean that we may not have them. We shall have them, and abundantly. There is nothing wrong or sinful about having money—even millions of dollars. There is nothing wrong about owning yachts and diamonds, or enjoying all the luxuries that can be afforded. In fact, I believe that we shall have a greater abundance of things, and

[1] Matthew 6:19.

218

enjoy them as a more permanent dispensation, when, instead of reaching for them, we stand back and realize, "This consciousness which is God is the creative principle of all, and it will appear in whatever form is necessary for me at the moment."

The sense of separation from God is the cause of all sin, disease, death, lack, and limitation. The realization of conscious oneness with God restores harmony, peace, joy, and abundance. If, instead of attempting to acquire something out here in the world or believing that safety and security are to be found outside of ourselves, we were to gain the sense of God as our individual consciousness, as our life eternal, of this truth as the Rock of Ages, and then relax—we would find our lives unfolding harmoniously every day. If it were a position we needed, we would have it. If it were a home, we would have it. Certainly, as we advance in this consciousness, our business, our home, our relationships will grow progressively better. I do not mean this in the sense of wishing, or "rubbing the lamp," and having the earth open with miracles tomorrow. That could happen, I am sure, but that has not been my experience. My own unfoldment was a gradual one, a slow, steady unfoldment of this truth. But then I have never been in a hurry. I have not been concerned as to whether or not I gained financial independence yesterday, today, or tomorrow. But this I have gained, even if but slowly: I have gained a consciousness of the truth that God is the Spirit and substance of my being; and that God is forever revealing Itself, unfolding Itself as everything necessary in my experience. I learned the truth from

God, his own consciousness of supply, been the substance of what appears to human sense as gold? Moses drew manna from the sky—from his own consciousness. Then his own consciousness of supply must have been the substance of that which appeared to his world as manna. Jesus drew transportation out of the world; but it must have been his own consciousness of the omnipresence of God that appeared outwardly as his transportation.

Your consciousness of good will appear outwardly as your manna, as your water, as your wine, as your meat. "I have meat to eat that ye know not of."[1] That meat is divine substance, and that substance is the consciousness of my being. From now on, when the world says there is not any meat, or there is not any water, or there is not any wine, my realization of this truth that I have the substance of all form, that my consciousness is the substance of all form, will, in one way or another, appear to me *as* the manna or the meat or the water, or the automobile, or a seat in an airplane or in a bus or in a streetcar, or a parking space. Whatever the need may be at the moment, my consciousness will appear as that form.

My consciousness will not attract some form to me from out here in the world. My consciousness will not attract your money to me. My consciousness will appear as money to me. If, at the moment, it seems to come *through* you, I can assure you that it is not coming *from* you. Watch and see if any money you spend for spiritual development ever comes out of your own pocket. No matter how much you spend,

[1] John 4:32.

give, or contribute, watch and see at the end of the year if it actually has come out of your pocket. I can tell you from years and years of experience, that not one dime of it will ever come from you. It may come *through* you, but it will not come *from* you. In one way or another, it will be made up to you.

Everything that happens in your experience must happen as a conscious activity of your own consciousness or mind. Unless you consciously bring the truth to your own awareness, the truth is of no benefit to you. It is like having a big bank account across the street in the bank, and not knowing it is there. You may be a millionaire with a checking account, and be hungry in your home, unless you are consciously aware of the presence of that bank account. So it is with truth; it has to be a part of your conscious awareness or it is of no benefit to you. Therefore, we have the Master's statement about the truth. It is not simply that the truth will make you free. That is not what he said. He said, "And ye shall know the truth, and the truth shall make you free."[1] This is the truth of being. But you must *know* this truth; you must consciously remind yourself of it, be aware of it, make it a conscious activity in your thought, and then you bring it forth into manifestation.

Go Within

God is truth, but God must be known. "Seek ye first the kingdom of God . . . and all these things shall be added unto you."[2] You seek; you search; you make this truth a conscious activity of your being;

[1] John 8:32.   [2] Matthew 6:33.

and then it must manifest, because Truth and its manifestation are not two separate things. *Truth and its manifestation are one.* You cannot have truth in your consciousness without having it express as all the forms necessary to your fulfillment. There is no such thing as God *and* a man. There is only God appearing *as*—the Word made flesh. There is no such thing as truth *and* the demonstration. Truth, entertained in consciousness, *is* demonstration. Truth is the substance of all form. Therefore, know truth, and truth will appear to you as the form necessary to your every experience. But it must be a conscious activity of your consciousness. That is why you cannot sit back passively and say, "Let God do it."

Anything that is in the external world is not permanent, and therefore, you cannot have it forever. However, once you consciously realize that God is consciousness, that Truth is consciousness, that Truth is the substance of all form; then when you have the Truth, you have the form, since they are one. Again we go back to our teaching of oneness. You cannot have Truth *and* a demonstration of truth. You can only have Truth manifested or expressed *as* demonstration. But they are one. Wherever you find Truth, you find It manifested as form.

For that reason, we have the injunction, "Pray without ceasing."[1] We have to pray without ceasing, until consciousness becomes transformed; until we die daily to the human being that we were, without a sense of separateness from God; until we are reborn of the Spirit; and until our consciousness is filled with the reminder and remembrance of God's

[1] I Thessalonians 5:17.

223

presence. Throughout the day we must acknowledge all of this. Then we bring this conscious activity of consciousness into form as effect, as what is called demonstration—as food, clothing, home, companionship, and all of the other things that are necessary.

Never go out and try to find a friend, get a husband or a wife, a bankroll or a business. Do not *seek* these things. Go within. Realize God as the substance of your being, as the real nature of your being. Realize God as law, as life eternal. Realize that "I live; yet not I. . . ."[1] It is the Christ that is living—the immortal, the eternal Christ within you. Then you find that the conscious activity of your consciousness will appear as all forms of good. Do not go back to your old metaphysics. Do not try to demonstrate something or someone outside. If you catch yourself thinking about wanting something out there, stop at once. Do not reach outside, even mentally, for person, place, thing, circumstance, or condition. Once you are on this path, there is not a person, place, or thing that is worth going after in that way, because, should you get that which you are seeking, it would turn to dust in your hands. This is all right for the person not on this path who thinks that he wants honors, place, position, or money. After he gets them, he still hugs to himself these tatters, and thinks he has something in his hands: he cannot see that they have already turned to rags or dust.

On this path, however, the moment that you do acquire something in the external, you should recognize that which you have as nothingness, because even a glimpse of this truth makes as nothing

[1] Galatians 2:20.

224

the things of the outer world. And yet, nobody in the world can be as appreciative as we are of the good that comes to us, when it comes, as it does, as the realization of this truth. In other words, the slightest thing, the smallest thing that comes to me, or the biggest thing, I appreciate, I enjoy. I enjoy the good things of life. I like to see them unfold. I like to see them appear, but only for one reason: I know that there is no longer any mental activity or any reaching out to get them. Whatever comes, comes as the grace of God. This form of living is living by grace. This is living without taking thought. This is living so that all life, all beauty, and all good, come as the gift of God, as the grace of God. It is a beautiful way of living, because you have everything to make life full and complete, but you have it only with the love and joy people find in giving it to you. You have not taken anything away from anyone nor have you deprived anyone of anything, but in receiving some good from or through a person, you rejoice in the knowledge that his own good has also been increased. It is a beautiful way of living—this living through grace:

"I live, yet not I, but Christ liveth in me."[1] Christ, now, is the invisible substance, and my world is that Christ or invisible substance appearing outwardly as form. The Word becomes flesh. Christ, the law and substance within, becomes the visible or tangible without.

Do you perceive the significance of that principle? Do you see its wonder and beauty? Christ, the

[1] Galatians 2:20.

225

invisible Substance; Christ, the Word; Christ, the infinite spiritual Consciousness of my being appears tangibly and visibly as form.

Whatever is going on within becomes visible outwardly. It is not necessary to broadcast it to the world. Actually, it is impossible to conceal this good; you cannot hide the Christ. Once you have taken the name and nature of the Christ, and once you have accepted this meat "that ye know not of" as the reality of your being, the invisible substance, the infinite invisible substance, it will appear outwardly in all its fullness, even as the joy and glow on your face.

Spirit is reality. Spirit is the underlying substance of that which is permanent, that which is eternal and immortal. If we want eternal health, if we want eternal substance and supply, we can only get them as Spirit. So Spirit, or divine Consciousness, now becomes the reality. If you have a consciousness of the reality of Spirit, you do not have to be concerned with forms, whether they come or whether they go. It really made no difference that Jesus was crucified and buried in a tomb, because his conscious awareness of himself as Spirit made him reappear immediately in the same form. The Crucifixion only proved the reality of Spirit.

So with us, each one of us must remember that it is not too important to try to save our own lives: our lives are already saved. Your life is Spirit, and if, for any reason, it seems to be lost or buried, do not believe it, and do not be disturbed about it. You will rise right up out of that tomb. There never was any grave that could hold Spirit, consciousness, life eternal, the Christ. And so, the consciousness of Spirit becomes your awareness of life eternal, of life immortal, of eternal substance, supply, and all good. Then let Spirit be a reality to you. Begin to see and to feel Spirit, out of which you draw your universe, out of which you draw your daily experience.

God is Spirit. Spirit is Soul. Soul is consciousness— yours and mine, individually. And out of that great Invisible, that Infinite Invisible, comes all form. So let us make a reality of Spirit, and let us stop using the word Christ, as if Christ were something of 2,000 years ago—something separate from us. Christ is still the Babe; and Christ is still being born in the manger of our human belief, of our human thought. Yes, Christ is a living reality, and It is the substance of all form. But mark this: only our *conscious awareness* of the presence of Christ makes It appear as visible form. Do not think that this is a lazy man's work. Do not think that praying without ceasing means doing a little mental work for ten minutes in the morning and another ten at night. "Pray without ceasing" means what it says. It is to live constantly and continuously in Spirit.

CHAPTER FOURTEEN

CHRIST CONSCIOUSNESS

"PEACE I leave with you, my peace I give unto you: not as the world giveth, give I unto you."[1] In the human picture, we have to earn our good. We have to be worthy of it; we have to be deserving of it. We have to work for it and work hard for it. In the human world, we are constantly making a physical or mental effort to bring about some good in our experience. And yet, the promise is, "My peace I give." But this promised peace does not come through the use of either physical or mental effort, nor does it come from those things that the world can give, such as money, position, or place.

In our healing work, we do not use physical means, but there are many students of metaphysics today who still use a great deal of mental effort. In The Infinite Way, however, we are learning to rise above the need for even mental work in healing to the point where healing comes by grace as that Christ peace. For example, if I were asked for help, and then immediately began to think thoughts, know the truth, or make declarations of truth, that would be mental effort. Of course, knowing the truth is our foundation, our beginning, in this work. We do know

[1] John 14:27.

the truth. We remember what we have learned about treatment, beginning with God, and following through to the realization of God. True, that was a mental effort; but that correct letter of truth forms the foundation of our work, because without it our healing work might be the result of a blind or ignorant faith. There are many times when a blind faith might not prove strong enough to withstand the suggestions of the world.

If, however, you know the truth of being, you know that God is individual life, and that therefore, the life of the individual is just as permanent as the life which is God; you know that the divine Mind, or God, is the mind of the individual, and therefore, there can be no mental aberration or lapse from intelligence; you know that God, the divine Soul, is also the Soul of the individual. You know, too, that there can be no sin; sin cannot exist as a reality; it cannot exist as an inherent or enduring part of individual being. When you really know that your supply is not to be found out in the world, in coins or dollar bills, but that your supply is your own consciousness—God, your own consciousness—appearing to you in visible form, then you have the practical knowledge of truth which is the basis of healing.

When you have imbibed the letter of truth, or the knowledge of truth, and when you have that fixed firmly within you as a basis, you come to a place in consciousness where you no longer think or require thoughts to bring about your demonstration. Your daily experience becomes yours through grace, through the Christ peace. That state of peace is brought about, not by something you do or think, but by something that the Christ is and does.

The Reality of the Christ

Let us remember this. There is something called the Christ. The Christ is not just a name given to some intangible or nebulous thing. The Christ is a divine reality that is a living presence, and it is omnipresent. It is right where you are and right where I am. Christ is not a person. Christ is a principle. It is a principle of life. It is a principle of God, which forms the reality of your being. But because of the prodigal son experience we understand what physical might is, we understand what mental might is; we know what it is to work hard ourselves; but we have not yet learned how to stand still and let Christ work. We have become, in belief, separated from the very Christ of our being. It is much the same as if we lived in a house with the blinds drawn and had become accustomed to walking around in darkness, semi-darkness, or in a room artificially lighted. As time passed, we actually forgot that there was such a thing as sunshine and that outside our drawn shades was the bright, warm sun. In our humanhood we have done just that. We have had the blinds drawn—our mental blinds. This is what Jesus meant when he said, "Having eyes, see ye not? and having ears, hear ye not?"[1] Those spiritual faculties have been closed, so that we are not aware of the fact that just beyond the range of our humanhood there is the divinity of our

[1] Mark 8:18.

230

being called the Christ, the Spirit of God in man.

Step by step in our study, in our practice, and in our association with each other, we develop an awareness of this infinite invisible Power or Presence called the Christ. We find that there is an actual Presence with us, which performs our work for us; It performs through us; It performs as us. That was what made it possible for Paul to say, "I live; yet not I, but Christ liveth in me."[1] Remember that He performeth that which is given me to do; He perfecteth that which concerneth me; or as the Psalmist says: "The Lord will perfect that which concerneth me."[2] This is the Christ, and that Christ is the principle or spirit of God present in you, as, let us say, your integrity, your loyalty, your fidelity, your trustworthiness. Those are qualities that you recognize to be present in you; and you recognize them, not because you have ever seen or heard them, but because of their effect in your experience. Your honesty and your integrity have won for you the respect of your business associates. Your loyalty and your fidelity have made of you good citizens, good husbands, good wives, good children. Those are the effects of the qualities of integrity, loyalty, fidelity, honesty, and trustworthiness. But there is something even greater than any of these, something greater than all of them put together; and that is the conscious awareness, the conscious recognition, of this Christ, which can and will create these qualities in us, even if, and when, they seem to be lacking.

The Christ in us is our divine intelligence, our spiritual wisdom. This is not human wisdom:

[1] Galatians 2:20.   [2] Psalms 138:8.

231

human wisdom can make mistakes; human wisdom can be misled. Our human wisdom is often based on past experience or common sense; but the Christ—this spiritual intuition, this spiritual wisdom, guidance, and power—never makes a mistake; and It causes us to do things that humanly we may not think wise, or that humanly we might not even think of doing. We may not even know what step we should take; but this Christ, opening up our consciousness, takes the step for us even before we are aware of the need. Christ is a reality. Christ is that upon which you can depend: you can turn your ear and listen to It and through It find your inspiration, your guidance, your direction. Christ is a healing consciousness; and when we are called upon for healing of ourselves or of others, if we have touched this Christ, there is no longer any need to rely on statements of truth or on any activity. This Thing, called the Saviour, the saving Principle, the healing Presence, or the healing Christ, takes over. It restores; It renews; It reconstructs; It builds.

Christ is a reality. Christ is not merely a name, a term for some intangible thing. No, Christ is as tangible in your experience as anything you can see or touch. It is as real as a personal teacher or a book—only more so. If we all could know the reality, the omnipresence, and omnipotence of the Christ, we would understand why all reliance can be placed upon It; and how It goes before us to do all that is necessary for us to do. But the Christ is even more than that! It is a unifying influence. Christ is the cement, the unifying influence, that brings us together in understanding.

mind. Therefore, it does not make any difference whether you ask me for help or ask somebody in New York or Capetown: you are calling on the one Mind, which is the mind of your own being.

This much most of us understand; but did you ever realize that that is only one facet of the omnipresence of the Christ. In the past, many of us have been taught to believe that it is necessary to be present physically, in order to receive a spiritual teaching. Today, in the light of our greater unfoldment, we know that not only can you ask for help at a distance and receive it, but by raising yourself higher in consciousness, you can even be taught spiritually while you are sitting in your own home or while on a trip to Europe. Why not? It is not your body that is being taught. It is not your brain that is receiving truth. It is your consciousness, and you have already learned that your consciousness is not in your body. You have already learned that you exist as consciousness. You exist as that one mind, and that mind is not confined to your body. But this great truth has more than an abstract value. You have found it practical in the healing work, so practical that many of you during your travels have, at times, wired or telephoned to your practitioner for help and have received it. Now you are going to find that whenever and wherever you open your consciousness to truth, you will find it there with you. You can be on a train, on a sinking ship, or on a falling airplane, but if you open your consciousness to truth, you will find it there. Christ is the thread that exists between what appears as an infinite number of men and women. If the Christ,

Truth, is in any one spot in the world, then It is wherever you are. That invisible Thread, that invisible Omnipresence, makes truth available to you.

This explains how some of the great healings—I mean great spiritual healings—have taken place in cases where those healed were not students of truth. Some person reached out, prayed to his concept of God with a great longing, a great intensity, a great faith, or a great need. It may not have been faith; it may not have been hope; it may not have been even a religious feeling. It may have been something like: "Oh, God, help me!" Something like that could have brought help. In that opening of consciousness the Christ registered.

Where was that Christ? It was right there. Right where you are and right where I am, the Christ is. Today the leading scientists of the world recognize that time and space are not realities. The very spot that I am occupying, you are occupying. You cannot be localized in time or space, because you are mind, you are life eternal, you are Spirit, Soul. It is only as long as you think of yourself as the body you see in the mirror and think that that body is you, that you might think of yourself as being separate from others. But when you stop and use the word "I," you certainly know that "I" is ego, or consciousness. Consciousness is omnipresent; and therefore the *I* that I am, which is the *I* that you are, is omnipresent. It is wherever you are, and it is there in Its fullness. Never forget this. There is not a little bit or a part of God here. God, the infinity of intelligence, of love, and of life, is expressed in all, is expressed in all Its perfection, right where I am and right where you are, since we are the one same consciousness.

Open your consciousness at any time, in any place, and under any circumstance, and see if truth is not right where you are, ready to impart itself to you. Once you have had the experience of that type of enlightenment, you will then know that wherever consciousness is—and it does not make any difference where, in time and space, it may seem to be —that is where this truth is available. All those who are on this path, all those who are opening their consciousness to this truth, have the whole of truth available to them now.

Throughout the world, at this very second, there are people who are opening their consciousness to spiritual power that they may play some part in world peace, in universal prosperity and harmony. As they open their consciousness to this truth, it is flowing in to them. That does not mean that we are sending it to them. It means that we are receiving it at this moment from the same Source from which they are receiving it, and that Source is the Christ. When you begin to understand the impersonal Christ, you will understand the thread, the invisible thread, that binds us together, not only all of us, but all men bent on this spiritual path.

If you should feel the need of some truth for the healing of yourself or someone else, it is not necessary to go through any mental processes of thought. Just open your consciousness to the light, to truth, to grace, to the peace that passeth understanding, to the Christ peace. As you learn to do that, the illness will be dispelled and the healing will come, whether it is yours or someone else's.

You may do the same thing for supply. Do not sit down and think of supply; do not take thought for supply. We do not demonstrate supply; but wherever there seems to be an absence of it in some form, we may sit down and open our consciousness to the Christ presence for the revelation of supply, as did the Hebrew prophet when he asked the Father to open his servant's eyes that he might see. When the servant's eyes were opened, he beheld the supply all around him. So it is with us. In Truth, there is no lack, no limitation. In reality, there is no more a lack of dollars in a room than there is a lack of air. Supply is here in its infinity and in its abundance. We may, however, find it necessary to pray that the Father will open our eyes so that we may behold it, because, although we have eyes, we do not always see. Then the Father, the Christ, this gentle Presence, this Influence, will open our eyes and we shall see that the whole room is full of dollar bills or million dollar bills, or whatever is the need. Open your consciousness to this truth—this inflow of Christ. Let the Christ show you the dollars, or whatever it is you may need.

Up to a certain point, we do use thought. Using thought, however, might be likened to a stepladder or bridge which carries us to the place where we no longer need such aid; thought carries us to that point where we open our consciousness, and then let everything flow out from it. When we open our consciousness to truth, remember that the same truth that is being revealed to us is also being revealed to all those who have their consciousness open. That makes of us a united group throughout the world—a united group of those who are seeking nothing for themselves, but who are seeking only enlightenment for the world.

The peace that "*I* give" you is not the peace that the world gives; it is not the kind of peace that any organization established for the purpose of working toward a peaceful world can give. The peace that "*I* give" can come only when you open your consciousness, not for something for yourself, but for light—for light for the world, for your patient, for your student, for your nation—that the glory of God may shine undimmed. That is the real purpose of the Christ. It is not to glorify you or me with anything of a material nature. The purpose of the Christ is not to show forth an infinity of health and wealth; it is to reveal the glory of God:

Let me be glorified with God's glory. Do not give me health, so that I can show how strong and well I am. Do not give me abundant supply just so that I can say, "See what my understanding has done for me." Give me health and give me wealth, not for me or for my glory or for my understanding, but only as an evidence to the world of what the infinite glory of God is when I open my consciousness to it. "Glorify thou me with thine own self with the glory which I had with thee before the world was."[1]

[1] John 17:5.

It is a miracle and a mystery, but this golden thread, or silver thread, actually does exist. It is in reality, of course, neither gold nor silver; it is neither tangible nor real to the human sense of substance. It is as invisible and as intangible to our physical senses as Spirit, Itself. Yet, it binds us together in an indissoluble union, so that whenever a seer, sage, prophet, or any individual gains some glimpse of truth, that glimpse of truth automatically makes itself available, and travels from one to another as fast as the speed of light, or faster. Each one on that thread receives the same light and the same intuition, the same guidance and the same direction.

There are no new truths. Please believe me, in my entire experience I have never found a truth that I have not seen stated in ancient scripture. I have never known a truth that cannot be found in ancient philosophy. I have not yet come across anything that is new in any of the metaphysical teachings. Everything that is, always has been; and everything that is now, always will be. It is always available, but it touches consciousness—it comes into consciousness at some particular time—and then it spreads. It is now spreading throughout the world. Those who are unable to grasp it with the inner fiber of their consciousness will not understand it. It is not sensible to the human mind; but nothing spiritual ever is. If that which is spiritual and true were sensible to the human mind, every sensible person would have an understanding of spiritual truth, but we know that this is not the case, perhaps because the

239

wisdom of the spiritual world is foolishness to men.

Spiritual truth is found only in the consciousness of those who have risen above common sense or mere human intelligence. How many Hebrews saw the risen Christ after the Crucifixion? If all those in the Holy Land had seen Him, then Judaism as a whole would have been supplanted by Christianity, because, having seen such evidence, they could not have denied Him; they would have had to accept Him. But very few of the Hebrews saw the resurrected or ascended Christ. Only those saw, who had already risen above human sense, above human intelligence. Only those few Hebrews who had already achieved a measure of Christ consciousness, who were in tune with the Infinite Invisible, who were part of this universal silver cord—only they saw; and they formed the nucleus of what is now Christianity.

So it is today. The inspired revelation of spiritual truth is so practical that in three-quarters of a century, thousands, hundreds of thousands, have experienced healings of the body and of the mind and soul. They have experienced physical, mental, and moral regeneration. Would you not think, with this Christ visible in the world today, that the whole world would be followers of the Christ? But there are very few who follow the Christ, who have learned to lean on the Infinite Invisible and trust It.

"I Have Chosen You"

The Christ is not only resurrected; the Christ is risen. It is risen above every sense of limitation.

But the Christ must be *realized*. The Christ cannot merely be preached: the Christ must be realized. When It touches your consciousness and mine, It makes us one with every individual in heaven, on earth, or beneath the earth. It makes us one with all life. From that moment, we are forever receiving from the Infinite Invisible. You would be surprised to know that not only does It come from human teachers who speak the Word to you, but It comes from invisible teachers, teachers hidden within your own consciousness. There is at this moment within your own consciousness *the* Teacher, *the* Revelator, because since your consciousness is infinite, nothing can exist outside of your consciousness. Therefore, opening your consciousness to the infinite Revelator, to the infinite Teacher, the infinite Healer, you find yourself one with It. You find yourself one with this universal Principle, and you find It operative and operating in your experience.

No one can influence the Christ. No one can ask anything of the Christ. No one can decide what he would like to do, or be, or what part he would like to play in the world. It is the Christ that determines that for us. All we can do is to open our consciousness to Its inflow and then let It have Its way with us. It will make of some of us practitioners, some teachers, some lecturers, some writers. Others it will not take into the depth of this spiritual work, but it may so enlighten us in the ways of the world, that we may play a more constructive part in human affairs. Many great men and women have been inspired by the Christ; certainly George Washington and Benjamin Franklin were. Throughout history, there have been those who have been inspired by the Christ and led to the particular role they were to play in world events. Joan of Arc is an example of a simple young girl, who, under divine inspiration, played a significant part in one phase of human history. She could not have chosen that particular part. No one can ever choose to be a Joan of Arc, a Benjamin Franklin, an Abraham Lincoln, a George Fox, or whoever it may be who acts under divine guidance, or divine inspiration in this, the human world. "Ye have not chosen me, but I have chosen you. . . ."[1]

It is always the Christ that touches consciousness and forces Itself through into recognition. The human being never seeks the Christ. The Christ has already touched your consciousness and mine in some degree, and only the depth of the density of humanness prevents it from coming into full and complete manifestation. But It has touched us. It has already manifested in us and to us and through us, and It has carried us through every step we have taken to bring us to our present state of development. The same Christ that has brought us to this point, will take us further. All that is expected of us is that we be receptive and responsive to It, that we recognize It openly and consciously. Recognize the presence of Christ, and you may be assured that in ever greater degree It will take hold of you: It will reveal and unfold Itself more and more in your experience, leading you to whatever place there is for you to occupy in the spiritual plan.

As spiritual identity, we are a part of God's plan.

[1] John 15:16.

We are a part of a divine universal Principle, which is the creative Principle of this spiritual universe, the governing Principle, and it is always in perfect operation. In this spiritual universe there is no sin, no disease, no discord, no war. All there is, is perfect harmony, peace, and love. This same state of peace can and should be enjoyed by everyone on earth. There is no monopoly of it; no one person or group of people invented or created it. But it descends upon those who, in some way or another, open their consciousness to it.

Wherever we are—on the earth, in the sky, or beneath the ground—we are one and are of one consciousness. We have only to think of each other, and instantly, whatever truth is manifesting in one, immediately becomes available to all those who contact it and tune in to it. Thus we shall carry each other into eternity. Why? It will not be through any human power, but because of the Christ and the opening of our consciousness to the Christ, which races along this invisible spiritual thread, making us all of the household of faith. And so it is. It is not that we would not bless all the world the same as we would bless each other, that is, bless those of us who are of the household of faith. It is only that many of the people of the world are not willing to open their consciousness at this present moment to feel that invisible thread which binds us all together, making us one in Christ Jesus.

CHAPTER FIFTEEN

MEDITATION AND HEALING

MEDITATION is the secret of this entire work. If you succeed in catching the vision of The Infinite Way, you will find that meditation will be responsible for at least ninety percent of that success. You will find that meditation is not only that which opens up consciousness, but meditation, ultimately, is the the mode and means of bringing the Christ into manifestation.

Many people are afraid of meditation because it has always been closely associated with the Orient. In the Occident, in our Western world, there is no such practice as meditation except among the Quakers. They have, of course, practiced meditation from the beginning of their organization. But aside from them and the various Oriental groups, meditation is practically unknown in the Western world. Yet meditation is your point of contact with Divinity. The kingdom of God is within you, and it is within you, yourself, that you must find God. For although you can be led back to the kingdom within by means of teachers and teachings or even books, these serve a purpose only as they lead you back to the depths of your own being, and it is there you must find God, through meditation.

Organizations perform a valuable function in the world, but that function should be to provide a teacher or a book which would be of help in helping students find the kingdom of God within their own being. In addition to teachers and books, organizations can also provide a place where students can go for meditation and communion, while they are in the transitional stage; while they are seeking God, while they are seeking the kingdom.

As I see it, there is no reason why some religious organizations should not exist forever. I do not see any reason in our age why they should be discontinued. But I do say that their purpose in the early stage of our search for God is to provide us with books, teachers, teachings, services, or whatever it is that we need that will help us find the kingdom of God. The function of a church or an organization is to lead us to the kingdom of God. Then when it has revealed God to us, it will have served its purpose, and we should be free to go our way, inside or outside the church, as we choose.

The work of The Infinite Way is to reveal the kingdom of God within your own being. I have never met anyone yet who has achieved the fullness of the realization of God, but in a measure and by degrees, we are making greater progress year after year. For that reason, then, it is right for me to tell you and to share with you all of these things about truth, as I have been doing. But if I do not help you to attain the ability to meditate, you will not arrive at that final step of meeting God face to face. And that is what you must do. You have to find God; you have to meet God face to face.

The Purpose of Meditation

Therefore, we do not practice meditation just for the sake of sitting in the silence, or just for the sake of attaining a steady, one-pointed attention on that which we call God. Our meditation is for the purpose of finding an inner stillness so that the presence and power of God can be made manifest in, or as, our individual consciousness; and then that enables us to live our lives as Paul lived his. "I live; yet not I, but Christ liveth in me."[1] Through meditation you will find the presence and power of the Christ, and It will live your experience. Remember this: It is not wise to spend too long a period in meditation; it is not wise to sit for as long as an hour or two. It is apt to dull perception rather than to sharpen it. It may take us an hour before we achieve a stillness or quietness; but when we do, and feel that silence, then let us get up and bring the meditation to a close. Usually, we should be able to find ourselves in this stillness and this quietness in two, three, or four minutes. Sometimes it may take ten or fifteen minutes, if the pressure from outside is very strong. But by the end of ten or fifteen minutes, we should have achieved a sense of inner peace. Then, after having taken another minute or two to let this Presence manifest or announce Itself, we should go about our business.

In other words, meditation is not an end in itself. It is a means to an end. It is merely a vehicle through which we attain an awareness of the presence of God. There are some people who use

[1] Galatians 2:20.

meditation as an end in itself. All they want to do is to sit for an hour or two or three in the silence. Do not do that. Use meditation as a means to an end, as the means of being quiet for a moment to feel the presence of God, and that is all.

If you have a problem, whether it is your own or whether it is a patient's, do not take the problem with you into meditation. When you give a treatment, the purpose of your treatment is to remind yourself of the truth of being, and thereby lift yourself to a state of receptivity, to a degree of consciousness in which you can be still and let that mind which was in Christ Jesus be also in you.

When you get the signal that you have touched that mind, or that that mind has touched you; when you hear that answering response that says to you, "All is well," or "It is done," or "I am here"; when you feel that a weight has dropped off your shoulder; or when you feel a sense of lightness within; this is the evidence that He is with you. This is the He that performeth that which is given you to do—that gentle Presence, that Christ within, that Spirit of God. Once you have felt that "click," it is as if you had released It; and then like a radio beam, It goes out and covers the whole world, so that whatever has to be achieved for you, is achieved by that Spirit, which has been contacted or realized. It is as if you had pressed a telegraph key here, and then the next instant the message was received at the other end in New York or London or Paris.

The moment you touch this inner Key, this inner Being, It goes all over the world to perfect and to perform that which is necessary to the fulfillment of your demonstration. If it is necessary to make a contact with somebody in Asia in order to bring him to you, It will. If it is necessary to make a contact with somebody next door, if a teacher or a book is needed, or if it is to protect you from danger or to open up the roadway for you when you are driving, It will do all of those things.

Building a Spiritual Foundation for Healing Work

This teaching has one prime purpose: to bring you to a place of actual contact with the presence and power of God. The letter of truth gives you a solid foundation on which to build the Spirit or consciousness of truth. In fact, once you have built this consciousness of truth, once you have touched the Christ, you can forget all about the letter of truth. When you actually get the feeling of that Presence, then it will make no difference whether you ever use a treatment, or whether you ever learn what a treatment is. The great spiritual seers throughout all time have had the Spirit, but very few of them knew what the letter of truth was. In our day, the letter of truth serves for those of us who were not born with the Spirit fully developed; it serves as a foundation, but after we have built our foundation, after we have erected the superstructure of the Spirit of that temple that is not made with hands, that spiritual understanding; then, if we like, we can discard the treatment, or letter of truth.

In most of my healing work, very little of the letter is used, but as yet I have not been able entirely to eliminate treatment. I have never been able to let a single day go by without a treatment in some form, about some subject. It plays less and less of a part in my healing work, but a greater and greater part in the teaching work. There are too many truth students who have not been well-grounded in the letter. They do not know what the principle is that they are trying to demonstrate. They do not know what the basis of our spiritual existence is. The time has come when all students must know more about this principle. If you do not know the basis which forms the foundation of your treatment, then your treatment is of little value. If you do not know the premise that God is the reality of your being, that all that is true of God is true of you, and that only that which is true of God is true of you, you have no spiritual foundation. And yet how few practitioners know that principle! For that reason I pray, and I pray diligently, earnestly, and sincerely, that everyone learn the letter of truth—learn the principle on which this work is based.

After you have learned the letter of truth, meditate until you have actually caught an inner awareness, a feeling of the Presence. When you have that awareness, you have the healing agency. "I can of mine own self do nothing";[1] but when you have caught the awareness of that Presence, you have that with you which can go out and heal any manner of disease. The awareness of the Christ can overcome any phase of lack or limitation. It can make any type of relationship harmonious—family, community, national, or international. It can do all of those

[1] John 5:30.

things for you, since It is the very mind or principle that healed and fed the multitudes of old. This was done, not only by the Master, but the same things were done by Moses, Elijah, Elisha, and many other prophets and seers.

Gain the conscious awareness of the presence of God; gain the conscious feeling of this inner voice, of this inner Self, of this inner peace, and then behold what happens. It rushes right out to the very person of whom you are thinking. It rushes right into the part of their bodies that is affected, and It heals it, changes it, or corrects it. It goes to the uttermost ends of the earth. It searches the bones, the marrow, the spirit, the whole structure from top to bottom. What does? The Christ—when you have caught It, when you have felt It, when you have touched It, and when It has touched you within. Then you can say, "Ah, It performeth the things that are given me to do. It perfecteth that which concerneth me. It goes before me to make the crooked places straight. It walks beside me. It comes up behind as a rear guard." This It we are talking about is the Christ, the He who performeth all things. We are not talking about a *He* in a book, or a *He* to whom you pray—there is no such a He. The only He or It there is, is something that you contact within your own being. That is the only place you can contact it. The kingdom of God is within you. "I can of mine own self do nothing[1] . . . the Father that dwelleth in me, he doeth the works."[2] There is a principle that heals, that saves, that actually is a way of spiritual living. There is a principle that will

[1] John 5:30.   [2] John 14:10.

live your life perfectly for you, that will lead you into green pastures.

Let those who are emerging from the traditional concept of God use right thinking and use statements of truth in whatever way they want to use them. But you who have come to this point should begin *now* to touch, or be touched, by that Christ, by that inner Power and Presence. "Let this mind be in you."[1] The only way you can be touched by the Christ and let this mind be' in you is to open your consciousness and let it come in. When it says "let," it really means *let. Let it come in!*

Open consciousness. Learn in your meditations to keep your ear open so as to let It come in. Wait until you feel It within, and then suddenly It will be right there—perhaps over your heart. Then you will be able to say, "He perfecteth that which concerneth me. He performeth that which is given me to do." You will know that He, because the *He* you are talking about is a He that you have actually contacted within, a He that you have actually realized and felt.

Do you begin to see the importance of meditation in this work? In meditation you take yourself out of the picture long enough to let that He, that mind that was also in Christ Jesus, come in. Just be still. Just be silent long enough, and some day you will find that God reveals Itself, not only *in* silence, but *as* silence. *God is the great silence.* It is a feeling, an awareness, a state of being—a wonderful, joyous state of being.

[1] Philippians 2:5.

251

Neither Good nor Evil Thoughts Are Power

The Christ is not a mental activity. It cannot be induced by any kind of mental legerdemain. It is useless to try to bring It into expression with thoughts; thoughts will not do it. Thought is not power: good thoughts are not power and evil thoughts, malpracticing thoughts, erroneous thoughts are not power. They will not hurt anyone except the individual who gives them power. Do not treat yourself for anything. The only treatment that is legitimate is a treatment which leads your thought to the realization of God as omnipresent and results in your feeling the Presence. Your treatment is never against rheumatism; your treatment is never against resentment, dishonesty, or injustice. If you treat too strenuously against these qualities, you are likely to engender them. The more a person treats against envy, dishonesty, and other undesirable characteristics, the more of these he has to meet. When you treat, treat for the presence of God, for a realization of the presence of God as your individual being. And when you have treated, be patient for a while, and let this feeling come. The evil thoughts of the world are not power. Evil is not a power. Sin, in any form is not a power; it is not a presence; and your recognition of that is the healing agency.

When we say that disease is an illusion, it does not mean that the illusion is out there in time and space, and that you as a practitioner or a metaphysician are being called upon to destroy it. There is no illusion out there. The illusion is in the mind of the believer, and that is the only place where it needs to be destroyed. You never remove growths from anybody; there are none to remove. That is a belief, and your recognition of the truth that it exists only as a belief or as an illusion is the healing agency. Do not go outside your own being to heal somebody. There is nothing wrong with the patient. You are entertaining a false belief about him. Correct that in your own thought. This evil, then, this wrong thought, is not a power; it exists only as false sense; and your recognition of it as a false sense is the healing agency—not knowing a lot of truths about it, or knowing that it is a lie, or that it does not exist in mind, or that it is not true. There is only one thing that it is necessary to know in healing work, and that is the non-existence as an entity, or power, of any form of error.

In the same way, a good thought is not power. If a good thought were power, I do not suppose any of us as children would lose our parents; and I am sure parents would never lose a child, because all they would have to do would be to think enough good thoughts and end all this nonsense of sin, disease, death, and imprisonment. Thinking good thoughts, however, will not do it. Good thoughts and Truth are entirely different. Truth is not a thought, and it is not a statement. Truth is a state of consciousness. It is a state of awareness, an understanding of the non-power of that which appears as good thoughts and bad thoughts. It is a touching of the Christ. That is Truth. Truth and Christ are synonymous. Therefore, Truth is not anything you can read in a book. Truth is not anything you can hear with your ears. *Truth is the Christ*, and the Christ is this inner awareness, this inner consciousness. Therefore, when you have

sense of the word awareness, since consciousness becomes a conscious awareness without a process or effort or mental procedure. It is like saying that we are conscious of our integrity, but without our having any awareness of having developed it, or brought it about. We are conscious of integrity; we are aware of integrity, but we never consciously *think* of it, except when it is absent. So consciousness is not only a synonym for awareness, but much more: it is an established sense of awareness *without a process*.

In my writings, I make a distinction between the word "consciousness" and the word "mind." Correctly understood, mind is not a synonym for God, because mind implies a mental process or mental activity of consciousness, a mental activity of awareness, which, of course, God is not. God just *is*. Rightly speaking, mind, then, would be a human agency and it could not be synonymous with God. On the other hand, God is consciousness, and because consciousness is awareness without a process, it is a much more comprehensive term than mind. Mind can be thought of as a facet of consciousness, as an instrument or activity of God, Consciousness, but never as God.

Many people believe that thoughts are things and that thinking can change the human picture. In this teaching, when we say "thoughts are not things," we mean that thought is not a creative principle. Regardless of how much thinking you do, you cannot create anything with your thought. All you can do with your thought is to become aware of that which *is*. With your thought, or through your thought, you become aware that two times two are four, or you become aware of the blue sky, or the ocean, or the high mountain, or the deep valley; but your thinking will not create these things. You can become aware, at least in a measure, of the very presence and power of God. But are you *creating* the presence and power of God? Can you create the presence and power of God? No! God is the infinite, all-knowing Intelligence, that knows your need long before you do, and it is Its good pleasure to give you the kingdom. Therefore, you are to take no thought for those things which you need, but let this all-knowing Mind, Life, Truth, Love, Soul, know what your need is without your telling It, and let It have the pleasure of providing it for you. Then you become a beholder of the activity of God, the divine consciousness of your being at work.

God is not a thought. God is divine reality, divine being. While I am thinking about truth or thinking about religion or thinking about God, the divine idea manifests itself, and through thought I become aware of it. Did I create God? Did I create truth? Did you ever create love, or life? No, those are divine ideas. They are divine realities that have existed since before time began, and we become aware of them. Always remember that there is not a manifested thing in the world; there is not a manifested truth in the world; there is not a divine idea in the world, that you can create. But you can become aware of every truth and every idea. And this is accomplished through meditation.

CHAPTER SIXTEEN

HEALING AND SILENCE

FROM the time a patient asks for help, the responsibility for the healing lies with the practitioner. It is the practitioner's responsibility to live, move, and have his being in and as divine Presence; and his life must be lived according to that standard. He must have grown into that state of consciousness in which he realizes his oneness with God in full measure, so that he does not look to person, place, or thing for anything and never permits such things as envy, jealousy, malice, or lust to enter his consciousness.

We do not set ourselves up as healers of disease; we are followers of the spiritual way of life, in which, if you seek first the kingdom of God, all these other things will be added unto you. It is a most marvelous thing that a grain of this truth does so many wonders. Very often people who are not on the spiritual path can easily be healed by a practitioner. Nevertheless, even the Master found those he could not heal because of their unbelief. Many times he asked people if they believed that he could heal them. When he spoke of belief and faith, he really meant a belief and faith shown forth in actions. He knew how many are invited to the spiritual feast and how few come: they are too busy with other engagements.

No practitioner can take the responsibility for

bringing about a healing if the patient is continually filling his mind with the pleasures and pursuits of this world. If the patient insists on listening to the radio or watching television from morning until night, or sitting at a card table or cocktail table, hour after hour, he is separating himself from his good, because, having ears, he cannot hear what Spirit is saying. He would not get a healing if it were sitting on his door-step, because he would not be at home. "Having eyes, ye see not, having ears, ye hear not." Certainly the patient does not hear or see if he is so busy with worldly things that he does not have time to listen for the voice of the Lord which thunders in the silence. In such cases the patient must not blame the practitioner.

The practitioner does not ask for cooperation in the sense of insisting that the patient follow a pre-scribed course of action set up by the practitioner. The patient is not asked to read so many pages in a book, to buy some book, to tithe, or to go to a certain church. The practitioner merely says, "Drop it at my feet as long as you feel that this is your way and that you can be helped; drop it; I will take care of it."

The practitioner does assume the responsibility, but he gives no guarantee of healing. That does not lie within the practitioner's province. I can well remember how many times I did not receive a heal-ing from practitioners—even good practitioners, consecrated ones—and later learned some lesson that I would rather have had than the healing— a lesson that might not have been learned had I not had to stay close to truth. We, ourselves, cannot judge as to why anyone's healing is delayed, or why it is slow, or why it does not come. It may well be that there is something driving that individual on to higher realms, and that this very delay may be the means to greater unfoldment. That, however, must not be an alibi for failure. We must shoulder the responsibility for each healing, and if it does not come, we can only acknowledge, "Well, if I had gone a step higher, I might have achieved it."

On the other hand, we who accept the words of the Master, should remember that he said, "And whosoever shall not receive you . . . shake off the dust of your feet."[1] There are many who come to us and would like to be healed by us, but they are not receiving us. They are not even listening or trying to understand the message. All they are interested in is, "When am I going to get this healing? When is the pain going to stop?" Our work is not primarily that of a healing agency. That is not our work. Our work is to show forth the kingdom of God and let these other things be added.

The Holy Ghost

In our present development, we seem to need eyes for seeing and ears for hearing, but these senses are only necessary in our present, limited concept of life. The moment we grow into a higher awareness, we shall find that we are conscious of the entire universe without the aid of the senses of hearing, seeing, tasting, touching, or smelling.

The Holy Ghost is that actual spiritual awareness

[1] Matthew 10:14.

or spiritual consciousness. When you spiritually discern anything, you can refer to that as the Holy Ghost or the descent of the Holy Ghost. The Holy Ghost is a religious or scriptural term for the coming to consciousness of spiritual awareness. Your spiritual awareness, your spiritual consciousness, must reveal to you the Christ, because with your physical senses of seeing, hearing, tasting, touching, or smelling, you could not be aware of it. That higher sense, which is actually spiritual illumination, is necessary.

To some extent, every metaphysician has touched or tasted the Holy Ghost. Every metaphysician who has ever brought about any healing, has, of necessity, touched the Holy Ghost, since all healing is done through spiritual discernment. I mean *spiritual* healing. All spiritual healing is done through spiritual discernment. Through spiritual sense, you bring about the healing. That is the Holy Ghost. Without this spiritual sense, you would merely be seeing something and be believing what you were seeing. Spiritual healing is the discernment, the inner vision, which enables a person to look at sinning, mortal humanity and say, "Here is the Christ." It is that which enabled the Master to say, "Father, forgive them; for they know not what they do,"[1] because he could see right through the appearance to the very heart. Nearly everybody in the world has eyes and can see humanity with all its frailties and faults, but the important thing is: having eyes, can you *really* see? When you have eyes that really see, there is no longer any criticism, judgment, or

[1] Luke 23:34.

condemnation of sin; and what is more, there is no fear of disease.

When we are called upon for help, most of us automatically begin thinking. We get a thought of some kind; it may be an affirmation or it may be a denial, but some kind of thought comes. Now let us do just the reverse of what we would ordinarily do when called upon for help. Let us remember the basis of this work: "I can of mine own self do nothing.[1] . . . Which of you by taking thought can add one cubit unto his stature."[2] God's thoughts are not your thoughts. Your thoughts are not God's thoughts. Now, when someone asks for help, the first thing I say to myself is: "Well, Joel, at least you know enough to know that you, yourself, cannot do anything about it." That stops any such nonsense as believing that a human being can heal anything or anybody. Now, what do we do? Where do we go from here? "The Father that dwelleth in me, he doeth the works."[3] So we turn inward and listen for the Father. If the Father gives the treatment, the healing takes place. If the Father gives the treatment, manna comes from the sky, water flows from the rocks, the dead are raised. When human beings give the treatment, it has to be given twice, three times, four times, sometimes seventy times seven; but if the Father gives the treatment, that is it. It is done.

To Heal without Argument, Listen

As you sit down to give a treatment, say, "Father, you give the treatment this time instead of me."

[1] John 5:30.   [2] Matthew 6:27.   [3] John 14:10.

Then, instead of thinking thoughts, listen. It may be that, in some cases, you will actually become aware of some thought or some quotation. But that does not necessarily follow, and do not be discouraged if it does not happen to you. In my own experience, ninety-nine times out of a hundred, I do not hear anything. There is a feeling within, a sense of release—I call it a "click." It is almost as if a weight dropped off my shoulders, or a feeling of lightness came in my chest. To me, that is the signal of the conscious awareness of the presence of God; that is the signal that God is on the field, and my work is done.

This kind of healing is called "healing without argument," or "healing without treatment." It is much simpler than using argument or treatment. However, even if you attain the ability to heal without words or thoughts, it does not mean that you will not use treatment, on occasion. We all have to do that at some time or other. In the course of your practice, you may have to give many treatments, but you will never again give a treatment to a patient.

Let me remind you that in this work all treatments are self-treatments. Never give a treatment to a patient under any circumstances. It may clarify this point for you, if you will try to think of how you would treat, or what kind of a treatment you would give to an animal. Would you expect a cat or a dog to catch your thought or respond to it? Suppose that you are taking care of a garden. Would you give a treatment to the flowers and plants? Would you give a treatment to the garden or to the earth? No, you give yourself the treatment about the plants. So it is in your work with patients. If you are going to give a treatment at all, give the treatment to yourself about your patient. Always honor your patient by acknowledging that, as a matter of truth, he is the living Christ, the Son of the living God, and, therefore, he needs no treatment. If you see any evidence of sin or disease or lack or limitation about him, you are the one at fault. The error is in you; correct it in yourself. Give yourself the treatment about your patient. Acknowledge to yourself: "Father, here is the Christ, but I am beholding the Christ in a limited way, mortally and materially. Give me the true vision about this individual."

If you are faced with a condition of paralysis, for example, you must realize, "Wait a minute; the divine Mind is the source of all action, and therefore, it is not possible for the body to be paralyzed, inactive, or under-active." You have proof of that in looking at your hand. Your hand will remain right where it is unless you move it. It cannot move of itself. No part of your body can move of itself. The entire body is controlled by mind or intelligence. Therefore, the feeling or sensation is not in the body; it is in the mind; it is in the consciousness. It is the same with other organs and functions of the body. The blood pressure and the heart, in and of themselves, can never be under-active or over-active. When they seem to be functioning abnormally, it is only because the human world has accepted the belief that there is life and power in the body.

Let us suppose that somebody tells you that he is poor. Do not acknowledge his poverty, but, within yourself, know immediately that he is joint-heir with Christ in God; all that God has, he has. Always give the treatment about the appearance to yourself. Remember, out here is only the Christ. We are entertaining either the spiritual vision that says, "Thou art the Christ," or "Whom do men say that I am—Christ, or sick and sinning mortal humanity?" What takes place outwardly is determined by the state of spiritual consciousness that is maintained. If there is a consciousness which looks out and sees sick and sinning and poor mortal humanity, then nothing changes. The same old picture goes on repeating itself year in and year out. But when consciousness beholds only the Christ, it can say, "I do not believe appearances; I do not judge by appearances; with this Holy Ghost, or inner spiritual vision, I know that right here is the Christ, the Son of the living God." Then the changes begin to take place.

Let the Christ Interpret Itself

In this work, we are not so much healers as we are expanders of consciousness, opening consciousness to the nature of our true being. The whole secret is: "Whom do men say that I am? . . . Whom say ye that I am?"[1] If you are mortal man, of course, you will say, "He is just one of the old Hebrew prophets come back to earth again." But if you have been touched by the Holy Ghost, if you have developed one bit of discernment; you will look right through that human picture, and you will say,

[1] Mark 8:27, 29.

"Thou art the Christ, the Son of the living God."[1] That is a universal truth. It was not only the truth about Jesus, but it is the truth about you and me, and about everybody. It does not make any difference what human beings outwardly appear to be. At the very heart and soul of their being, they are the Christ. When we begin seeing each other in that way, ultimately, we reach the place where we do not have to use treatment.

There is a difference between healing through treatment or argument, and healing by spiritual awareness. When you use argument or treatment, you are voicing something which is true, but which you do not know is true. There is nothing wrong with that, as long as you know what you are doing and why. There is nothing wrong at all in reminding yourself, "I am Spirit. I am Soul. I am that place where God shines through. God is the life of my being." There is no harm in that as long as you do not go around repeating, "I am spiritual; I am spiritual," or reciting the Lord's Prayer twenty-five or a hundred times. As long as you are merely reminding yourself of your true identity, or of the truth of being about God, man, and the universe, that form of treatment is legitimate, and it will eventually lead to an expansion of consciousness in which treatment is unnecessary.

Ninety-nine times out of a hundred my own form of treatment is merely a closing of the eyes and a listening attitude. Sometimes I pay no attention to what has been said on the telephone. I am listening to get that feeling of awareness, and when I get that,

[1] Matthew 16:16.

the patient gets the results. It does not do any good for the patient to tell me that a certain part of the body is causing trouble, because I do not take that into my consciousness. As the patient is describing his problem, whether in person, by telephone, mail, wire, or cable, I am listening for that still small voice —for the Christ to interpret itself to me. The Christ *is*, but to me—that is, to my human eyes—It appears to be sick and sinning humanity. There is no use of my sitting down and saying, "Oh, no, I know you are spiritual; I know you are God's perfect child." I will accomplish nothing with that, and I doubt that you will either. But if I let the Christ interpret what is out there to me, then there is a healing. If a patient calls for help, instead of my repeating a lot of words, I stop for a moment, so that there is almost a vacuum created, and then the Christ interprets Itself.

You are the Christ. Therefore, It is what you are, interpreting Itself to me through spiritual vision. The moment a claim comes up, instead of responding to it with an affirmation or denial, reverse it with, "What is that to me! I can of my own self do nothing, no matter how good my thought is. And now, Father, you give it to me!" Let the Christ interpret the situation to you, and then will come the spiritual sense of it. Presently, you will receive a call from your patient, telling you, "Oh, it is really wonderful. I feel fine."

Neither you nor I, with all the truth we know, with all of the books we have read, can change material appearances, or heal diseases. We ought to be very honest about that. There is nothing that we, intellectually, can do about them that is powerful enough to bring about healings. But there is *something*, and that something can be called the Holy Ghost. You can call it "spiritual discernment," or "spiritual consciousness," or "the Father within"—anything you like. It is something that is greater than any degree of humanhood, but it is necessary that you open your consciousness to It. It is a higher form of healing work to be able to heal through the Spirit than it is to heal by means of mental argument, because it leads you into that place where, ultimately, you learn to live without taking thought. You learn to live without taking thought for what you shall eat or what you shall drink, or wherewithal you shall be clothed.

Begin now to practice being still, without making affirmations or denials. That does not mean that you will try to blank out your thoughts, because you cannot do that. Sit and ponder the idea of God, if you like, but do not make affirmations or denials about your patients. Ponder the idea of God while you are asking the Christ to interpret the scene to you. You may ask the Christ to interpret the truth about those of your relatives who are here or who have gone on, if that is what you are interested in. The Christ can reveal the truth about world situations, national affairs, local affairs. The Christ works on any and every level of human affairs; we cannot do it humanly. It is only this Spirit within which can interpret the scene. It interprets it to me, not by *saying* something to me, but by giving me that *feeling* of the divine Presence. Then the Christ is released; it is as if It jumped out into the whole world and touched everything that was a part of the demonstration. We do not direct It and send It to any person. We sit and realize It and then, since It is the all-knowing Mind, It goes to that very place and does the very thing that is necessary for It to do.

We shall not succeed if we are merely trying to save a human being's life. If we try to hold on to that human sense of life, we lose it. Let us be willing to release the human sense of life, and become receptive to the divine sense, to the infinite sense of eternal life. Let us stop thinking about a life caged up in a little body. "Loose him and let him go."[1] That is the answer. Loose anything, loose any condition, and let it go. Do not hold it in the grasp of treatment. Do not hold it in the grasp of affirmation. Loose it and let it go. And it will disappear.

See the Rope as a Rope

This can be summed up by an illustration from Hindu Scripture of the man who went into his bathroom and was badly frightened when he saw a snake. As his eyes became accustomed to the semi-darkness and he looked more closely, he saw that it was not a snake, but a coiled rope. He lost his fear; the color came back to his face; and everything was normal. As strange as this may sound, even to those of us who are old students in truth teaching, the snake that you are looking at is a rope. That evil condition which you are looking at, is not an evil condition at all, and your attempt to get rid of it is what is perpetuating it. You must release the condition, whatever it may be. Loose it and let it go, and then you have harmony;

[1] John 11:14.

the snake disappears, and only the rope remains.

Everyone of us in this work is tempted to believe that there is some condition to be removed or changed. Everyone of us is sometimes tempted to try to heal something, overcome something, or get rid of something. I have never known anyone in this work who has not come under that temptation at some time or another. And in succumbing to that temptation lies our failure. There is no better healing treatment in the world than the remembrance of the snake and the rope: the snake is not a snake at all, but a rope. You may be thinking, "When you say that, you are virtually saying that disease is something good." No, I did not say the snake was a rope. I said that what you *saw* as a snake was a rope. There was no snake there to be a rope. I do not say that disease is of God. I say that what you have looked at and said was disease, is of God. That is quite different. What you are seeing as a snake—in other words, the mirage—is actually a rope. So, where you are seeing sin and disease, there, actually, the presence of God is, but through finite sense, you are seeing it incorrectly.

Let the Christ, that is, the spiritual awareness, interpret the snake and the rope, and It will say to you, "That is not a snake; that is a rope." It will not remove a snake; it will not cure a snake—or gall-stones, either. It will not heal cancer or consumption. It will interpret this spiritual scene to you and say to you, "Stop your worrying. Stop your fearing. God is all there is, and that very thing that you are trying so hard to get rid of and overcome is not there."

The whole purpose of the use of the letter of truth is to develop spiritual consciousness. How do you

269

know when you have achieved spiritual consciousness? Only when you can look at a rope and see a rope; when you can look at any and every person and see the Christ, instead of seeing a sick or sinning human being. When you can do this, you will know that your Christ-self is taking over the personal self. When you can look at a person without envy, jealousy, malice, lust, hate, greed, or revenge, you have developed spiritual consciousness, because you know then that that person is the Christ, that you are the Christ, and that both of you are the fullness of the Godhead bodily. Then you know that you have the Christ vision, or the Holy Ghost. You can look out on this world without fear and realize:

There is no power out there except the power that comes from God. All power is given unto me. Dominion was given to me in Genesis, and it is my fault if I have not carried it all the way from Genesis to Revelation. It is a dominion over the things of the earth and the water and the skies and everything that is in the world. This dominion is mine by virtue of the realization that God is the only presence and the only power. God is the only creative principle.

Once you loose the condition and let it go, through the understanding that even that which is appearing as your particular snake actually is the rope itself seen through finite sense, then begins the development of spiritual consciousness. Then you can loose everything in the world and find it literally true that all that the Father hath of harmony, peace, joy, power, and dominion is thine.

CHAPTER SEVENTEEN

THE EVER PRESENT CHRIST

THERE is a power called Spirit, or the Christ, and It does the work. Talking about the Christ will not bring God or the Christ to bear upon your problem. The Christ must be realized, must be felt. Then we really can say, "I can leave it with God. I can leave it with Truth." As we become convinced within our consciousness of the truth, that conviction, which is realization, makes the demonstration.

Our object is to develop this awareness, this consciousness of truth, this sense of omnipresence. As this is developed, we no longer work specifically on problems; as a matter of fact, we do not have specific problems on which to work. Life begins to unfold in a normal and harmonious manner. We have only to maintain ourselves in that atmosphere of the Spirit for that flow to come through, the flow of divine Life. When we are confronted with problems, then, it is necessary to get back within ourselves, until we get that feeling of the Presence.

As you think of God, the one Life, omnipresent as your own life; God, the one Mind, omnipresent as your own mind; you will not have the sense of twoness, or even the customary sense of God as omnipresent—God and you over here somewhere, separate and apart from It. In thinking of Omnipresence, think of It as your own being—the allness of God, the infinity of God, omnipresent as your individual being. Then there is no sense of separation or division.

The Christ is something which is controlling your being and your destiny. All you have to do is to realize this Christ, or gain the conscious awareness of It, since everyone has It. You do not have It within you, and you do not have It without you: you have It as being. When you talk about the activity of the Christ, you are not talking about a within or a without. If it acted just within our consciousness, there would be no reaching from one to another. It is a within, and it is a without.

What Is Sin?

In spiritual teaching, of course, there is no such thing as sin, in and of itself, because there is only God, expressing Its infinite being. Sin, therefore, is a human term and defines, more or less, a violation of a code of conduct. Rightly speaking, sin is the violation of any law. That law might be a moral law, or it might be a legal law, inasmuch as we consider stealing a sin. If we understood our spiritual identity, everything would flow through; and if it did, there would be no need of having personal possessions or personal ownership; in which case, you would be welcome to whatever I had, and I would be welcome to whatever you had; and that is all there would be to it. It would be a recognition that "the earth is the Lord's and the fullness thereof,"[1] and "Son . . . all that I have is thine."[2]

[1] Psalms 24:1.   [2] Luke 15:31.

The Master recognized this when he walked through the field, plucking the corn. When he was rebuked for it, he referred to David in the temple, eating the shewbread, which was also against the rules: I suppose that he meant that the corn in the field was for the use of the disciples or anybody else who had need of it.

Another human code of conduct relates to marriage. Marriage has been established as a human institution, because it is a protection to society against the unpredictable nature of men and women. Such laws are designed to protect men, women, and especially children. Under spiritual dominion, there would be no need for these laws, for the simple reason that under the government of Spirit, no one would ever do anything contrary to spiritual right.

That leaves us with the question, "Then what is sin?" If we forget human law and consider only spiritual government, we would have to say that sin is anything that takes us outside the government of God, government by spiritual instinct, intuition, or spiritual law. In other words, sin violates the truth of spiritual oneness. If we should desire money, that would be sin, since that would be a violation of the spiritual truth of the omnipresence, the oneness of God, appearing as the fullness of individual being. To believe that we are separate and apart from the infinity of our supply would be a sin; it would be a sin against the Holy Ghost; it really would be a sin even to desire supply. In fact, desire, in any form, would be sin, because it would be an acknowledgment of less than Self-completeness—and, of course, "Self" spelled with a capital "S" really means God or all-completeness, here and now, individually expressed. Any sense, then, of lack or limitation is sin.

Any sense of separation from good would be sin. You might say that any unhappiness would be sin, since it would be based on a sense of our own incompleteness; and spiritual truth reveals that we are already complete. We are the fullness of God's glory. If we say, "I am the fullness of God's glory made evident," and then are unhappy, or desire some thing or some one, we have nullified the sense of completeness, and in that we have sinned. We are taught that the word "sin" comes from the Greek word meaning "missing the mark"—missing the mark of spiritual perfection. That is exactly what this would indicate, that sin is any sense that we entertain of a separation from good.

God Appears As

Let us consider the word "God" in relation to cause and effect. To illustrate, let us think of a mahogany piano. We would not say that there is mahogany in the piano: mahogany is formed, or appears *as* a piano. Or we might take as another illustration a solid gold fountain pen. Again, we would not say that there is gold in the fountain pen. No, gold is formed as a fountain pen. You might say there is ink in the fountain pen. Yes, but the ink and the fountain pen are not one and the same. If you say, God *in* effect, it is like saying that there is ink in the fountain pen, or gas in the gas pipe. You have two substances. Therefore, in that sense, there is no God in any effect. That is the objection to the term, "God in man." Certainly, there is no God *in* man.

When Jesus spoke of "the Father within me," he was not making of himself some kind of a hollow tube in which God was located. He did not mean that statement in a literal sense. It was his way of referring to God *as* his consciousness, God *as* his being, God *as* his life; but not God *in* his life, not God *in* his body, not even God *in* his mind. How can you get infinity *into* anything? It is literally impossible to incase infinity *in* anything. You could not get infinity *in* this whole world; but infinity can *embrace* the world, or infinity can appear *as* a world.

To state that God appears *as* individual being is to have God and individual being as one. It is like saying that whatever the quality of gold is, that is the quality of the fountain pen, since the gold and the fountain pen are inseparable and indivisible. They are one, as essence or substance, the fountain pen appearing as the form into which the gold is molded; or in the illustration of the piano, all that mahogany is, the mahogany piano must be, since mahogany and piano are one. But you certainly would not say, "There is mahogany in the piano." The only way you could say that is if you had a piano and then put a little piece of mahogany into it. But then you would not necessarily have a mahogany piano. Nor can you say, "I and my Father are one," if you merely mean that there is a little bit of God somewhere in us.

God, infinite Life, individually appears as the life of your being and of mine. God, Life, is not *in* your life; nor is God, Life, *in* your body. But God is the *substance of* your being. God is not visible; God is not definable; God is not a limited being, person, essence, or substance. God is the totality or infinity of spiritual being. Let no one try to reason out what God is, because it cannot be done. On the same basis, let no one try to reason out what man is. It cannot be done. It is playing with words, and it is cheating yourself of any hope of ever finding heaven or harmony. The only way you will ever know God is through spiritual sense; the only way you will ever know man is through spiritual sense. Trying to reason out the truth, fathom it with the mind, or think it out, is pure nonsense, and only defeats your purpose.

Spiritual Consciousness, the Seventh Sense

It is not that we are to accept anything blindly, but we are certainly not to seek God through intellectual reasoning. The things of God are foolishness to man; that is, to mortal man. "Cease ye from man, whose breath is in his nostrils: for wherein is he to be accounted of?"[1] Do not look at a mortal man and hope to find God. If you do, you will not find healing, because the spiritual world does not heal human beings. The spiritual teaching reveals the Son of God, the Christ being, and it does not do that through human reasoning or thinking. The Son of God is revealed through spiritual intuition. Do not permit yourself to be cheated out of the wonderful glories of heaven on earth by a reliance on the intellect. You

[1] Isaiah 2:22.

cannot achieve heaven on earth with the thinking process. Beyond the five physical senses, beyond the sixth sense which we call intuition, there is a seventh sense which operates even above the intuition—that seventh sense is spiritual discernment or spiritual consciousness.

That is why, in our treatment, instead of voicing statements, we listen for that still small voice, and it reveals to us spiritual being—God appearing as an individual. What does He look like? I have never seen Him with my eyes, but I have felt Him in my innermost being. I have felt the God-being of many people, many times. If this healing work could be done humanly or with human thinking, there would not be so little of it in the world, and instead of a few dozen practitioners, we would have millions of them. Jesus, himself, could not train more than a few to go out and do healing work. Why? Because it took a specially developed power. And that power is the power of the Spirit, not of the human mind.

John beheld a wonderful vision of heaven. He saw the heaven while he was here on earth, right while he was here with us. He saw an incorporeal universe; that is, a world without physical structure. He saw this through spiritual sense. He was able to see through what appears to us as a structural universe to that which is, and he saw it as it is in all its perfection. He saw it with that seventh sense, spiritual consciousness. His vision revealed that this is a spiritual universe, that we are spiritual beings, and that this body is spiritual. This body is the temple of God, the temple of the Holy Ghost, just as it is

277

described in the New Testament. This body is the temple of God, and it is indestructible. It is not our body that ages or changes. Our body is just as indestructible and spiritual as it was before Abraham was, and as it will be until the end of time. The change takes place, not in our body, but in the human concept of body.

Removing False Concepts

Everyone, to some extent, is under the claim or belief of human consciousness. Remember, however, that you do not have a human mind of your own, nor a human consciousness. The human mind or human state of consciousness is a universal sense of separation from God. Actually, there is only one mind, the instrument of God. But there is a false or limited sense of that mind, which we call the human mind or human consciousness. It is not really mind or consciousness, but a *limited sense* of the one infinite Consciousness. Through that limited sense, you look at the body and see the changes that that limited sense depicts.

Let us suppose, for example, that you see a diamond, and, looking at it, you mistake it for a rhinestone. Yet, all the while it is a diamond. Where does the rhinestone exist? Nowhere; there is no rhinestone. What you are calling a rhinestone represents a finite or false concept of a perfect diamond. You accept your concept of the stone as truth until a diamond broker appraises the stone and tells you that it is a diamond. What happens to your rhinestone? There never was a rhinestone; the stone is now and always has been a diamond. Your rhinestone has disappeared. But from where has it disappeared, since it never had any existence? There was really nothing to disappear, since there never was a rhinestone; the rhinestone's only existence was as a belief or false sense.

In the same way, we are told that all of mortal experience—everything we see, hear, taste, touch, and smell—is illusion or a false concept. Does that mean that there is a real world and an unreal world? No. It means that this world is the world which was envisaged by John, except that John had risen above the finite concept, so that he no longer saw it through the misperception that would mistake a rhinestone for a diamond.

That is the basis of spiritual healing. The person who calls himself a patient is actually the Christ, the presence of God, spiritual man, standing in all the fullness, all the glory, of spiritual being and identity, actually God made manifest. Just as you were falsely seeing the diamond as a rhinestone, so you see this universal picture of mortal man, that "man whose breath is in his nostrils," and who, according to Isaiah, "is not to be accounted of."[1] Your first reaction is to attempt to heal that man. The moment you seek to do that, it is as if you were to say, "I should like to change that rhinestone into a diamond." But you cannot do that, because there is no rhinestone there. The diamond is *already* a diamond. The healing takes place when you, yourself, recognize that the patient is not out there as an individual to be healed. The patient is a false

[1] Isaiah 2:22.

279

concept in universal belief. The minute you know that truth, your patient should be healed. Ultimately, your patient is healed through knowing that truth. Sometimes when you know that truth the first time, he is healed; but sometimes, for one reason or another you have to know it a hundred times.

Among many metaphysicians, the belief persists that you must heal something or somebody, or change him, or reform him, or correct him. The only healing, reforming, or correcting, which has to be done, is that which is done in the thought of the beholder. That means in your thought and my thought. If we could catch this point, then, regardless of the name or nature of any form of error—and error actually has no more existence than the snake in the rope, or the diamond appearing as a rhinestone—healing would be instantaneous. Some day, we who remain with this long enough will develop this spiritual sense sufficiently to bring about quick healings, and, ultimately, instantaneous healings, since all that it requires is this awareness.

There is only one thing that will compel us to refrain from giving somebody a treatment: that is to realize instantly that, no matter what the picture is, it is not true, since Christ, the spiritual man, the Son of God, is *all* that is there. When that is your reaction, you have instantaneous or quick healing. Nothing less than that is spiritual healing. Spiritual healing is not using the power of God to get rid of sin or disease. Spiritual power is the realization of God, omnipresent as individual being. When once you can recognize that God is omnipresent as individual being, you will never give a treatment to the appearance, but you will instantly be alert to recognize, "I am not deceived by appearances."

Christ interprets Itself. The vision of The Infinite Way is that we do not go out into the world trying to correct it or improve it. Let us not have any fear of or for the world, or any sense of the world's needing saving or reforming, since all that has to do with the universal concept of a world. We are not asked to leave the world; we are asked to be in the world, but not of it. We are to be in the world, but we are to be no part of its fears, its hates, its enmities, or its jealousies. "Ye are the light of the world."[1] No one can be a "light of the world" who has any fear, doubt, criticism, judgment, hate, envy, jealousy, or malice. The "light of the world" is that individual who, through spiritual discernment, has seen that the universe is spiritual, perfect, and harmonious. This, he can only see or feel through an inner spiritual light or spiritual discernment.

The attempt to reform or to govern and control other people's lives will not work. You were not ready for spiritual teaching, and I was not ready for it until the time came; and no one could hasten that readiness by preaching at us, or by shoving books in front of us and asking us to read them, or leaving them on the table for us, hoping we would pick them up and read them. What we are called on to do is, not to preach the gospel in the sense of going out and talking it, but to preach the gospel in the sense of *living* it, showing forth what it is doing in our experience. Then, strangely enough, we do not have to tell anyone about it. They can see it in our whole

[1] Matthew 5:14.

being; and, certainly they can see any health or supply that we show forth. So we never really need to speak. When we find our God in secret, that secret will be shouted from the housetops.

Let us, then, begin with that knowledge. Let our relationship with God be a sacred and secret one. Let it be made manifest outwardly only through the appearance of the new harmony of our being and of our body. Not only do we bless the world that way, but we bless the entire spiritual movement. The world is hungry for truth. It is merely looking for someone to show it forth so that it, too, can find it.

Spiritual Power

Spiritual power is a power that is generated or made manifest through our awareness of God as one power. One Power, good—that is the only power. In other words, spiritual power comes with your recognition, not that you are going to give a treatment to remove the snake from the rope, but that the rope is a rope, and there is no snake there. You need not say a prayer or give a treatment to remove a snake when all the time it is a rope. That is spiritual power. In individual experience, then, that means that as we walk up and down the world, realizing God as the infinite nature of our being, we do not look out at the world and strive to save it, or change it, or reform it. Our spiritual power consists in looking through the human being to the divinity at the center of his being, and, thereby, greeting the Christ as individual being. You never have to say that aloud. You do not have to mention it to anyone. In a store, on a streetcar, in an automobile, or wherever you may be; if you do not pay attention to the outer appearances, but always realize Christ, God, as the center of all being, the reality of all being, and realize that behind that mask is the real man, the man of God's creating—that is spiritual power.

Let us add to the great sum total of spiritual power that is abroad in the world. It is almost incredible when you think back on the experiences of some of the early workers and realize how many people they healed as they walked up and down the streets. They did not wait to be asked to give a treatment. As soon as they met with deformity, dishonesty, or alcoholism, they looked right through it to the center of being, and there beheld the Christ; they knew what was appearing as this human being was a false concept, an illusion, but not an illusion out there. The appearance out there did not fool them; and in that way they brought about healing.

That is exactly the same way in which a lecturer or a teacher on a platform brings about healing in his audience. He does not take pity on someone he sees in the audience who is sinning or is ill; he does not recognize the error by saying, "Well, now, we will just bring God down here to do something about that." That is not a healing state of consciousness. That is not the Christ state of consciousness. The Christ state of consciousness looks right through the sinner and right through the disease and says, "What does hinder you? Pick up your bed and walk." It beholds spiritual being out there where the false concept seems to be, and it knows that the false

283

concept is not out there. Do you remember the illustration of the mirage on the desert? The person who sees a mirage on the desert as if it were an actuality to be surmounted is afraid to go forward through that which appears to be water. The one who recognizes that the mirage is but a belief in thought, an optical illusion, drives right along in his car and pays no attention to the water on the road.

When you begin to realize that, since God is the only creative principle of the universe, you are not dealing with sinful, diseased, or dying humanity, you, then, have the vision of Paul. Spiritual being is the house not made with hands, eternal in the heavens. You deal only with that false concept which we recognize to be a complete illusion in mortal thought, and not an entity or identity out there. Then are you the "light of the world."[1] Then are you the healing Christ. Then do you bring spiritual power to bear in this world.

When one practitioner can bring about the healing of many hundreds of people through individual awareness, can you not realize what would happen if there were a million of them? Think what a million practitioners could do—a million practitioners, all motivated by spiritual power, that is, by the power to recognize that God is the center of all being, the actuality and reality of all being. We read in newspapers and magazines about spiritual power, and about utilizing spiritual power in this age. We shall never utilize any of it, however, if we think of it as a *good* power that we are going to apply to an evil person or condition. This is just as benighted

[1] Matthew 5:14.

284

an idea as it is to pray to God to reform a bad man, or offer up a prayer to heal a sick child. It is a lot of nonsense. If God knew anything about the evil man or the sick child, He would have done something about it long before anyone did any praying.

Spiritual power lies in the awareness of God as omnipresent, as the Presence appearing as individual being. You can begin to utilize spiritual power any moment that you like. All you have to do is to adopt the first commandment of Moses and the commandment that Jesus added to it, which is also an Old Testament commandment, revised. There is but one power. Acknowledge no other power but God, and see God as omnipresent, as all individual being. Recognize that good is the only power, and evil is not a power. Evil does not exist as power, but as an illusion. The second commandment, "Love thy neighbor as thyself,"[1] means that if you believe that you, yourself, are spiritual, or that your mother is, or that your child is, you should then "love your neighbor"—and that means the whole world—with the same love. Know that God is just as much the reality of this person's being as of that person's being. In other words, know that God is the reality of universal being, and that there is no being separate or apart from God's being. Then you are utilizing spiritual power. When you sit down in your home in the morning to do this work, you probably think of it in connection with yourself, your family, your business associates, your friends, or with anyone with whom you come into personal contact;

[1] Matthew 19:19.

and it is right that this should be so. Unless we can really begin to see this truth operating in our immediate circle, we shall not see it operate in the wider circle. We must be able to demonstrate it here where we are, before we can expect to see it demonstrated in the far-off places or in the deeper problems of human existence.

Some time during the day or some time during the night, sit down and give earnest thought to this great truth of loving your neighbor as yourself, recognizing God as the life of all spiritual being, recognizing the one mind as governing the spiritual creation. Stay with your vision of God as the actual reality, presence, and power of all spiritual creation, and then let that truth govern what we call the concept or outer condition.

Spiritual power begins with an individual and actually it ends there. If we utilize spiritual power for the realization of God as omnipresence, we then find that it appears here, there, and the other place, and gradually, spreads, until Its light eliminates the darkness on the face of the earth.

CHAPTER EIGHTEEN

THE INFINITE WAY

THE Infinite Way has two fundamental points which are basic to its teaching. One is the nature of God as individual being, which means God as your being. Unless we catch this idea of oneness, we miss this basic spiritual premise—that there are not both God *and* you. The only way we can realize oneness is to understand God *as* you. That is the first point in the teaching of The Infinite Way. The life which is God is your individual life; therefore, your life is just as immortal as the life we call God. That is the reason I am always so positive about saying that no one in the world has ever died or passed on at any time in the history of the world. If he had, he would have had a life of his own to lose, to give up; but *God* is life. God is life eternal, and God is one. Therefore life is one, and that means your life and mine.

Old theological beliefs have instilled in most of us a sense of duality. All those who were not born into some metaphysical movement or other and all those who have any kind of church background have been taught to look up to a God in heaven to be worshipped, or to think of God as something separate and apart from their own being. Of course, to all these people, it is almost sacreligious to say that I and the Father are one, that there is only one Being, and that that Being is God-being. Nevertheless, if we catch that point, we have caught the entire message of the Master. That was the whole of his teaching—oneness. "I and my Father are one"[1]— the Father within me, not a Father afar off, but a Father within me. "The kingdom of God is within you."[2] Remember the meaning of "within" as used in this context. It does not mean like ink in a fountain pen or water in a glass. It really means that God is the life, the mind, the substance, the Spirit, the Soul of your being; yes, even *the substance of your body*.

The question comes up, then, "How can that be?" Such a question is raised, of course, only because we are thinking of God in an orthodox way. If we were to understand God as consciousness, then there would no longer be a question of duality. We are consciousness; we know that all there is to us is consciousness. If I have a body at all, or rather, if I am conscious of having a body at all, it must be because of consciousness. If I am conscious at all that there is a universe, I can only know it through the consciousness which I am. This is not a consciousness which I have, however, since in that case, there would be an "I" and a "consciousness." If that were true, there would be that separation. The consciousness which *I am* rightly describes it. I am a state of consciousness. As consciousness, I am conscious of myself, of my individuality, of my being, of my body, of my business, of my home, of my universe. Except as *consciousness*, I could not be

conscious of them. Either each of us has a consciousness of his own, or there is one Consciousness which
is manifested as individual being. That is the explanation of oneness as taught in The Infinite Way, and
it is the same explanation given by Jesus and by
every great Master who caught the vision of oneness.

If you are seeking God, if you are seeking truth, if
you are seeking good in any form, if you are praying
for anything, you can know that you are deviating
from the teaching of oneness; you are "off the beam."
There is only one way of knowing that you are on
the beam, standing in oneness, and that is when you
can say, "I already *am*. All that the Father hath is
mine. All that God is, I am." Only when you make
an acknowledgment of your present infinity, of your
present identity as one with the Father—only then
can you know that you are following this teaching.
If you have a desire, if you have an awareness of lack
or if you have a sense of limitation, there is only one
way to meet it. Get back on the beam of recognition
that all that the Father hath is mine; all that God is,
I am.

The second point in the message of The Infinite
Way is the nature of error. Throughout all my
writings you will find chapters on the nature of
error. In this work there is only one error, which we
call hypnotism, suggestion, or appearance. We can
handle the entire human scene by calling it hypnotism, since it is a suggestion that is being presented
to our five senses, a suggestion that to our senses is
an entity or identity. If, in treatment, in the healing
work, you were to recognize quickly that any phase
of limitation, or any phase of sin, discord, disease,

unemployment, or any phase of insufficiency is a suggestion, then you would have a quick healing, since the nature of error is illusion. It does not exist as reality.

When you grasp these two points of The Infinite Way message, the rest of it is not difficult. The trouble has been that, for thousands of years, we have accepted the universal belief of a selfhood apart from God. Now we are training ourselves to acknowledge ourselves as the very presence of God, as God made manifest, the Word made flesh. There is no reality to disease. You do not have to find a cause for it, and you do not have to find a remedy for it. You merely have to recognize its nature as a non-existent illusion or suggestion.

The world needs to agree on the basic principle that I and my Father are one; all that God is, I am; all that the Father hath is mine. This is oneness—the single *I*, non-duality. Then we must come to an agreement that error of any nature, regardless of its form—sin, disease, fear, lack, limitation, war—represents only a false and finite concept of the world as it is. In 1932, I discovered that all metaphysical books were wrong which state that error is in our thought, and that we must search our thought to find out what it is. Error is not in *our* thought; error is in the *universal* thought, and we merely accept it. One person accepts it in the form of sin, one in the form of disease, one in the form of lack and limitation. But, in whatever form, it is a universal belief.

What is the basis of a successful practice? There are just three things: First, "I and my Father are one."[1] Regardless of his appearance, his background, or his sins, every person is God made manifest. The second point is that all error, regardless of its name or nature, is merely a false sense of the real; all error is impersonal. Error is no more personal than good is. Never forget this, in case you are ever inclined or tempted to think that some individual is good. No one in the history of the world has been, or is, what can be called good. The greatest Master of them all said, "Why callest thou me good? There is none good but one, that is, God."[2] So give credit where credit belongs. You are but the vehicle for the good of God. The third point is that all error and all good are universal. No matter who the sinner is, or what the sin is, do not accept the sin as his. Satan, evil, error are as impersonal in any individual as good was impersonal in the Master or anyone else who has ever been incarnated. That is one of the sins—glorifying people. How can we glorify people, when we know that all the good there is in the world is the universal good, and that everyone can be an avenue for that universal good. It is a matter of opening consciousness and letting it flow out into expression. That is all.

Prayer

A treatment is a statement or declaration of truth, and for that reason, I do not call it prayer. Prayer is that which takes place after the treatment has been given and the truth about God and the nature of individual error has been stated. As one sits in a

[1] John 10:30.   [2] Matthew 19:17.

receptive and responsive mood, suddenly he feels the "click," announcing the presence of God. That is prayer.

Prayer comes only when you are silent and are not voicing truth at all; when you are not thinking truth, or stating truth, or declaring truth. Why do we ever state the truth, affirm the truth, declare the truth, or give a treatment? The reason is that this reminder of the truth of being lifts us higher in consciousness to where, in a degree, we can overcome the fear of the condition. Actually, what we have done is to reveal so much truth within our own being that we have lost a great deal of the fear of the condition; and at last we can sit quietly and pray.

Prayer is listening for the still small voice, and prayer is communion. Prayer is the ability to receive from the infinity of our own being, which is God. And when we do that, the presence of God announces Itself—that presence of God, that Christ—and That does the work. That is what really heals. The treatment does not heal anything; it just lifts us to a state of consciousness where we can be receptive to spiritual truth. "Receptive" means "to receive." Receive it from where? From God, who is the very center of our being. It is from the infinite Source within that we feel that "peace, be still," or hear, "Knowest thou not that I am with thee? I am ever with thee." Or, if we do not hear a thing—if we just feel that great warm glow within, or that "click," or that deep breath—that, too, is all right. That is the presence of God, the Christ announcing Itself, and It does the work.

Illustrations that Reveal the Principle

You cannot heal anything with an effect. Therefore, in a treatment never use the words which you have heard or read. But, if you can catch these three main points and then voice them in your own words in an original way, if you can find some way of thinking about oneness without using as illustrations, Lake Erie and Niagara Falls, or the sun and the sunbeams, or the waves and the ocean; then it will be that much more powerful for you. Those three examples make the idea of oneness very clear. This, I know, because, for many years, I have seen the effects; I have seen the work that has been done in the world through a recognition of the truth found in these examples; but I can promise you that the work will be even more effective for you when you can find illustrations which are original with you.

For example, I have watched how people have lost their fear of sin and disease, of alcoholism, of drugs, the moment they have caught the meaning of the illustration of the white poodle. In my younger days in New York City, there was a vaudeville act, in which a hypnotist told the people he hypnotized, "Now you see that white poodle down there. We don't want it on the stage. Chase it off and into the wings." With that suggestion, the subject made a great effort to get the dog off the stage and into the wings, and in most cases, with a little shoving, succeeded. The white poodle has done great things for me; it has been a very helpful illustration.

I remember one day I had a patient in the office, to whom I was trying unsuccessfully to explain the

293

illusory nature of error. I was not succeeding very well. Suddenly, the vaudeville hypnotist came back to my thought, and after telling him about his act, I said to the patient, "Now, suppose we had a man up there on the stage who just couldn't get that poodle off the stage and into the wings; it just wouldn't go. Suppose this hypnotized man looked out into the audience, saw one of his metaphysical friends, and called to him, 'Ah, you can help me! Give me a treatment to get rid of my white poodle!' Now what form would such a treatment take? It would be just a laugh, wouldn't it? a smile and, 'Thank you, Father, there is no white poodle.' "

That is the nature of error. It does not exist; it is not there; it is a state of hypnotism. We know that because of all our years of healing so-called incurable diseases. There is not a form of disease that it is not possible to heal in this work. In our realization of truth, we know that error exists only as a white poodle—a non-existent white poodle or a state of hypnosis—and the healing agency is the realization that we are dealing, not with a white poodle, but with hypnosis. Try this when you are called upon to heal anything. Immediately see if you cannot say to yourself, "No, I am not going to try to get rid of the white poodle, because there is no white poodle. There is nothing here but hypnotism." Stand on that and see if you will not have some wonderful healings. Prove in your healing work that there is no disease— that everything that appears to you as disease is a state of hypnotism. If you can do that once, you will have proved the principle. From then on it is only the degree in which you can maintain this vision that will make you successful in this work. If we can go out and do this healing work through our understanding of this principle, then the whole world will come to us.

No practitioner of spiritual healing has the right to be a practitioner unless he has received some measure of illumination that reveals to him the allness of God. Everybody will tell you that God is all, and that that is the secret. And it is. But unless you can see that the allness of God precludes the possibility of their being any reality to error, then you see, you do not understand the meaning of the allness of God. You cannot have the allness of God *and* a sin or a disease. Do not fool yourself, it is an impossibility.

Treatment

Meditation is not a necessity. If you think that meditation is a necessity, then you are making a God out of meditation. Meditation is just an avenue, a vehicle, which helps us to arrive at the place where we hear these revelations and unfoldments of truth, and where we are able to feel the presence of God. But if, after we have made the contact, we could not meditate, we might get along just as well, have just as many healings, and have just as satisfying a life. Nothing is necessary to our experience in the realm of an effect, not even meditation, not even treatment. If you could not give yourself a treatment, you could be healed. If you were knocked unconscious this second, you would be healed, even without a treatment or anyone's giving you a treatment. Why? You are living in the consciousness of God's allness, and that acts as a treatment, whether you are conscious or unconscious, whether you are awake or asleep.

That is why I continue to refer to the injunction to "Pray without ceasing." If you are praying, if you are knowing this truth all the time, it does not make any difference, then, whether you give a treatment at this particular moment or at another moment. You are always living in your treatment. You do not have to declare it over and over again. If twelve people came into your office in one or two or three hours, you would not have to stop twelve times to give each one of them a treatment. The fact that you are living in your treatment *is* the treatment. All there is to this situation is God, and any other appearance is the suggestion of a white poodle; or you may think of it as the snake in the rope, except that there is no snake in the rope; it is a rope. If one thinks quickly of either of these illustrations, the treatment is complete, right there and then. That is treatment, but it is not the kind of treatment that many metaphysicians call treatment. In other words, it is not sitting down and rehearsing a great many statements of truth, affirming this and denying that, and then saying that God hooks up broken bones and knits them together or some other kind of wishful thinking.

While it is true that many of those things constitute treatment, the highest form of treatment is when, after having learned all that, you do not have to rehearse it any more, but just sum it all up in one sentence, "Well, that must be the white poodle." In other words, you are saying, "That is just a hypnotic suggestion, just a state of mesmerism." Then snap your fingers at it. However, I do not advise anyone to give that one-sentence kind of treatment until he knows the substance that belongs in a treatment.

You must come to the place where you can say to yourself, "Well, if there is any error, it is simply the hypnotic suggestion of a white poodle. Now, I am not going to give a treatment to get rid of a white poodle that I know does not exist. Neither am I going to give a treatment for the fleas on the white poodle." Yes, even fleas, because after you have a white poodle, you might just as well take all that goes with it! After you have accepted man as mortal, you have birth, accident, sin, fear, disease, change of life, old age, decomposition, insanity, death. But mortal man is non-existent, so why give a treatment for any kind of mortal man or any part of his body? If you do away with mortal man himself, then you have nothing left to treat. It is profound, and yet it is the simplest of truths.

The Limitation of Words in Expressing Truth

Let us consider the term "reflection." The fire that we see at the center of the diamond comes through each facet of the diamond. We might say that the facets reflect the fire that is within, but, of course, the facet is not a thing apart from the diamond itself. So actually the fire of the diamond is as much a part of the diamond as the facets. We do, however, refer to the facets of the diamond as reflectors of the fire within. In the same way, it is true that God is

297

infinite substance and that that substance is formed as the one body. But remember this: There is only one mind and only one body. That one mind and one body express individually as you and as me. Reflection is a term that is sometimes used to indicate the fact that body is individual in the sense of being your body or my body. We say that your body or my body is the body of God, the infinite body, infinitely expressed, or infinitely reflected. There is only one body in the same way in which there is only one diamond. The diamond may have a hundred different facets, but the diamond and the fire are really all one. There are not 100 diamonds to a single diamond: there is only one. All the fire, all the brilliance of the diamond, however, is reflected in each and every facet, because there is no place where those facets can be separated or divided from each other. They are all one.

Using the word "reflection," not in the sense of a reflection in the mirror, but in the sense that "I reflect integrity, loyalty, honesty, or fidelity," is not really incorrect. However, such a statement is not true. As expressed by the Master, in the spiritual language of the Bible, the correct statement is: "*I* am the way; *I* am the truth; *I* am the life." We could in the same way say, "I am integrity, loyalty, honesty, or fidelity." But to state this truth in that way, would not be very intelligible to the world, and so we say, "I express integrity, or loyalty, or fidelity; or I reflect it." The truth is that I am really not reflecting it at all. It is really a constituted part of my being, and of yours. It is all one.

Let me caution you not to be too much concerned about the use of words. Words are designed to convey ideas, but it is difficult to express spiritual truth in human language. It was the great spiritual teacher, Lao-tse, who said in effect, "If you can name it, it is not God. If you can define it, it is not God." That is true. Nothing you can know about God is God, since the knower of the truth is God. Yet we go right on teaching what God is, although, actually, it is impossible to teach what God is, since *I Am*. But that same *I Am* is you when you are saying "I am." In the final analysis, all that can ever be known about God is that *I am He*. That is the basic truth. Always the knower, the one who is knowing the truth, *is* the truth that is being known. But to convey this truth through words presents difficulties.

The use of the word "transparency" is also open to misinterpretation. Ordinarily when we think of the word "transparency," we think of a clean pane of glass letting the sunshine through, and we call that glass a clear transparency for the sun. If the glass is dirty, we say it is a poor transparency. If I were to speak of myself as a transparency for God and mean it in that sense, I would be wrong, because the sun and the pane of glass are two separate things. But God and I are not two separate things; and therefore, in that sense, I would not be a transparency for God. You remember Jesus' statement, "Why callest thou me good? there is none good but one, that is, God?"[1] In that sense, Jesus was the clear transparency through which the goodness of God was shown forth

[1] Matthew 19:17.

to the world. As with any form, words have their limitations. That is the reason that the deepest teaching is wordless.

God is the reality of being—the sum total of the reality of being. The individual "I" is that place at which the totality of God is made evident to you. In that sense, God, the Reality, which is my incorporeal and invisible being, appears outwardly to you as what you call intelligence, integrity, loyalty, fidelity, gratefulness, appreciation, cooperation. In that sense, I am a transparency through which that light of God-being is flowing. If you use the word transparency in the sense of their being a God and an "I," and God pouring through, you would be wrong. But if you can see integrity, spirituality, intelligence, love, as qualities of God, and then if you say, "My, what a wonderful transparency for good that individual is," you do not have two-ness any more than you have two when you are expressing faithfulness or fidelity. There are not two of you, you and the fidelity. Fidelity is actually a quality of your character, of your nature. It is ingrained; it is inherent in you. It constitutes your being. It is not wrong to say, "My, you are a wonderful transparency for truth," because that does not mean that truth is something that is separate from you, showing through: it means that you are a visible evidence of an invisible quality.

With enough of the light of this truth, we shall be at the place where, regardless of any phase of error which we meet, we can just snap our fingers and say "shoo," and think of the white poodle. Then, we shall be such a transparency for the truth of being

300

that we will heal automatically. Watch this. If, for any length of time, you can maintain that state of consciousness in which you do not take in any phase or any appearance of error, but instantly recognize, "I do not have to give a treatment to a non-existent poodle," you will be doing wonderful healing work.

You might say, "Well, will I heal all my own ills?" I do not know. It still seems necessary for us to help each other. Of course, with this realization many things will clear up for us, and with the gradual unfolding of consciousness, they will all clear up. But with problems that are particularly annoying, we still seem to have to call on each other and borrow each other's light for a little while. Some day, by living in this consciousness continually, so that we never indulge in gossip, hearsay, or false rumors, and never accept appearance as reality, we shall come to the place where our own flesh will completely disappear.

Just as the Master cautioned some of his followers to tell no man what things they had seen, so I caution you not to speak about this. Do not speak of it to anyone for weeks or months to come. Take it into your consciousness; practice it; train yourself in it. You now know what the principle is. You have only to look out and smile at the white poodle that does not exist, and you will have the sum total of the practice of this truth. But it must be practiced. Develop this consciousness of not loving, hating, or fearing error of any name or nature. Keep this inside your own being. Work with it every time you are confronted with error, whether it is yours or that of some friend, patient, or relative. Do not tell him

CHAPTER NINETEEN

THE INFINITE INVISIBLE

MEDITATION is our preparation for the inflow of the Spirit. It is the period during which we realize our oneness with the Infinite. That realization gives us the very presence of Spirit, Itself, with which to face the day. We have been inclined to believe that since God is omnipresent, always and everywhere present, that that is all there is to spiritual living and to the assurance of God's being at hand. But any such assumption is contradicted by a study of the history of the world.

The omnipresence of God is of no avail to any one except in proportion to his conscious oneness with it, his conscious attunement, his conscious feeling and realization of it. Without that we go out on the street as human beings: we may reach our destination or we may not; we may catch cold or we may not; we may get sick or we may not. All these things are happening to people all over the world; but they are happening to people because they are going out into the world without making a conscious contact with the infinite Source, with the infinite Power. The promise is: "He that dwelleth in the secret place of the most High"[1]—dwelleth, dwelleth, dwelleth in the secret place of the most High. He

[1] Psalms 91:1.

who dwells there, he who lives and moves and has his being in Spirit, is protected from the so-called evils of the world.

"Pray without ceasing."[1] Go into the inner sanctuary and there find your communion or oneness with God. A study of scripture on the subject of prayer will show you how important prayer is; and then a study of modern metaphysical writings will show you the nature of prayer. I suppose we know more about prayer in this age than did most of those who were responsible for writing the Bible; at least, we know more about how to reveal the nature of prayer. Many of them may have known about true prayer within their own being, but their concept of prayer, praying to God *for* something, has not done the world much good. The modern idea of prayer, which is individual communion with God, is what might be called "effective prayer." In some of the orthodox churches today the metaphysical idea of prayer is to be found. There are more modern thinkers in the orthodox church today than there ever have been before; just as there are more people in the world today who really believe in the possibility of conscious communion with God.

Conscious communion with God is pure mysticism. The word "mysticism" frightens some people because they do not understand its true meaning. However, when the word is correctly understood, there is nothing strange or disturbing about it. A mystic is one who consciously tunes in to God, who consciously receives impartations from the Father within. A mystical teaching is any teaching

[1] I Thessalonians 5:17.

304

which sets forth the possibility of individual communication with God, individual communion with God, the ability to receive impartations from God. Modern prayer—prayer as we know it today—is conscious oneness with God. Anything that will bring about our realization of conscious oneness, anything that will bring the actual Spirit to our consciousness, is prayer and meditation.

Our meditation is a quietness, a stillness, a state of receptivity, in which we open our consciousness to the impartation of the Spirit. Then, when the Spirit answers—when we receive the impulse that gives us that sense or awareness that God is present—the Spirit which we have touched, lives our lives. When the three Hebrews went through the fiery furnace, a Fourth was there with them. That Fourth was the Christ or conscious presence of the Spirit of God. If the three Hebrews had not been consciously aware of the presence of God, there would have been no presence of God visible or tangible. It was their *consciousness* of the Presence that was their protection. Moses was conscious of the presence of God, and that consciousness was shown forth as manna from the sky, the opening of the Red Sea, and water from the rock.

Always remember that "I can of mine own self do nothing"[1]; but the presence of God with me can do all things. "I and my Father are one[2] . . but my Father is greater than I."[3] To one imbued with the presence of God, all things are possible, whether it is healing or supplying or protecting—*all things are possible.* However, to rely solely on the blind belief

[1] John 5:30.   [2] John 10:30.   [3] John 14:28.

that God will do something, or that somewhere out in space there is a God to do it, is a dangerous thing. But if you ever feel, actually feel the presence and power of God, then all that God is, is right where you are. Without understanding this, you have only a faith or a belief, and usually it is a blind faith in God's presence. There must be a conscious awareness of the presence of God in order to have available the power, activity, safety, and security of God.

It is our conscious awareness of truth that acts as our saving presence throughout the day. That is the unseen Second One that is with us, the unseen Fourth One. The Infinite Invisible will be with you always in your conscious awareness, in your consciousness of the Presence. Meditation is one way of realizing the presence of God; and at first, it is almost the only way we have. After you have made your contact and have had your first awareness of God's presence, and after that has been repeated over and over many times in your meditation, you finally come to a place where God virtually is never absent or apart from you. I mean by that, that you are never outside of that conscious awareness.

Establish and Maintain Your Conscious Oneness

Another word on this subject of meditation. You may be meditating for your self, or it may be for a friend or a patient. Will you remember this? If you want to help some one with any problem he may have, when you sit down to meditate, immediately forget that individual. Drop the name of the person or the specific claim, and in your meditation turn within to make this contact with God. Do not think of the patient or his problem; think only of your own contact; drop the case right there. That touch, that contact with God, is the presence of God, working in, or through, or upon that problem to bring out the harmony of Its being. *Your contact* is the Presence that goes out to make the correction; and whether the patient is sitting in the room with you, or whether he is on the other side of the earth, makes no difference. You do not have to direct your thought to the person or to the problem.

That is clearly stated in *Conscious Union With God*[1], "My conscious oneness with God constitutes my oneness with all spiritual being and idea." When I meditate, I am not thinking of any one individually or collectively. I sit and make my contact with God. I feel the response; I feel that touch of the Infinite; I feel the whole surge of Spirit flowing through me. But notice this: that contact with God is also the contact with you, individually and collectively, since in God we are all one. As an example, we may use the telephone system. If I want to speak to you through a telephone in your home, I cannot do it unless I first make contact with the central office. When I reach central, I have entrée to any and every telephone in the world, through my contact with the central office. I can be tuned in to your home or any other home. As a matter of fact, I can be tuned in to twenty million homes—but only by first making my contact with central. Then, my contact with central

1 By the author (New York: Julian Press, 1962).

establishes my contact with everybody who is tuned in to central. In the same way, inasmuch as God is infinite divine Consciousness, my conscious oneness with the one Consciousness constitutes my oneness with your consciousness because it is one and the same Consciousness. Never do I have to project a thought toward you. Never do I have to inform infinite Consciousness of your problem, or what the solution would seem to be. All I have to do when you have said, "Help me," is to tune in to the one Consciousness. That one Consciousness, which is infinite Wisdom, knows the who, the what, the why, the wherefore, and the how.

Try that for anyone with any problem that comes up—just meditate. Find your oneness; and as soon as you feel that answer, release the whole thing and let it go. Then see what wonderful ways God has of working out your problem, whether the need is a sum of money or a ticket on the railroad. Whatever it is, tune in to the Infinite; but do not tell the Infinite that you need money or a ticket. It may turn out that the Infinite knows that you need something else or that you are to go in another direction.

The healing of mind, body, soul, spirit, business, and human relationships is an important part of our work; and this method of healing is, in the final analysis, the highest way. We have been all through the mental processes of treating, but remember that this is the final step that does the work after all the treating has been done. Establish and maintain your conscious oneness, and everything you need will flow automatically to you, as a rule before you know that you have need of it. We, on the spiritual path, are not interested in just the normal, natural, human health and success. The health, wealth, and success that we want—the harmony, peace, and joy—are those which we attain through the Spirit, through God. We bring this into our experience through the activity of truth in our consciousness.

The most important moment in your life is when you make a conscious contact with God. Nothing will ever come into your life greater than that moment. A realization of your conscious oneness with God will be the supreme demonstration, the crowning achievement of your experience. We are told that kings and emperors would have given all their earthly possessions for that realization. They would, but they could not achieve it, because their whole thought was on a world of power, money, place, position, and honor—everything that has to do with the external world. And God is not reached that way.

Before you retire, sit down quietly in meditation and consciously feel this Presence. If, after five minutes, or six or seven, you have not achieved the realization, forget it and go to bed. If you should wake up in the middle of the night, try it again at that time. Once you have accomplished it, you have entered an entirely new experience; you have entered a whole new plane of consciousness. This fourth dimension is the Infinite Invisible. The fourth dimension is the transcendental, that which no one can ever know through the senses, through seeing, hearing, tasting, touching, or smelling. It is literally the secret place of the most High, and that place is found in your consciousness.

Effects of Conscious Oneness

When you have touched this Presence, when you have felt It, you can give up all concern, all worry, and all fear, for the rest of your life. All of your worries are behind you. You have found Aladdin's lamp. But this is better than Aladdin's lamp, because you will not even have to wish. As a matter of fact, you will not even have to know what it is you want! You sit in silence and touch that Presence; It responds; and It literally tells you:

> "*I* am here; *I* am on the field; *I* will never leave you, nor forsake you. If you walk through the waters, you will not drown. If you go through the fire, the flames will not kindle upon you. If you walk through the valley of the shadow of death, not a bit of death will touch you. Walk through all the valleys you like. *My* Presence goes before you. *My* presence is with you.

But remember, you have that assurance only when you have made your contact with It—when It responds, and you feel that "click" in your system, that energy that rushes in, the still small voice, or whatever way It has of responding. To each one of us, it is something different, and sometimes, it is different each day.

If you make this contact, let us say, in the morning before you leave home, you can rest assured that your contact with It, God, is your contact with everything necessary to your unfoldment for that day. If it is a person, he will be there; if it is a place or a thing, it will be there; if it is a healing, if it is harmony, if it is joy or peace, or if it is a parking space —whatever it is, whatever the form in which it has to appear to you—it will be there. Your conscious oneness with It constitutes your oneness with every "it" that is necessary to your experience. But remember, it comes only as the activity of your own consciousness.

Do you understand, now, that when a practitioner is asked for help, it is the consciousness of the practitioner that does the work? Do you understand that it is not some far-off God? Do you understand that it is nothing more nor less than the consciousness of the practitioner—the consciousness of a practitioner who knows his oneness with God, and thereby has lost all hate, fear, or love of error? In the degree that your practitioner has consciously touched the Presence, in the degree that your practitioner neither hates, fears, nor loves error, in that degree, will healing take place. If that were not true, if it were some outside force or power doing the healing work, you could ask any practitioner for help and get the same results. But by now, you all know that you must have a practitioner who has some measure of the consciousness of the presence of God; who has in some degree lost the fear, the hate, or the love of error; and that that practitioner's consciousness, which is God consciousness, does the healing work. It will not do any good to ask "the man in the street" for help, unless he, too, is a student of this work; because his consciousness is not imbued with this Christ. He could say from morning until night, "I live; yet not I, but Christ liveth in me,"[1] and it would be meaningless. But

[1] Galatians 2:20.

311

the moment he is aware of It, he begins to show It forth by his healing works—by the bringing out of harmony and peace around him.

Success inevitably follows the consciousness imbued with the Christ, the Spirit of God. The moment, then, that you have made Christ, or the Spirit and presence of God, a reality; the minute you have touched It, and felt that impulse within you; you are on your way to success. It does not make any difference what your business is, or what your work may be; you begin to be successful in it, right where you are. Then, if necessary, you will be graduated from your present position into other work. But It will begin by making you a success where you are. It will lead you from that point forward.

The Christ goes before you, and It attracts to you anything and anybody necessary to your unfoldment; but you must make the conscious contact. Your success in life is the result of the activity of your consciousness. Your practitioner and teacher are merely helps on the way until you have been led back to the kingdom of God within your own being.

There is a difference between sleep after you have felt the conscious contact, and sleep which comes just from falling into bed and going to sleep. There is almost as much difference as there is between living and dying, because that sleep, which is a part of every twenty-four hour cycle, is almost extinction. But the sleep that comes after a realization of the presence of God is not sleep at all. It is a resting of the body, but consciousness is functioning just as if you were wide awake. In this state, your eyes will be closed and you will appear to be sleeping; but actually, your consciousness will be open, and then you will find that the most wonderful ideas of your life will come to you. That is when divine inspiration comes. That is when the great lessons of life are learned.

It is worth while even if you have to practice this awareness of God for six months or a year before you attain it; because, remember, when you have attained it, you will have solved every problem of existence. One by one, all the problems of human existence will fade away. Oh, it may not be that you will wake up some morning and find that you are completely in heaven, but, at least, you will find that you are on the road to heaven, and that, bit by bit, errors are disappearing and problems are being solved without too much anxiety and trouble; the good things of life are being experienced without any effort at all, without taking thought for what you shall eat or what you shall drink or wherewithal you shall be clothed.

A Conscious Realization of the Presence of God

Many students become so involved in the functional duties of a metaphysician that they forget to make their conscious recognition of God, to make themselves a law unto their experience each day. I have never permitted myself even for a day to forget my work; I consciously remember, not always in the same way, because I have no formula for it, but when I start out the day—and usually this takes place even before I am out of bed; and if not then, soon after, when I am sitting in a chair—I begin with a conscious realization of the word *I*:

313

I is God. *I* is infinite good. *I* is consciousness, life, being. This *I*, is the *I that I Am*, and because of all that *I* am, I am; all that God is, I am; all that the Father hath is mine; all of the wisdom, guidance, direction, spiritual love, spiritual life, spiritual soul, all of the love of God and of man, all that God knows of love, constitutes the love of my being. It constitutes the God-love which the individual needs. It constitutes my love for the universal God; and thereby, It constitutes my love for all mankind, for all whom I meet. And that immediately reminds me that that love must include enemy as well as friend.

God is the activity of my day: God is the activity of my work; and therefore, it is God, the infinite Wisdom, which is outlining my day's program. It is the one Intelligence, operating universally, which brings to my desk whatever is necessary for me to do. I know that the very God, Soul, or Consciousness, that formed me has saved out for me all of my activity and all of its fruitage, all of its reward. I know that, because of this truth, I am never dependent on man whose breath is in his nostrils. I am never dependent on the good will of any man, woman, or child. All my good flows from within to the without. The kingdom of God, of wholeness or harmony, is within me; and in the degree of my understanding of that, I can multiply loaves and fishes for all those who are not yet aware of the fact that they also are a law of multiplication. I realize, also, that because God is infinite, my being is infinite, since I and the Father are one. Therefore, in this

314

infinity of being, I include all of God's good, and because of that infinity, there is no room for error or evil or negation of any sort. Therefore, there are no laws to act upon me.

God is the law unto my being; God is the divine principle of my being; and therefore, that law is a law unto my universe. But nothing outside of me, whether of the past, the present, or the future, can act upon me as law, even for good. Nothing existing in the realm of effect can act upon me or upon my affairs as law, since God is the only law-giver. God, the divine Consciousness of my being, the very Soul of me, is the only law unto my experience. Therefore, regardless of what the world may call the law of cause and effect, the law of karma; regardless of what the world may call the law of the stars and the planets; none of that is law unto my being, either for good or evil, since my good is derived from the infinity of my own being, which is God. I lean not unto my own understanding, or on the understanding of any man, but on the infinity of God, pouring Itself through as my individual being.

I know that this power of love, which is God, is a law of attraction, and therefore, it can only attract to me those whom I can love, and those who can love me; those whom I can serve, and those who can serve me; since we are one in Christ. Because God is a universal law of love, only love is expressing through everyone on earth. Therefore, all men, all men throughout the world, not only throughout this world, but throughout what we call the world of those who have passed on, and the world of

315

those who have not yet been born—all those become a law of love and of life unto my being.

Our protective work is not hiding ourselves in a shell somewhere and saying, "Error, you cannot reach me!" Our protective work is the realization of God as individual mind, life, and Soul; but the life, mind, and Soul of all beings. This shows us the absolute nothingness of such appearances as accidents, disease, and carelessness. We realize that God governs, not only my driving, but that God sits at every wheel; that God is the only automobile driver anywhere in the world—or airplane pilot, or sea captain. The realization that God is the mind of every individual, and is everywhere present—that is protective work. That is protective work because it is a declaration to every belief of error: "Thou couldest have no power at all against me, except it were given thee from above."[1]

Establish that in your thought every day. Establish in your consciousness the great truth that God is the only presence and the only power; and that all this human belief in a selfhood apart from God is illusion—without presence, substance, law, reality, cause, or effect. *Establish this.* If you do not establish it, do not expect to demonstrate it. You can only bring forth as demonstration that of which you are actively conscious. That does not mean, however, that you should go around all day muttering statements of truth. But it does mean that at some time during the day, you must actively and consciously bring these truths of being to light. There should be

[1] John 19:11.

316

no reason for people on this path to experience the errors of human existence. To some extent, at times, everybody comes under human belief, because of the universality of the belief. But the experience should be mild; it should not be of long duration; and it should not be tragic.

Importance of Daily Realization

In this work you must learn that it is the activity of your consciousness that brings forth your demonstration. The thing to do is consciously to take the truth, learn to apply it in your experience, and then each day actually put it to work in your consciousness. Realize it; state it to yourself; remind yourself of your true identity, of your conscious oneness with God, of the illusory quality of anything of a negative nature; and maintain that, not just for a day or a week, or a month, but constantly. Even after thirty-two years in this work, I would not permit a day to pass without consciously knowing the truth. Even though it is not necessary for me to take thought about supply—it seems to be coming in of its own accord sufficiently to take care of all my needs—nevertheless, I never see money without thinking, "Thank you, Father; I know the Source, the infinite Source, of this good, and I know the purpose and use of that which appears as Its effect." Always, some time each day, I give recognition to that, and I am confident that this conscious awareness of truth is the activity that comes forth as manifestation and expression.

Again, let us realize this: There is no such thing as

truth *and* manifestation. The truth you consciously entertain does not produce a manifestation of good. The truth you entertain in your consciousness *appears as* your good. The truth you consciously entertain in your consciousness appears outwardly, tangibly, visibly, as your good. There is no such thing as truth's producing opportunity. There is no such thing as truth's producing health. The truth, entertained in your consciousness invisibly, appears visibly as health, wealth, harmony, happy relationships, peace, joy, dominion. This is extremely important. There can not be both truth *and* manifestation. There is truth entertained in your consciousness appearing visibly *as* manifestation. If you are not entertaining the truth of being in your consciousness, you cannot have the manifestation, because truth and manifestation are inseparable and indivisible.

It is up to you how much of demonstration you have, whether the demonstration is one of money, of companionship, of home, of success—regardless of what it is. It does not make any difference what business you are in or what your activity is. The success, the harmony, the peace, and the joy, will be there, and it will be there infinitely, if only you will entertain infinite truth actively in your consciousness. That truth, which is entertained in secret, appears visibly. Truth, entertained as the activity of consciousness, appears visibly. Truth, entertained as the activity of consciousness, appears as the visible and tangible manna of today. We do not live on yesterday's manna. There is nothing wrong in using what we have accumulated in the past, either of money or of reputation, but it is not necessary. Each day is a unit unto itself; each day is a day unto itself. If you were to begin today with nothing, that is, nothing tangible or visible, and if you entertained truth consciously, that truth would soon appear as your need of today.

Never be concerned about the things you had yesterday, but do not have today. Never be disturbed over the opportunities of the past that you have missed. Never be concerned for the years that the locusts have eaten. Do not be concerned even for the years of your past sins, or your wasted youth. Do not even regret that you did not know this truth ten years ago. Today is the only day in which you live. You cannot live yesterday, and it is a waste of time to try. You cannot live tomorrow, because, strangely enough, none of us ever sees tomorrow. It is always *today*. And it is always *this minute*. And it is always this minute in which I am the fulfillment of God. It is always this minute in which God is appearing infinitely as my individual being. That is all I have to be concerned with. All I have to be concerned with is the joy and peace and harmony and dominion of *this minute*. And if I live continuously in this consciousness, in this minute, then each minute that follows will be just as successful and joyous as this one—a steady and continuous unfoldment of good.

CHAPTER TWENTY

TRUTH UNFOLDING

WE cannot have a consciousness of truth *and* a demonstration; nor can we have a consciousness of truth *before* the demonstration, nor the demonstration *before* the consciousness of truth. First, there must be the consciousness of truth, and then, with it, comes the demonstration, because all demonstration is truth itself made evident—the Infinite Invisible becomes visible; the Word becomes flesh. There is no time lapse, or space lapse, between the Word and the flesh. The Word becomes flesh instantaneously. Truth becomes demonstration instantaneously, because demonstration is truth manifested.

Nothing takes place in our outer world except as the manifestation and expression of our consciousness, and if truth is not active in our consciousness, then our demonstration is not the activity of truth. If our thought remains barren of truth, no matter how fruitful in material things it may be, it cannot bring forth spiritual fruitage. If we sow to the flesh, we reap corruption. If we sow to the Spirit, we reap the fruitage of the Spirit.

Let us remember this: Our individual consciousness actually is God consciousness; God is our only consciousness. Therefore, all demonstration, all manifestation, is God consciousness expressed. It takes our knowing of this truth, however, to make that evident. All harmony in our experience is the direct result of the activity of truth in our consciousness. This activity of truth does not consist merely in making statements of truth, or in vain repetitions of truth, or in repeated affirmations of truth. That is not the activity of truth in consciousness. The activity of truth in consciousness is an awareness of the truth of being. As we learn to dwell on God, on God in Its infinite forms and varieties, on God as omnipresent, and especially on God as individual consciousness—your consciousness and mine—then the infinity of God appears.

The Infinite Way of life is actually an entrance into the fourth dimension of life, into spiritual consciousness. The personal sense of life gives way to universal life. In the personal sense of life, each of us is living his own experience, and each of us is interested in finding some way—materially, mentally, or spiritually—to enrich that experience. But The Infinite Way of life does not include any such self-seeking. The Infinite Way of life becomes our way of life, when we enter the spiritual path. On this path, we do not live for ourselves; we are no longer concerned with our own particular demonstrations; we have left all that behind in the realization of the great truth that God has created us in Its image and likeness for Its own purpose. The divine universal Consciousness has manifested Itself individually as you and as me for Its glory, for Its purpose, and for Its use.

The greatest sin in the world, for those on the spiritual path, is desire—even the desire for good—since this path is the realization of *grace*. All that the Father hath is mine—"not by might, nor by power, but by my spirit"—by grace, by an inner power. In that there is no need to desire anything or anybody. There is no need to move here, or to move there. If we rest in this inner peace, if we learn to live in this inner consciousness of "all that I have is thine[1] . . . it is your Father's good pleasure to give you the kingdom,"[2] strangely enough, whatever needs to be done is done—the sale that should be made is made; the purchase that should be made is made; the move that should be made is made; but always without taking thought, always without worrisome planning. That does not leave us with a life of inaction or a "do-nothing" life. On the contrary, it is a most vital life, since every day, in fact, every hour of every day, the Spirit is moving us on and on and on to greater degrees of unfoldment; moving us into more important places, greater activities, more significant work.

At times people are critical of the fact that The Infinite Way stresses the handling of error. "If God is all, why don't you leave it alone and forget this error business." But those very people often fail when they try to heal with "God is all, and God is love." It is important to understand the nature of error and to know how to handle it. Nobody would experience sin, disease, or lack, if it were not for some *claim* of a power apart from God. Actually, there is no power apart from God. Then why is anyone ever

[1] Luke 15:31.   [2] Luke 12:32.

sick? Why does anyone ever die? It is because there is a negative force operating as law which pulls us into sin, disease, lack, limitation, and war. It is only when we understand what it is, that we are able to nullify it.

What is this law? What is this claim of a selfhood apart from God which operates as sin, disease, lack, and limitation? Actually, it is our white poodle, which presents itself to us through hypnotic suggestion or world belief. Where it began, we do not know. I only know that in this world of ours, there is something operating that results in sin, disease, lack, limitation, false desires, false appetites, and, ultimately, death itself. It claims to be present as a power—as a power of disease, a power of death, a power of infection or contagion. But through this revelation of truth, we understand and know that horrible as the appearance may be, actually it is a non-existent white poodle; it is the non-existent snake in the rope. It is our recognition of that fact that results in healing. Never forget that. Never forget that you are *not* in the business of overcoming disease, or death. Your work is to understand that what appears as sin, disease, or death is nothing but an illusory picture caused by the universal belief of a selfhood apart from God; and your conviction of the illusory nature of the picture is the healing power. Peace, the Christ peace, is that state of peace which recognizes that the absolute fulfillment of God is here where I am and where you are. We do not have to look up or out for anything or anybody; but remember, as the poet, John Burroughs, said, "My own shall come to me." We have only to sit and wait and our own will come to us. While we are sitting and waiting, of course, we should also be working. The work that we do is the work that is given us to do each moment of each day. Whatever its name, whatever its nature, whatever call may come, we do that work without desiring that it be some other work, without desiring to be in some other place. Let us give up all sense of desire, except the desire to realize God. That is the only legitimate desire we should have.

Our Purpose in Life

Our life, at this stage of unfoldment, should become impersonal. We should be willing, at this point, to accept "my grace" or "my peace"—that peace which comes from the Christ—rather than the peace that the world can give us. The world can still give us a kind of peace: It probably could surround us with more of the world's goods. That would be one kind of peace that the world might give. At our stage, however, we should be able to say, "That is not the peace I am seeking. I am looking for the peace which comes of the Christ. I am looking for that peace which comes by grace, not by effort, desire, mental manipulation, trickery, treachery, lying, or deceit, but that which comes to me as the grace of God, as the gift of God."

We should be in the world, but not of it. We should enjoy anything and anybody that is in the world; but in enjoying them, we are not to enter into the intrigues of the world, or to employ the methods of the world. It is not necessary to use the world's weapons. It is not necessary to use the world's ways. We can achieve the harmony of our existence without utilizing the weapons of the world or the ways of the world. All that we are to do—our only purpose in living—is to show forth the effects, or the absoluteness, of the power of this principle. That is why we are living; that is why we are here. We are not here simply to earn a living, to eat three meals a day, to go to sleep at night, or to raise a family. All those human activities are but incidental to the main purpose, which is to show forth God as the central theme of the universe, God as the principle of all existence, God as the glory of individual life. That is our purpose here, and that is the purpose of the statement, "My peace I give unto you; not as the world giveth."[1] There is no room in spiritual living, in The Infinite Way of life, for personal glorification. There is no room for believing that one person has any power that is denied to another. The power is universal; the power is omnipresent; the power is *I Am*. All that is necessary for this power to become evident as our existence is our realization of that truth, our consecration to this purpose.

This all leads to the fourth dimension which is spiritual consciousness. It leads into that realm where we begin to realize this great truth of being:

> *I* am the life and the light of the world. *I* am life eternal. *I* am truth. *I* am the bread and *I* am the water. *I* am the Father; *I* am the Son, and *I* am the holy Ghost. *I*, in my infinite being, am all that

[1] John 14:27.

325

God is, since God has conferred upon me and upon you, Its own being, Its own glory, Its own life, as my life and as your life. This is a universal truth. *I* am the divine substance of the universe. *I* am the substance out of which the world is formed. *I* am divine consciousness. God is the only reality, the only consciousness, the only *I*, and *I* am That; and *I* am That in all Its glory, in all Its perfection. *I* am the mind of the universe. *I* am the soul of the universe. *I* am the infinite individuality of all being. Therefore, my universe contains only God in Its infinite form, God in Its infinite variety— God, my consciousness, appearing to me as the harmony of my daily experience. If I were not all that, then there would be an "I" *and* a "me," but I and the Father are one.

The wonderful part of this work is that those who are ready to receive this unfoldment through you, are always being prepared for you. In due time, they will come to you as patients, or as students, and you will reveal to them that which is already established as their consciousness. Never will you be able to give them anything new or anything you know, which they do not already know. Many, many times, in my experience, I have tried to share this truth with people who were not ready for it, and I can tell you that they were never able to understand it. They were just as much unaware of its meaning when they left as when they came. Only those who had already been prepared through the unfolding of their own consciousness were able to say, "I received something from the experience." Yes, they did, because the bonfire had already been prepared within them and all I did was to strike the match.

Good Is the Effect of the Activity of Truth in Consciousness

All of the good we expect in our experience from now on, we should expect to come to us as the result of the activity of truth in our consciousness. That gives new meaning to the statement, "The kingdom of God is within you," or to the truth that all good must unfold from within our own being. Do you see how foolish it would be to sit down and say, "Oh, the kingdom of God is within me"; and then stop with that? It would be useless, even were you to repeat those statements a hundred times. Do you see how foolish it would be just to say, "Well, all my good must unfold from within me?" It cannot unfold from within if there is only spiritual barrenness within. The kingdom of God *is* within you, and all good *must* unfold from within your own consciousness, but please be sure that you understand what that means. All good unfolds from within your consciousness of truth. The activity of truth in your consciousness appears outwardly as the harmony of your daily experience: it appears as your health, as your wealth, as your companionship; it appears as your wife or your husband or your friend.

Since salvation is individual, it is up to you, as an individual, to bring forth the amount of harmony that you would like to experience, by the measure of the activity of truth in your consciousness. Repeating truth, reading truth, or hearing truth is not necessarily the activity of truth in your consciousness. True, they are a part of it and serve as aids along the way. In fact, every time you open a book of spiritual inspiration or scripture, you are making truth active in your consciousness. Every time you attend a lecture, every time you attend a class that is based on spiritual truth, you are making truth active and keeping truth active in your consciousness. But those are only avenues leading up to the final one, and that is the actual activity of truth as your consciousness. At that stage of unfoldment, you ponder these statements of truth, meditate on them, see through the letter of them to the Spirit. When you read the Bible, and you read that God saved out a remnant of 7,000 for Elijah, instead of saying, "Wasn't that a blessing for Elijah?" you read it again and again until you find that the principle is that God, my individual consciousness, has likewise saved out for me all that is necessary—the complete number, the completeness of everything, necessary for my unfoldment. That is the activity of truth *as* consciousness.

Keep Truth Active in Consciousness

God is the one and only consciousness, and It is infinite. Out of that infinity *appears* the infinite form and variety of this universe, but God is *individual consciousness*, which means that God is *your* consciousness. Therefore, your individual consciousness is infinite. Out of that consciousness must appear your daily experience; and that experience must be infinitely good, infinitely harmonious, joyous, successful, and prosperous. Unless you can realize, acknowledge, and claim God as your consciousness, you cannot claim an infinity of good in your experience. Unless you can understand that God appears as your individual consciousness, you can never bring forth the fullness of eternality and immortality, or the infinitude of divine Being. Out of your consciousness springs your universe. And since God is your consciousness, your universe is infinite; and it is infinitely good. It becomes your duty and your privilege to remind yourself of this truth every single day. It is necessary that you recognize each day, that because of the infinite nature of your consciousness, there is no law outside of your consciousness. There is no belief outside of your consciousness which can enter to defile or make a law. Nothing can act upon you for good or for evil, except God, God appearing as your individual consciousness; and this becomes a *law* unto your universe. It makes you the master of your destiny through God-given dominion.

It is not that I, of myself, am anything, but through God, all dominion is given to me over everything on the earth and beneath the earth and above the earth. All things are possible to me through Christ, through this truth of the realization of God as my real being. Unless you make this a law unto yourself by conscious realization, you permit the world beliefs to handle you, to act upon you as if they really were laws. They are not laws: they are beliefs, world beliefs; they are universal beliefs; and they will foist themselves upon you, if you are not alert, if you do not pray without ceasing, if you do not make truth active in your own consciousness.

Keep truth active in your consciousness: this is your defense against the thoughts and the things of this world. Remember, individual or collective thought is not power, in and of itself. It is power only as you, through ignorance, permit it to be a power. Scripture does not tell you that there are no evils in the world, but it tells you that these evils will not come nigh you, *if* you live and move and have your being in this divine consciousness of Truth. "He that dwelleth in the secret place of the most High"[1]—he that dwelleth in this secret and sacred consciousness of Truth—finds in it a sure defense, a fortress, and a rock. This truth, entertained in your consciousness, becomes the rock on which you stand. It becomes the fortress, and so the Word of God becomes your defense.

To Each of Us a Work Is Given

The Word of God is your sure defense, but it is your offense, also. The Word of God becomes your very life and being. You do not need this Word to be steel lined. You do not need this Word in an underground tunnel. You do not need this Word in concrete. You need this Word established in your consciousness. You need this Word of God with you from morning to night, and from night to morning. You need Its assurance and reassurance continuously.

[1] Psalms 91:1.

You need the association of those who are on this path. You need the cooperation of all of those who are travelling in the same direction in which you find yourself going. And you need to remember that because God is infinite in being, God has established you in such a way that you can show forth your infinitude without infringing on anyone else's good. You need not hate, or fear, or knock, or compete with another person. God, active as your consciousness, and God, manifesting as the consciousness of your own being, is your demonstration; and because of that, you will always be successful in your particular work and in your particular way.

To each of us is given some work. As you enter this fourth dimension, as your consciousness is opened for light and guidance, ultimately, that inner guidance directs you to your work. For one, it is in one field, and for another it is in another field. Each has his own individual work—a work which can be carried on wherever we are. When the need comes for us to be in some other location, circumstances take us to that place. We need never seek it any more than we need desire it.

The whole message of the fourth dimension is this: "I have meat to eat that ye know not of."[1] I have a wellspring of living waters within—not water that the world gives. No, this water comes from the Spirit; it comes from the Soul. I have meat—a substance that ye know not of. And that meat is my very consciousness. No longer do I have to look out to man whose breath is in his nostrils, or even to a

[1] John 4:32.

331

man's book, or to man's scriptures. Those are given to me only as guides to help me reach the center of my own being, where I can rest and say:

Father, I am home. Now, I will live by grace. "All that I have is thine . . . my peace I give unto you"—this inner peace, this inner substance. I have meat the world knows not of. I do not have to strive for the world's goods, or strive for the world's recognition. Right where I am, all that God is, I am. The place whereon I stand is holy ground.

This is the activity of truth—the Word—constantly maintained in my consciousness:

The Word of truth is my secret place of the most High. It leads me beside the still waters. If I make my bed in hell, It is there. As I walk through the valley of the shadow of death, It is there. And It—this It—is the divinity of my consciousness. It is that *I* within me that makes me the offspring of God and not of man. It is that within me, which recognizes that I was not born of woman. The *I* that I am is an infinite, divine, consciousness that formed this body for Its own use, as a vehicle for carrying out God's purpose on earth.

Give up as fast as you can the personal sense of existence. Stop believing "I cannot do this," or "My understanding is not sufficient for this," or "It's too late at my stage of life," or "I am too young to embark on this." When you say, "I," speak that word *I* as you would the word God. Then all things are possible unto you, through the God-being which you are. "I can of mine own self do nothing[1] . . . my doctrine is not mine but his that sent me."[2] Through Christ, you can do all things. As the offspring of God, you are joint-heir with Christ to all of the heavenly riches. Therefore, speak not as man. Speak as Christ-being, as the Son of God, or as God made manifest as your own being. Keep this consciousness of truth: it is your responsibility to keep consciousness so imbued with this truth as to make of your consciousness a sure defense against the arguments of the world.

And now remember this: *My peace I give unto you* —not as the world giveth. Stop looking for some good that the world giveth. Right here and now stop looking for some good that the world has to give you, whether it be fame or fortune. Turn within and be willing to accept the grace and the peace that God has—that spiritual peace. Then stand to one side and behold what it does for you out in this world.

"My peace I give unto you."[3]

---

[1] John 5:30. [2] John 7:16. [3] John 14:27.